MOTIVATING VOLUNTEERS

How the Rewards of Unpaid Work Can Meet People's Needs

Larry F. Moore
Editor

i

The publication of this book was made possible through grants received from:

The Samuel and Saidye Bronfman Family Foundation

The Laidlaw Foundation

The Leon and Thea Koerner Foundation

The Hamber Foundation

An Anonymous Donation

The Vancouver Volunteer Centre's publication program is funded in part by a grant from the B.C. Ministry of Human Resources.

Our thanks to the following organizations for their cooperation in obtaining photographs for this book:

Arts, Sciences and Technology Centre
B.C. Blind Sports
Cartwright Street Gallery
Crane Library, University of B.C.
Design Projections Limited
Greater Vancouver Information and Referral Service
Kinsmen Rehabilitation Foundation of B.C.
Lower Mainland Wildlife Rescue Association
Rogers Cable 10
Stanley Park Children's Zoo
St. John Ambulance Brigade
United Players
Vancouver Aquarium Gift Shop
Vancouver Museum and Planetarium

CONTENTS
Preface and Acknowledgements

PART ONE: INVITED CHAPTERS

PART TWO: SELECTED PAPERS

PREFACE AND ACKNOWLEDGEMENTS

This book was developed to provide a comprehensive look at the perplexing question of why volunteers volunteer. The aim of this publication is to assist managers of volunteer programs in motivating volunteers by developing interesting, creative, and challenging assignments for people who are motivated to work for reasons which are far more complex than a paycheck. At a time when volunteerism faces fierce competition from the strengthening attraction to paid jobs due to economic and other pressures, gaining insight into the reasons why people volunteer is essential if a program is to operate with minimal volunteer turnover and maximum volunteer satisfaction.

We hope that this book will assist community groups in: (1) identifying volunteers' motivations, (2) perpetuating volunteers' interest in their jobs, and (3) keeping those people, who work for much more than money, involved in the community.

Financial assistance for *Motivating Volunteers* was received from the Samuel and Saidye Bronfman Family Foundation, the Laidlaw Foundation, the Leon and Thea Koerner Foundation, the Hamber Foundation, and an anonymous donation.

We are grateful to Larry F. Moore who originated the concept for this book and who, as Editor, gave much of his time and energy in shepherding the project to its conclusion. Additional kudos go to Verni Brown who volunteered for the monumental task of typing the manuscript, to Graham Brown who is responsible for the graphic design, to Peter Martin who provided the photographs, to Tess Little, Jill Murray, and Kirstine Griffith for much insightful feedback, to the United Way of the Lower Mainland for the use of their work processing equipment, and to the V.A.R.C. Publications Committee.

Valerie A. Ahwee
Managing Editor

Part One
INVITED CHAPTERS

Chapter 1

MOTIVATION IN THE CONTEXT OF VOLUNTEERISM

Larry F. Moore

It has been estimated that the difference in performance level between the best and the worst workers in many organizations can be 100% or more. That is, the best workers sometimes produce between two and three times as much in a given time period (*Lawler, 1973*). Quite commonly, industrial workers performing under a direct monetary incentive system, such as piece-rate, produce at levels at least one-third higher than similarly qualified workers on straight salary. Business managers have long been aware that motivated workers perform better and have spent much effort in looking for ways to raise the motivation levels of their employees. Improved performance is not the only consequence of understanding and enhancing job motivation. Work attendance can be improved, lateness and turnover can be reduced, and overall work satisfaction can be increased.

This book is dedicated to the premise that obtaining and maintaining high levels of motivation is just as important in settings where volunteer work is performed as in paid work settings. In fact, securing a high level of motivation in a volunteer work setting may be much more difficult because of the absence (*by definition*) of a monetary incentive. On the other hand, volunteers clearly expect to obtain some type of reward for their participation and performance. When asked why they engage in volunteer activity, people give a delightfully wide range of reasons, of which the following are pithy examples:

1

"I really love any kind of work related to medicine. I'd consider myself a perfect candidate for our Red Cross Blood Clinics. My supervisor is a wonderful person, deeply involved with her job and I believe it shows constantly — not only in her work, but also in her person. My volunteer work leaves me with a feeling of accomplishment I cannot possibly put into words, and it is a job I love doing. Even in this little way, knowing the blood we collect is helping to save lives, brings out the pride in me — it is so worthwhile a cause — and so very needed."

"I was chosen as the Big Brother of the Year, one year ago, and because selection was based on a letter from my little brother, I felt quite good to know he thought as well of me as he did."

"As a member of the Elizabeth Fry Society, I am part of a team which visits the local jail weekly. Anyone who has ever spent any time in an institution of this sort will surely appreciate the hours of boredom that inmates must spend — rising at 6:30 a.m. or so and bedtime at 10:00 p.m. — with little to do. I feel, therefore, that any diversion is an asset and so our visits, if nothing else, provide a change in the day for both inmates and staff. Of course, we also hope that we can be of more practical aid in counselling and advising re legal aid, etc."

"Just being able to provide a service once a week to help cheer those less fortunate."

"I have never felt my volunteer involvements needed to give me a 'sense' of satisfaction. That comes automatically with a job well done. Rather, I have been privileged to have the energy to be helpful outside my home in a variety of ways during the past twelve years. I enjoy being busy and take pride in being able to handle home and volunteer involve-

ment."

"I'm only a gift shop staffer, and also help the treasurer of the hospital's Ladies' Auxiliary. We try to keep it staffed at all times for patients and visitors. I enjoy meeting people and have lived here all my life, so working here is almost like an evening out."

"To experience (1) growth in the organization and the formation of new groups, (2) new awareness for members of St. John's Ambulance of their widening roles of service in the community, (3) having all the members of the organization become aware of the need for continuous, challenging training, (4) fitting someone into a role for which he or she is well-suited and (5) saving a person's life by applying training principles."

"I have done volunteer work in many communities in many different agencies and hospitals for the past thirty years. My most stimulating and challenging volunteer work has been as a board member of the Family Services Association under the direction of an outstanding executive director. This is a very active board and I have been fortunate to actively participate in some of the work the agency does and help formulate their policies."

"I like meeting people and over these past years, I have met a lot of fantastic people."

"The need — as one grows older — to keep active. There is always someone who needs help. You don't have to look for problems. They are always around."

"It would be very difficult for me to give just one reason. Every single day that I work is different. I am unable to isolate just one experience. Every time a child responds to me and actually learns what I am trying to teach him is a satisfying experience."

These testimonials tell us some very important things about volunteer motivation. First, motivation, in the context of volunteer workers, is more complex than one might think. Second, there usually is a mixture of several reasons why a person engages in voluntary activity. Third, pure altruism rarely, if ever, provides a satisfactory explanation of volunteer motivation (*Smith, 1981*). Finally, the motives people have for doing the things they do may not be very clear, even to themselves.

THE NATURE OF MOTIVATION

Clearly, if we are to begin to understand human motivation and to examine the nature of motivation in the context of volunteerism, we need a framework for organizing our thinking. Such a framework can be arrived at by defining what is meant by the term "motivation" and then considering briefly several of the current motivation theories applicable to volunteer work.

There is no standard definition in existence at present on which all students of motivation can agree. One of the most complex definitions says:

> ...motivation has to do with a set of independent/ dependent variable relationships that explain the direction, amplitude, and persistence of an individual's behavior, holding constant the effects of aptitude, skill and understanding of the task, and the constraints operating in the environment. (Campbell and Pritchard, 1976)

One of the most simple (however incomplete) attempts at definition refers to motivation merely as the "force to behave." One of our chapter authors, Professor Craig Pinder (1984), distilling the best of several earlier writers' attempts, has recently provided a particularly lucid definition of work motivation as:

> ...a set of energetic forces that originate both within as well as beyond an individual's being to initiate work-related behavior and to determine its form, direction, intensity, and duration.

Several important characteristics of these attempts at definition deserve our consideration. First, motivation, as energy, is

4

goal-directed or purposive. Even the most primitive impulses to action (e.g., scratching an itch; blinking the eyes) have a purposive quality about them, and are designed to alleviate an inner state of disequilibrium. Second, motivation is derived from complex sources, such as how a person was raised, how he or she has been treated at work, personal energy level, and need state. Third, motivation is a feedback process involving a chain of events. That is, the individual experiences an inner state of disequilibrium which results in the calling into consciousness of a goal which, if achieved, is expected to remove the state of disequilibrium currently being experienced. The accompanying behavior is thus goal-directed and is linked back to the original inner mental state.

The process of motivation may be affected by or linked to a wide range of organizational variables including job or task design requirements, financial and non-financial rewards, co-workers, performance levels, choice processes of many types including "to participate" and "level of effort," training or conditioning, imposed leadership style, acceptance of transfer or promotion or responsibility, turnover, absenteeism, and loyalty.

A fourth characteristic of motivation is that motives cannot be seen — only inferred. Motives are products of the human mind and thus are not directly visible or measurable. We do not and perhaps cannot ever know exactly how motives are developed by individuals. On the other hand, it is apparent that any single act can express several motives. Motives may be disguised either consciously or subconsciously by an individual. For example, one person may help another out with a particular computer problem. Perhaps this is an act of kindness, but perhaps it is done to keep the first person ignorant of the data, misinformed, and powerless. Motives change and may be in conflict. Goal attainment may reduce or enhance motive strength under varying conditions. And finally, cultural variation may significantly moderate modes of expression of motives.

In summary, motivation is a pervasive influence in organizations and is linked to many work variables in complex ways -particularly to work performance and satisfaction. Therefore, as administrators working within the voluntary sector, we join with managers from industry in sharing a disparate need for good motivation theories to help us explain and predict human reaction and behavior in our organizations. In reviewing the available theories of motivation, one is reminded of the fable about a group of blind men describing an elephant. Each, because of his reduced sensory exposure to a small portion of the elephant's anatomy, produces a description of an elephant which, while accurate in a limited way, differs greatly from the descriptions of the others. Furthermore, after much bickering and arguing, the blind men fail to reach a consensus on exactly what an elephant is. Similarly, although scientists, particularly psychologists, have developed several theories of motivation, they are often very different and deal with varying facets of the subject. We will now review some current theories of motivation which seem potentially useful in improving our understanding of volunteers. This initial discussion will be brief and definitional, since several of the theories are developed in detail in subsequent chapters.

SELECTED MOTIVATION THEORIES

Need Theories

Very early in the history of psychology it was believed that humans, as well as other animals, behaved in response to primary drives necessary for physiological survival; that is, humans are driven to respond to hunger, thirst, cold, heat, and so on. Later, it became evident that humans, in fact, are attracted to many outcomes which are unrelated to physical survival or well-being. Thus, the concept of need came into use. Simply put, the attraction potential an individual has for a given outcome can be expressed as a need. Numerous needs have been defined. For example, Murray (1938) was able to list and construct definitions for 49 separate needs, but was unable to say much about the relative importance of them. Maslow (1943, 1954) contributed a great deal to our understanding of needs by theorizing that needs are ordered in a hierarchy based on their relative strengths (prepotencies). The most prepotent needs must be largely (but not necessarily completely) satisfied before the less potent needs become aroused to the point of providing motive force. Maslow's hierarchy, in ascending order of importance, consists of five need categories: physiological, safety, social, esteem, and self-actualization. Although recent theorists (cf. Alderfer, 1969) have questioned the five-fold hierarchy and the exact nature of the prepotency hypothesis, the hierarchical concept of needs has received much attention among people interested in organizations. Need theories allow us to identify which need or needs may be most active for individuals and to specify outcomes (e.g., rewards) which may lead to need satisfaction or frustration.

Expectancy Theory

This theory, sometimes called instrumentality theory or valence-instrumentality-expectancy (V.I.E.) theory, is based on the premise that motivation is the result of (1) the strength of belief (expectation) that a specific outcome or outcomes will follow a given behavior, together with (2) the personal value (or valence) a person attaches to the outcome. Thus:

$$\text{MOTIVATION} = \text{EXPECTANCY} \times \text{VALENCE}$$

If, for example, a potential volunteer believes that there is a high probability that delivering meals to the elderly will lead to a more comfortable existence for many elderly persons and attaches great personal importance to this outcome, then we could anticipate that this volunteer would be strongly motivated to choose to volunteer with Meals on Wheels rather than seeking alternative uses of his or her time. On the other hand, if either the expectancy probability associated with achieving an outcome or the valence of the outcome itself is low, then the motivation to achieve that outcome over others will also be low.

This theory will be developed more fully in later chapters, but we can easily see its potential for understanding how beliefs, expectations, and values play important roles in determining whether volunteers will choose to participate in or reject various activities or assignments and in explaining or predicting the level and direction of effort which may be expended.

Goal Setting Theory

Earlier, in considering motivation as a process, we noted that an inner state of disequilibrium results in the setting of a goal, the achievement of which is expected to restore balance and psychic harmony. Edwin Locke (1969) has proposed a comprehensive theory of motivation in which people's conscious goals are the primary determinants of their actions. Thus, the type of goal or goals that are set have a primary influence on human behavior. Incentives of various types, such as monetary reward, advancement, formal recognition, reassignment to more interesting or challenging work, training, etc., have an impact on future behavior depending on how they affect the person's goals.

Research by Locke and his colleagues (Locke et al, 1981) has shown that goal setting is very important to job performance and that:

1) within limits, the more difficult the goal, the higher the level of performance achieved,
2) the more specific the goal, the more positive the effect on performance, and,
3) goal acceptance is positively related to performance toward the achievement of that goal.

Goal setting theory has been employed successfully in many organizations and appears to offer many implications for improving the performance of volunteers, particularly in settings where goals for volunteers have been left vague or ill-defined and where volunteers are not encouraged to engage in the goal-setting process.

Reinforcement Theory

In contrast to need theory, expectancy theory, and goal setting theory where the focus of attention is on the thought (cognitive) processes of individuals, reinforcement theory directs our attention to the processes of learning and/or the ways rewards and punishments influence behavior. Simply put, any behavior which results in pleasant consequences (positive reinforcement) is more likely to be repeated. Behavior which results in unpleasant consequences (punishment) is less likely to be repeated. B. F. Skinner (1969), the most well-known proponent of reinforcement theory, emphasizes the importance of structuring work environments in order to provide a reinforcing stimulus when a job is well done. For example, the volunteer program director, using this approach, might verbally praise a new volunteer who has performed some function in a correct manner, thus raising the likelihood that the volunteer would repeat the performance.

While the logic of reinforcement theory is quite simple, its application can be quite complex. The timing and scheduling of rewards are crucial to the overall application of the process. Actual rewards available for use as reinforcers may be limited in volunteer settings. Finally, the approach requires conscious effort on the part of an administrator to control, manipulate, and shape the work environment in order to produce desired outcomes. Ethical issues regarding human freedom are important considerations in employing any motivation technique or approach designed to influence the behavior of people in organizations.

In sum, the four motivation theories briefly mentioned here are the major ones which the chapter authors in this book draw upon, but many other theories about motivation and rewards exist in various forms in the current literature in the fields of sociology, economics, psychology, anthropology, and political science.

RATIONALE AND ORGANIZATION

This book consists of two parts. The first part contains invited chapter contributions from a number of authors well-known in the fields of motivation and/or voluntarism.

Chapter 2, by Vicki Schram, focuses on the challenge of motivating volunteers to participate. Schram reviews a number of reasons suggested by various motivation theories, then she examines the results of three national surveys before developing implications for practitioners and for further research.

Having attracted volunteers into a program, how can their needs be satisfied? How can need frustration be avoided? In Chapter 3, Craig Pinder develops in detail the need theory of motivation and provides a serious look at possible sources of need frustration in volunteer settings.

Chapter 4, also by Craig Pinder, explores the role of

beliefs, expectations, and values and their interlocking effect on the choice process and the performance of volunteers. Use of the expectancy model of motivation is demonstrated with an example drawn from a volunteer environment well known to us. Several excellent suggestions growing out of the model are provided.

Ivan Scheier, in Chapter 5, describes certain methods of improving volunteer motivation through the way in which work is designed. The significance of these methods is in defining broad alternatives in job design which may be useful in volunteer organizations.

Motivation and goal setting is treated by Ronald Burke and Lary Lindsay in Chapter 6. The extensive research of Locke and others furnishes the theoretical base of this chapter which provides a number of excellent operational guidelines for improving the personal goal setting practices of volunteers in order to provide personal challenge and direction. The importance of personal commitment to program goals is stressed.

Chapter 7, by Eva Schindler-Rainman, discusses ways in which the competence of volunteers can be enhanced so that they give better service and continue to feel highly motivated.

Finally, in Chapter 8, Valerie Ahwee examines a number of important societal trends and changes which are likely to have considerable significance for the motivation of volunteers over the next several years. The chapter suggests many challenges for those of us seeking personal satisfaction through our efforts in the voluntary sector and for volunteer coordinators and administrators charged with enhancing the performance of their people.

Part Two of the book is a series of papers selected by a review panel in response to a call for papers sent out in the spring of 1982. Most of these papers report results of research which has recently been conducted on various aspects of the motivation of volunteers. An attempt has been made to sequence the papers so that there is some relation to the chapter organization in Part One. Unfortunately, some large gaps in topic coverage are quite noticeable. Thus, we may quickly conclude that much research work remains to be done in the area of volunteer motivation — providing many challenges for researchers and practitioners alike.

REFERENCES

Alderfer, Clayton P.
1969 "An Empirical Test of a New Theory of Human Needs," *Organizational Behavior and Human Performance* 4: 142-175.

Campbell, John P. and Robert D. Pritchard
1976 "Motivation Theory in Industrial and Organizational Psychology," in M. D. Dunnette, ed. *Handbook of Industrial and Organizational Psychology*. Chicago: Rand-McNally.

Lawler, Edward E., III
1973 *Motivation in Work Organizations*. Monterey, CA: Brooks/ Cole.

Locke, Edwin
1969 "What is Job Satisfaction?" *Organizational Behavior and Human Performance* 4: 309-336.

Locke, Edwin, K. N. Shaw, L. M. Saari, and G. P. Lathan
1981 "Goal Setting and Task Performance: 1969-1980," *Psychological Bulletin* 90: 125-152.

Maslow, Abraham H.
1943 "A Theory of Human Motivation," *Psychological Review* 50: 370-396.
1954 *Motivation and Personality*. New York: Harper.

Murray, Henry A.
1938 *Explorations in Personality*. New York: Oxford University Press.

Pinder, C. Craig
1984 *Work Motivation: Theory, Issues and Aplications*. Glenview, IL: Scott Foresman.

Skinner, Benjamin F.
1969 *Contingencies of Reinforcement*. New York: Appleton-Century-Crofts.

Smith, David Horton
1981 "Altruism, Volunteers, and Volunteerism," *Journal of Voluntary Action Research* 10 (1): 21-36.

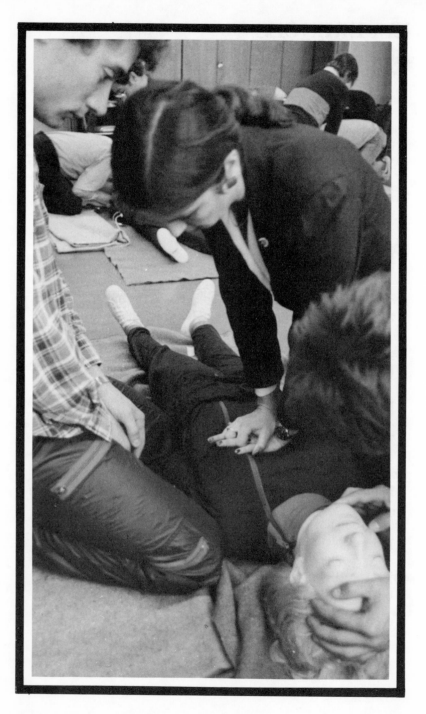

Chapter 2

MOTIVATING VOLUNTEERS TO PARTICIPATE

Vicki R. Schram

Motivating volunteers to participate in volunteer work is especially challenging in today's world. The demand for volunteers has been growing, especially in the United States. As the federal government has relinquished some of its human service activities, voluntary associations have helped to fill the void. With the expansion of clientele, their need for volunteers has increased as well. Meanwhile, the availability of people for volunteer work has been changing. Traditionally, women have been the largest group of volunteers. With many more of them in the labor force, their time for volunteer work is much more limited than in the past. While the pool of available women has been shrinking, the number of elderly available for volunteer work has increased. Their time is much less constrained than working women, but their physical ability for volunteer work can be somewhat limited. Also, their motivations to participate are different. Other segments of the population, too, are possible volunteers and may not have participated much in the past. Thus, volunteer administrators and others working with volunteers are faced with a demand for more volunteers and a changing supply of volunteers with motivations that could be quite different from those of the volunteer of the past.

The crucial question in volunteer motivation is why people volunteer in the first place. A related question is what motivates them to continue to volunteer. In this chapter, discussion of motivation will be concerned with both types of motivation, but primary emphasis will be on the motivation to participate in volunteer work. The chapter is organized with a discussion of theoretical frameworks useful in explaining motivation to participate. Following this discussion is a review of national survey data to examine what reasons people give for volunteering and how these empirical findings relate to volunteer motivation theories. Based on these theories and data analyses, practical applications are suggested in the final section.

WHY PEOPLE VOLUNTEER — SUGGESTIONS FROM THEORY

Motivation, that is, energizing and sustaining behavior, can be studied from a variety of theoretical perspectives. In any event, Lawler (1973) indicates that the primary task of any motivation theory is "to explain the voluntary choices people make among different behaviors" (Lawler, 1973: 5). Understanding the goals that people have and how they feel about these goals is imperative as a first step. Several theoretical frameworks follow which can help in this understanding.

Altruism

Altruism has long been thought to be the major reason for participating in volunteer work. Smith (1982), however, indicates that altruism may be one of the multiple reasons that a person volunteers and that altruism plays a minor role in why any one person volunteers.

The traditional view of altruism reflects unselfish behavior or sacrifice for others. Smith argues that this absolute altruism is rare, if it exists at all. Rather, altruism is relative. Further, persons who say they volunteer for altruistic reasons just do not admit that they have some sort of self-satisfying reason for volunteering. With this relative volunteerism in mind, Smith indicates that a definition for altruistic behavior applied to the volunteer might be that the individual volunteer gets satisfaction by attempting to enhance another person's satisfaction; at the same time, the volunteer does not consciously expect the other person to reciprocate. Thus, a person volunteering for altruistic reasons would be motivated to participate in volunteer work where other people can be helped in some way.

14

Utility Theory

With Smith's definition for altruistic behavior of the volunteer in mind, it might be argued that motivation in this sense is not altruistic but rather motivation due to utility maximization. Economists indicate that a person allocates his/her resources in such a way that optimum utility is obtained (Leftwich, 1970). That is, you get the most for what you spend, be it time, money, energy, etc. Thus, a person might spend an hour in volunteer work because that is where he/she gets the most utility or satisfaction for that particular hour.

Smith's definition is simply a specific application of this theory that says that the satisfaction is obtained by attempting to enhance another person's satisfaction. Utility theory is more general, however, in that satisfaction can be from a variety of sources, not just from enhancing another person's satisfaction. Further, the satisfaction obtained can be for one's own self or for one's family.

Unlike work in the market sector, an individual or family does not have to supply any volunteer work to receive benefits (i.e., utility) from the voluntary sector (Mueller, 1975). Rather, it is possible to be a "free rider"; for example, in a youth group, not all parents are involved in providing leadership or volunteer time. But, when the amount of available services is not enough, the family might be motivated to provide the services. Or, volunteer work might enhance the family's utility when a family member receives special favors because another member is a volunteer. For example, a child might be a "star" in a youth-group play when one of the parents is a leader of that group. Of course, specific costs and benefits vary by individual so which specific inducements would be motivators are difficult to identify.

Human Capital Theory

Human capital theory is a special form of utility theory with the return/cost relationship, in this instance, involving investments in human capital. Becker (1964: 1) defines human capital investments as those "activities that influence future monetary and psychic income by increasing resources in people." Examples of such investments are on-the-job training, schooling, medical care, migration, and searching for information about prices and income. According to Becker, these investments "improve skills, knowledge, or health, and thereby raise money or psychic incomes." Volunteer work can provide many of these human capital investments (Schram and Dunsing, 1981). Thus, people might be motivated to volunteer to obtain these.

On-the-job training and work experience are important human capital investments because they are known to increase wages. For those people who are not in the labor force, participation in volunteer work can help to build and/or maintain their job-related skills. Volunteer work can enhance job-related skills of others who are already employed in the labor force by giving them opportunities to learn new skills or to exercise abilities which their current jobs might not use.

Further, volunteer work can provide people with an opportunity to obtain information about the job market, especially information about different kinds of jobs and salaries. Volunteers frequently work with paid employees, and such contact could provide this information.

In addition to developing skills and knowledge applicable to the labor market, volunteer work can help to develop skills and knowledge useful in the home. Organizational skills learned in volunteer work, for example, could be transferred to the home and result in increased home productivity. Work areas and time might be better organized to provide more efficient meal preparation. Volunteers who are youth group leaders often are trained to work with children which ought to promote a more satisfying relationship with their children at home. Those who volunteer in hospitals would have access to health care information which could increase their capabilities of providing nursing care for family members who are ill.

Volunteer work could enable people to acquire wider knowledge about community resources and thus increase their levels of living. Information about prices charged, for example, would enable them to buy from the cheapest source and raise their command over their resources. Information about the political system would increase knowledge about the effect of different political philosophies. This type of knowledge could effectively raise real incomes and provide a motivation for participating in volunteer work. Indeed, any type of identifiable skill or knowledge that the volunteer can get from participation can serve as a motivator.

Exchange Theory

Derived from economics and behavioristic psychology, exchange theory (Homans, 1974; Thibaut and Kelley, 1959) is similar to utility theory in that consideration of costs and benefits of one's activities is assumed. The benefits are referred to as rewards. However, unlike utility theory which indicates that resources, including time, will be allocated so that benefits will equal costs for maximum return, exchange theory posits that activities will be chosen where rewards are greater than costs. Thus, behavior is profit-motivated. This profit can be either monetary or non-monetary in nature.

Whether the individual could be induced to volunteer would depend on whether the organization offered the appropriate reward for the individual volunteer as well as the value of the perceived rewards and costs to the individual. Rewards could be a variety of things while costs are primarily time, energy, and out-of-pocket expenses. It becomes quite difficult to recruit volunteers on an exchange basis since rewards and costs vary by individual, but rewards can be motivators for participation and costs can inhibit participation.

Expectancy Theory

Like utility, human capital, and exchange theories, expectancy theory (Lawler, 1973) is based on some type of return. In this instance, the emphasis is on forward-looking beliefs about what will happen as a result of one's actions. In volunteer work, people have expectations about satisfactions they will get from the work, types of interactions they will have with others, their contribution to the organization and community, the work environment, etc. Motivation is influenced not only by the expectations they have but also by the probability they feel that the expectations will be met.

Need Fulfillment

Maslow (1943) indicates that each of us has various needs arranged in levels resembling a pyramid and that fulfillment of these needs motivates behavior. Once a need is met, it is no longer a motivator, and the individual is motivated by the next higher need. These needs in ascending order are: (1) physiological needs: need for food, water, shelter, etc.; (2) safety needs: a need to be safe from harm or to have security; (3) social needs: need for love, acceptance and friendship; (4) self-esteem needs: need for self-respect and respect from others; and (5) self-actualization needs: need to fulfill one's potential; being all that one can be. Fulfillment of the needs suggested by Maslow can be obtained in volunteer work, thus becoming motivators for volunteer work.

Socialization

Throughout the life cycle, individual behavior is socialized by family and peers. Initially, socialization occurs when parents and peers transmit their values to children and, thus, shape the child's behavior.

Although childhood and adolescence are the stages when socialization takes place to the greatest extent, socialization continues into adulthood and usually occurs through organizations such as employment, school, and voluntary associations. It is possible that people are socialized for volunteer work; that is, they come to believe that it is part of their role to participate in volunteer work or that it is their duty to volunteer.

Socialization for volunteer work can occur during childhood and adolescence (Whiren and Schram, 1983). Parents who participate in volunteer work provide a model for their children. That activity becomes part of the adult role to which the child aspires. We know, too, that children are influenced by their peers. Thus, to the extent peers volunteer, so will the children. Since volunteerism has long been a part of American life, it seems logical to assume that socialization can be credited for this continuing phenomenon.

If the adult was not socialized for volunteer work as a child, adult socialization is possible. In either type of socialization, the motivation stems from attitudes and beliefs acquired by the individual rather than what the volunteer work can give to an individual.

Summary

There are several theoretical frameworks which can help us to understand motivations people have for participating in volunteer work. In actuality, the combination of these might be the best predictor. Additionally, there may be other theoretical frameworks just as appropriate as the ones presented here. However, the limited space does not allow an exhaustive review, and the ones chosen help to examine the data used. In the next section, the reasons people themselves give for their participation will be examined to determine some of the validity of the frameworks presented here.

WHY PEOPLE VOLUNTEER — SURVEY RESULTS

National surveys of volunteers were conducted in the United States in 1965, 1974, and 1981. These surveys investigated the amount and type of volunteer work done by volunteers, characteristics of volunteers, and reasons for participating in volunteer work. Since these were national surveys, they give the broadest possible picture of the American volunteer. Also, comparisons over time are more easily made with these surveys than with other studies. Reasons that volunteers indicate for participating and continuing to participate in volunteer work in these three surveys will be compared. First, to enhance interpretation of the results, a brief discussion of the methodologies used will be given.

In 1965, the Bureau of the Census conducted a national survey on volunteer work for the Bureau of Labor Statistics (U.S. Department of Labor, 1969). The sample of respondents consisted of almost 9,800 individuals from 4,000 households. These 4,000 households were drawn from the 17,500 households who participated in the monthly labor survey conducted by the Bureau of the Census. Questionnaires were completed by those household members present at the time of the interview. Questionnaires for absent household members were left to be completed. The response rate for the survey was almost 96%. Estimates of volunteer work for the civilian non-institutional population of the United States were determined. This survey examined organized volunteer services; individual volunteer effort was excluded.

A sequel to the Bureau of Labor Statistics survey was conducted by the Census Bureau in 1974 (ACTION, 1975). Of these people participating in the April 1974 Current Population Survey, 24,795 received the volunteer survey. The number of valid interviews obtained was 23,731. As in the earlier study, estimates for the civilian non-institutional population were determined. Volunteer work was defined as "any unpaid work performed for or through an organization."

The third national survey was conducted by the Gallup Organization in 1981 (Independent Sector, 1981). It had a broader definition of volunteer work; that is, "working in some way to help others for no monetary pay." Personal, in-home interviews were conducted with the youngest man aged 18 years or older in each household. If no man was home meeting this criterion, the oldest woman aged 18 years or older was interviewed. This method was used to approximate the age distribution in the population. The number of respondents was 1,601. As in the other two national surveys, all respondents were aged 14 years or older.

Reasons for participating or for continuing to participate in volunteer work were solicited in slightly different ways in the three surveys which might influence results obtained. Thus, results should be interpreted with caution.

In the 1965 survey the respondent was asked the question, "What are your main reasons for doing unpaid volunteer work?" In reporting the results, the responses were categorized by others who may have had a different interpretation of the answer than the respondent intended. This can be a problem when using the open-ended type of question. Further, the names given to the categories may not be very meaningful in understanding volunteer motivations.

In the 1974 and 1981 surveys, the respondents were given several reasons for volunteering and asked to indicate which ones were their reasons for volunteering. In this instance, by answering from a list of possible reasons, some respondents might have been "led" to select an answer which they otherwise might not have given or they might not have volunteered a reason which did not appear on the list. Reasons for continuing to volunteer were handled in the same closed-ended manner.

In all three surveys, more than one reason for volunteering or continuing to volunteer could be given. Given the total responses, many people gave more than one reason. Further, these surveys did not ask for the most important reason for volunteering or for a ranking of the reasons for volunteering. Thus, no conclusions about which motivations are most important can be drawn.

Participation in Volunteer Work

Volunteer work participation rates varied in the three surveys. During 1965, 16.1 percent of all the civilian, non-institutional population participated in volunteer work. This increased to 26% in 1974. Volunteer work participation was highest in 1981 with 52% of American adults volunteering. Some of the increase since 1974 can be explained by the much broader definition for volunteer work that was used. Also this may explain some of the differences in reasons for doing volunteer work in the latter two surveys.

Reasons for doing volunteer work given by the respondents in the three national surveys are in Table 1. In 1965, slightly more than 35% indicated that they volunteered "to help people" while slightly more than 30% volunteered because of a "sense of duty" and because they "enjoy doing volunteer work." Less than 10% of the respondents indicated any of the other reasons. In 1974, additional reasons for volunteering were given; however, the same three categories had the most responses but with slightly different percents of respondents indicating these reasons than before. In the 1981 survey, "sense of duty" was not one of the choices given respondents. Of the two remaining reasons reported most frequently in the earlier surveys, 45% indicated that they volunteered "to help people" while slightly less than 30% "enjoy doing volunteer work." One response not measured in the earlier surveys was "had interest in activity or work," and 35% of the respondents gave this as a reason for doing volunteer work. Thus, reasons for volunteering do not seem to have changed that much over time. Some variations might be due to the slightly different ways of asking questions and categorizing responses in each survey. As indicated earlier, definition of volunteer work could be influential as well.

Two categories in Table 1 might be indicators of altruistic reasons for participating in volunteer work. These are "to help people" and "sense of duty." In both instances, the reasons seem to indicate participation with no expectation of return. The two reasons were the most frequently given reasons in 1965 and 1974. "To help people" was the most frequent response in 1981. Slightly more than 20% said they volunteered for "religious concerns" in the 1981 survey, but this response was not reported in either of the other surveys. This, too, could be interpreted as participation with no expectation that the other party will reciprocate similarly. If these three categories do represent altruistic behavior, then altruism is one of the motivators for a large proportion of volunteers. However, there is always the possibility that respondents give reasons which are "socially acceptable," and altruistic reasons for volunteering might fall in this area.

The three national volunteer surveys included a large percent of people who volunteered for reasons that could indicate utility maximization. Thirty-one percent of the respondents in 1965, 36% in 1974, and 29% in 1981 participated because they "enjoy doing volunteer work" which seems to be a good indication of satisfaction obtained. Further, 22% participated in 1974 because they "had a child in the program" and 23% in 1981 because they "had a child, relative, or friend who was involved in the activity or would benefit from it." This is an indicator of family utility maximization suggested by Mueller (1975). The latter category seems to indicate that utility is enhanced further by the participation of more family members. Another utility-maximization indicator is the response, "thought my volunteer work would help keep taxes or other costs down" (5%). Here the utility maximization involves a trade-off between the volunteer time and an indirect return in the form of money savings. Still, overall utility is increased. A small percent of respondents in the 1974 and 1981 surveys volunteered because they "had nothing else to do." Obviously, the volunteer work had a higher utility value to them than other activities. Given this interpretation of the categories in Table 1, people seem to be motivated to volunteer in order to increase their individual or family utility. Alternatively, these same responses may flow from exchange theory if the time expenditure is profit-motivated. Whether utility maximization or profit motivation underlies the reasons given for volunteering is not clear.

Only a small percent of the respondents in any of the surveys indicated that they volunteered to increase their human capital. In the 1974 survey, slightly less than 5% hoped that the volunteer work would lead to a paid job while slightly more than 10% in 1981 gave reasons such as "wanted to learn and get experience; work experience; help get a job." It is possible that these results vary by age, sex, and education of the respondent. Those people who need human capital skill development might be women, young people, and those with less education. Thus, they might be more likely than other groups to report human capital development as a reason for volunteering. Too, opportunities for skill development in volunteer work may have increased over time so that many more volunteers are using volunteer work as a way of getting job and other skills. Certainly, these results seem to indicate that a few people, at least, are motivated by human capital investment possibilities.

TABLE 1

Reasons for Doing Volunteer Work[a]

Reasons for Volunteering	Percentage of Respondents		
	1965	1974	1981
To help people	37	53	45
Sense of duty	33	32	—[b]
Enjoy doing volunteer work	31	36	29[c]
Had interest in activity or work	—	—	35
Asked to volunteer; could not refuse when asked[d]	7	15	—
Had a child in program	—	22	23[e]
Hoped would lead to paid job	—	3	11
Had nothing else to do; had a lot of free time[f]	—	4	6
Religious concerns	—	—	21
Thought my volunteer work would help keep taxes or other costs down	—	—	5
Other	4	—	1
Don't recall	—	—	5

[a] Reasons are for any volunteer work in 1965 and in 1981. In 1974 reasons are first non-religious volunteer work ever done.
[b] -- indicates that this reason was not reported.
[c] Includes "feel needed."
[d] Reasons assumed to have same meaning though reported differently in the two years.
[e] Stated as "had a child, relative, or friend who was involved in the activity or would benefit from it."
[f] Similar meaning assumed.

Expectations individuals had about volunteer work were not measured in these surveys. The reasons given for participation could be assumed to represent expectations, however. All the reasons given would measure motivation then.

Some people seem to participate in volunteer work because of need fulfillment, though this is somewhat hard to determine from the way the reasons were recorded in the written reports. In the 1981 survey, "feel needed" was combined with "thought I would enjoy doing the work." Slightly less than 30% of the respondents indicated reasons falling in this combined category. It is questionable whether these two reasons can be combined into one category indicating need fulfillment. Those who indicated that they wanted to help people also could be fulfilling their need to feel needed as Maslow has identified. Though some may participate for need fulfillment reasons, the data are too limited to indicate the extent of this motivation.

Socialization for volunteer work also seems to be present as a motivator. This can be represented by such reasons as "sense of duty," "asked to volunteer," and "could not refuse when asked." "Sense of duty" had the largest percent of respondents reporting of any of these reasons, but only in the 1965 and 1974 surveys. If people continued to volunteer for this reason in 1981, they apparently indicated it in some other way since this was not one of the choices for respondents.

Based on these data, then, people seem to volunteer for a variety of reasons, some of which vary over time. To understand better the motivations of people, cross-tabulation of volunteer characteristics by reasons for participation in volunteer work is needed. The limited analysis here has served to indicate that a variety of theoretical frameworks is useful in helping to explain why people participate in volunteer work. In fact, people apparently are motivated by several factors simultaneously. In all probability these factors vary in importance. Continuation in Volunteer Work

Continuation in Volunteer Work

Of the theoretical frameworks discussed earlier, expectancy theory has the greatest potential to explain why people continue to volunteer. When rewards of volunteer work fail to match the expectations that the volunteer had initially, a discrepancy results.

The worker's motivation to continue in such a situation is lowered. Thus, to keep volunteer workers, the level and nature of the rewards should fit their expectations. Alternatively, their expectations could be altered to fit the volunteer job.

In the 1974 and 1981 national surveys, respondents were asked their reasons for continuing to do volunteer work during the year (see Table 2). Reasons given were the same as those given for participating initially. If the reasons given for participating initially

TABLE 2

Reasons for Continuing to do Volunteer Work During Current Year

Reasons for Continuing to Volunteer	Percent of Respondents	
	1974	1981
To help people	60	49
Sense of duty	38	—[a]
Enjoy doing volunteer work	49	28[b]
Am interested in the activity	—	35
Could not refuse when asked	11	—
Had a child in program; work helps child, relative or friend[c]	16	21
Hoped would lead to paid job; am getting job experience	2	6
Had nothing else to do; had a lot of free time[d]	2	5
Religious concerns	—	20
Work helps keep taxes or other costs down	—	4
Other	6	1
Don't know	—	9

[a] -- indicates that this reason was not reported.
[b] Includes "feeling needed."
[c] Similar meaning assumed.
[d] Similar meaning assumed.

are assumed to be expectations and reasons for continuing to volunteer to be received rewards, then expectancy theory is helpful in explaining motivation to continue volunteering. The percent of respondents giving each reason varied only slightly between the two surveys. Since the discrepancy between the responses was small, it can be assumed that expectations were met.

IMPLICATIONS FOR PRACTITIONERS AND RESEARCHERS

The foregoing theories and empirical data indicate some useful information for those working with volunteers. However, there remain unanswered questions about why volunteers participate.

A better way of assessing motivation would be helpful since the data reported here are somewhat limited. Rephrasing questions is one suggestion. An important contribution would be to test the theoretical frameworks in terms of their predictability in identifying potential volunteers and appropriate motivational strategies. Since different voluntary organizations utilize volunteers with varying characteristics and possibly differing motivations, this type of research would help them to develop recruiting strategies based on the motivations of their potential volunteers. Another possibility would be for voluntary organizations to survey their volunteers about their motivations for participation. Potential volunteers could then be offered inducements appropriate to their wishes and needs.

With the exception of those socialized for volunteer work, individuals seem to participate in anticipation of some sort of return. And, even those who volunteer out of a sense of duty probably have other self-serving reasons. Voluntary organizations offer several types of inducements which can serve as rewards or benefits to the volunteer. There could be increased potential rewards including opportunities to interact with others, to feel a part of an organization and the community, and to meet others; to accomplish something worthwhile, etc. Types of training that could be rewards include technical job skills, first-aid and related health skills, arts and crafts skills, and communication and management skills. Many organizations seek volunteers with these skills already. It might be useful to recruit trainable volunteers who desire these skills. A chance to get a needed skill might motivate someone to volunteer.

Care should be taken that the appropriate benefit is offered for the prospective volunteer. For example, if the organization uses primarily elderly volunteers, offering opportunities to develop job skills will not be much of a motivator for them. Emphasizing the opportunity for interaction with others would be more likely to motivate them. A carefully detailed set of questions when volunteers are interviewed for placement would help to identify individual motivations and enhance placement. Consideration of Maslow's hierarchy of needs can help in matching benefits and volunteers. If recruiting from low-income groups where lower needs are not always being met, the voluntary organization must help meet these needs. For example, volunteering in a soup kitchen could entitle the volunteer to a certain number of meals.

Maslow's hierarchy of needs is also important in retaining volunteers. As the volunteer job helps the individual to meet his/her lower-order needs, other needs become apparent. The volunteer job will need to be changed to help the individual meet these needs. Otherwise, they may be sought elsewhere. Also, the need fulfillment originally sought in volunteer work may be met outside the volunteer job which would indicate the necessity of modifying volunteer jobs occasionally to increase volunteer retention. In sum, Maslow's hierarchy indicates that a person's situation is not static; therefore, the volunteer should not be placed in a job and left there if retention is desired.

Most voluntary organizations have numerous returns for the volunteer, but the potential volunteer may be unaware of them. In fact, some volunteer administrators are not fully aware of them. It would be beneficial if the staff of the voluntary organization would brainstorm to identify potential benefits. Asking current volunteers to participate in this session would be useful. Next, the benefits need to be conveyed in recruiting volunteers. Here, a good public relations campaign is a must. This strategy has an additional benefit. By helping the individual become more aware of the available benefits, he/she can judge more accurately if the volunteer job matches his/her expectations. This, in turn, will enhance volunteer retention since the expected and received benefits will be more likely to match.

Utility and exchange theories encompass the idea of a cost to one's choice of activity. Such a cost could be a disincentive, thus inhibiting motivation to participate in volunteer work. To enhance recruitment and retention of volunteers, something can be done to reduce the known costs to volunteers. Since time is an important cost, volunteer jobs could be set up so that fewer hours could be spent. Also other activities compete for an individual's time so some way to merge volunteer work with those other activities would be useful. To meet other costs, day care could be provided, and transportation expenses reimbursed.

The voluntary organization also has costs in motivating volunteers. The organization should try to locate the most important motivators and use these to recruit and retain volunteers. As indicated earlier, it is important to find out the most important reason for participation as well as the individual's own ranking of the reasons for participation. This will help the organization to maximize use of its monetary resources. Such research could be conducted by the organization itself. Alternatively, future studies of volunteer work participation could easily incorporate this type of questioning into the survey instruments used.

Hopefully, this examination of motivation will stimulate much discussion and generation of ideas for motivating participation. The theoretical frameworks presented provide direction for motivation strategies and further research. Utilization of the motivational strategies discussed and other strategies devised by voluntary organizations should help to cope with the increasing demand for volunteers and the changing nature of volunteers.

REFERENCES

ACTION
   1975 *Americans Volunteer 1974*. (ACTION Pamphlet 4000-17) Washington, DC: U.S. Government Printing Office.
Becker, Gary S.
   1964 *Human Capital: A Theoretical and Empirical Analysis, With Special Reference to Education*. New York: Columbia University Press.

Homans, G. C.
　1974 *Social Behavior: Its Elementary Forms*. (rev. ed.) New York: Harcourt Brace Jovanovich.
Lawler, Edward E.
　1973 *Motivation in Work Organizations*. Monterey, CA: Brooks/Cole Publishing Co.
Leftwich, Richard H.
　1970 *The Price System and Resource Allocation*. (5th ed.) Hinsdale, IL: The Dryden Press.
Maslow, A. H.
　1943 "A Theory of Human Motivation," *Psychological Review* 50: 370-396.
Mueller, Marnie W.
　1975 "Economic Determinants of Volunteer Work by Women," *Signs: Journal of Women in Culture and Society* 1: 325-328.
Schram, Vicki R. and Marilyn M. Dunsing
　1981 "Influences on Married Women's Volunteer Work Participation," *Journal of Consumer Research* 7: 372-379.
Smith, David Horton
　1982 "Altruism, Volunteers, and Volunteerism," in John D. Harman, ed. *Volunteerism in the Eighties: Fundamental Issues in Voluntary Action*. Washington, DC: University Press of America.
Thibaut, J. W. and H. H. Kelley
　1959 *The Social Psychology of Groups*. New York: John Wiley.
U.S. Department of Labor, Manpower Administration
　1969 *Americans Volunteer*. (Manpower/Automation Research Monograph No. 10) Washington, DC: U.S. Government Printing Office.
Whiren, Alice, and Vicki R. Schram
　1983 "Family Socialization for Volunteer Work." Paper presented at the Annual Meeting of the American Home Economics Association, Milwaukee, WI.

Chapter 3

NEEDS, COGNITIVE FACTORS, AND THE MOTIVATION TO VOLUNTEER

Craig C. Pinder

Mary Snow, a 45-year-old housewife who does volunteer work for a disease-related society in Vancouver, B.C, summarizes her feelings about her work this way: "I'm having a ball!" In fact, Mary — who has worked for twenty years for this society in a number of voluntary roles — is now the coordinator of more than thirty other volunteers, most of whom are women who quietly and reliably work two or three days a week performing clerical tasks. Mary is aware of the fact that most volunteer coordinators working for other similar agencies in the city are paid for their time, but she cheerfully continues to organize the staffing of the many behind-the-scene jobs that keep the society functioning. When she is asked why she spends her time in this capacity, particularly without concern for remuneration, Mary smiles and says things such as, "Well, I don't know ... it gives me something to do, I suppose ... I'm not really sure why. I just seem to enjoy helping out." In fact, Mary has given little thought to why she serves as a volunteer coordinator, or to *why* she enjoys her work so much.

The question of what motivates people to volunteer their time and effort to work for health care agencies and other types of voluntary organizations is a complex one, probably much more complex than the question of why people work for pay. Moreover, although it has been the focus of a few empirical investigations (e.g., Anderson and Moore, 1978; Briggs, 1982; Pearce, 1983) and some conceptual analysis (e.g., Smith, 1981; Vroom, 1964), the question of what "motivates" voluntary work activity has received considerably far less attention from behavioral scientists than has the issue of work motivated by pay and other forms of remuneration. The papers in this volume seek to redress this disparity somewhat, and the purpose of this chapter is to explore, on a conceptual level, the issue of volunteer work from the perspectives of one of today's most popular current approaches to understanding work motivation — the theory of human needs.

The chapter will consist of two parts. In Part One, we will examine the nature of human needs, both in general terms as well as in terms that reveal how they may be related to voluntary work behavior. Then, in Part Two, we will discuss frustration - the situation in which goal-oriented behavior that is initiated by needs is blocked, preventing the individual from behaving in ways that have led to need satisfaction in the past. The major implications of the analysis for the particular problem of managing a volunteer workforce will be presented as the discussion proceeds. To begin, let's take a look at the nature of human needs.

PART ONE: NEEDS AND MOTIVATION

Over the years, psychologists have explored the role of a variety of different factors in the origin and direction of human behavior. Two of these types of factors, instincts and drives, attracted considerable attention during the early years of this century, but, for a variety of reasons, are less important in current theory and research. A discussion of the history associated with the rise and fall of instincts and drives in thinking about human motivation is beyond the purpose of this chapter; the interested reader is referred to thorough treatments by Atkinson (1964) and Cofer and Appley (1964). Instead, we will focus here on human needs, since they have played a major role in modern thought about the origins of behavior, particularly work behavior.

THE NATURE OF NEEDS

But what are needs? The term "need" is used frequently in everyday parlance to refer to people's desires, aspirations, yearnings, goals, and values. Generally, when someone says, "I need a new car," we understand what he means. But to a psychologist the term has a particular meaning, one that is more precise than any of the others just noted. In this chapter, we will adopt the definition of human needs first advanced by Henry Murray (1938: 123-124). According to Murray, a need is:

> ... a construct (a convenient fiction or hypothetical concept) which stands for a force ... in the brain region, a force which organizes perception, aperception, intellection, conation and action in such a way as to transform in a certain direction an existing, unsatisfying situation. A need is sometimes provoked directly by internal processes of a certain kind ... but, more frequently (when in a state of readiness) by the occurrence of one of a few commonly effective press (or features of the environment) ... Thus, it manifests itself by leading the organism to search for or to avoid encountering, or when encountered, to attend to and respond to certain kinds of press.... Each need is characteristically accompanied by a particular feeling or emotion and tends to use certain modes ... to further its trend. It may be weak or intense, momentary or enduring. But usually it persists and gives rise to a certain course of overt behavior (or fantasy) which ... changes the initiating circumstances in such a way as to bring about an end situation which stills (appeases or satisfies) the organism.

The length and complexity of this definition requires that we examine a number of its features. First, needs are hypothetical entities, not physical in nature; we cannot speak of their mass, shape, or color, and we cannot observe them directly. Instead, we must infer the existence of particular needs by observing the behavior of people who we believe possess them. In practice, this inference process can be tricky.

A second aspect of this definition - one that is of particular interest in connection with the question of the motivation of volunteers — is that needs can be induced by features of the environment. The term "environment" refers here to the context(s) within which behavior occurs, and the point is that certain facets of these contexts (such as, for example, the opportunities they provide for affiliation, growth, or the exercise of power) may activate or arouse needs which otherwise are not operative.

Another feature of the definition is that it helps us understand both approach behaviors and avoidance behaviors; that is, why some things attract a person whereas others may repel him.

A fourth important feature of the definition is that needs can be either strong or weak, and either momentary or enduring. This means that different people are motivated to respond to satisfy different needs, at different times and in different circumstances. In fact, although there is a finite number of needs which may account for most goal-oriented acts, there are nearly an infinite number of ways these needs combine and interact to arouse and direct the behaviors of different people. Moreover, the needs that account for the behaviors of a particular person at one point in time may not be as important as other needs for that same person at other times. So, for example, one set of needs may be responsible for causing a person to investigate the possibility of working on a voluntary basis for a political party, while another set of needs may increase in importance after the individual has started to work for the party and becomes more familiar and more proficient in her new role (cf. Katz, 1980). The point is that individual differences abound in the comparative importance of various needs, differences both between people as well as within given individuals over time. Further, although goal attainment usually leads to a reduction in the comparative importance of many needs in accounting for behavior, there are certain needs — especially some that appear to be involved in voluntary work behavior — that often increase in comparative importance once their satisfaction has been attained. For example, we will discuss the need for self-actualization in a later section of this chapter; it is one need that is believed to increase in importance the more people are successful in attaining the things that satisfy it.

A related feature of the definition that is of importance to us here is that needs give rise to behavior and/or fantasy. This feature has several implications. One is that there is no simple one-to-one correspondence between needs and behaviors. Therefore, the same need may instigate one type of behavior in one individual and a totally different type of behavior in another individual. Thus a woman with a strong need for achievement may seek to satisfy it through improving the performance of her work at her job while another woman, for any of a variety of reasons, may attempt to satisfy the same need by perfecting her squash game or organizing a fund-raising group for a local charity. Moreover, the lack of simple correspondence between needs and behaviors implies that many (or most) behaviors are driven by more than one need, and voluntary work behavior is no exception (Smith, 1981: 25). For example, the woman who elects either to play squash and/or raise funds for charity may simultaneously satisfy her social needs and even her need for power (if she has one) by engaging in either of these activities. In short, the same voluntary activity may satisfy different needs for different people who do it, whereas even if they are heavily motivated by a common basic need, two prospective volunteer workers may seek out and prefer different types of voluntary (or non-voluntary) activity.

Where does fantasy fit into this? People's abilities, interests and occupations often limit their capacity to meet certain of their needs through behavior, so fantasy often serves instead of action. Needs for power and sex are two specific examples of needs frequently served by fantasy, but we often find human needs for esteem, social interaction, and even self-actualization also frequently serviced by fantasy when the objective circumstances of a person's life (such as his or her job) make satisfaction of them through behavior difficult. The importance of the role of fantasy in need satisfaction for a discussion of voluntary work behavior is that participation in such activity can provide a *behavioral* outlet for powerful human needs that otherwise have been frustrated and/or satisfied primarily through fantasy.

Needs and Values

Before we turn to an examination of a number of specific needs, two other general points must be addressed. First, distinctions must be made between the concepts of need on the one hand and both goals and values on the other.

Let's consider needs and goals. As defined above, needs are inherent characteristics of individuals, whereas goals are end-states or objectives people pursue for the sake of meeting their needs. The distinction is more than a matter of semantics. To say that a person "needs to get ahead in life" or that she "needs constant attention" is incorrect, strictly speaking. Getting ahead is a *goal* that some people pursue for the sake of impressing others (thereby serving a need for esteem), whereas it is a goal that may or may not satisfy the need for self-esteem among other individuals. Likewise, "constant attention" is a goal that may serve the need for succor among some who seek it or the need for competence (to be discussed later in this chapter) among others.

What is the difference between needs and values? Again, needs are inherent characteristics of people that arouse and direct their behavior. Needs must be met (to a certain extent) in order for an individual to become or remain healthy. Alternatively, values are things (such as goals or commodities) that people believe will contribute to their welfare. A person may value a new stereo, but probably not actually need it. The point is that needs are not necessarily conscious, so they can instigate and direct human behavior without our awareness, making it difficult to determine precisely what needs "motivate" someone (or ourselves). If you ask a person what motivates him (to do volunteer work, for example), the answers received usually reflect goals and/or values; they rarely reflect an accurate view of the fundamental *need* profiles that can explain why different goals increase and/or decrease in value for the individual over time (cf. Smith, 1981: 25). Nevertheless, the things a person values are naturally influenced heavily by the nature of her needs, so that, in practice, both needs and values play a role in arousing and directing behavior (cf. Locke, 1976). Other characteristics of goals and goal setting will be discussed in Chapter 6 of this volume.

Need Satisfaction

A second general point concerns the nature of need satisfaction. Whereas we tend to think of satisfaction as the state that exists after the force associated with a need has been reduced (such as the pleasurable feeling one has after a restful sleep), the satisfaction of some needs consist, in part at least, of the experience associated with *removing* the need's tension. Thus many people derive satisfaction from acts such as falling asleep (as opposed to having slept), eating (as opposed to having eaten), and interacting with others (rather than having interacted). Moreover, to the extent that satisfaction comes from the process of reducing need-related tension, it follows that greater satisfaction results from reducing greater degrees of tension. Therefore, people are motivated to increase the force associated with their needs to a point which is sufficiently high so as to maximize the pleasure they will derive in the process of reducing it. Sexual foreplay and the common practice of eating lightly in anticipation of a feast are two physiological examples of how people strive to increase need tension levels so that greater pleasure results from the process of relieving their tension. We will see shortly that similar phenomena of increasing and reducing psychological stimulation are involved in the satisfaction of other, non-physiological needs.

In short, although the concept of needs is comparatively simple and widely understood by "the man on the street," the scientific meaning of the concept is much more complex and precise. Reliance on loose interpretations of this term, or of any terminology, makes our understanding of complex processes much more difficult than is necessary (Pinder and Bourgeois, 1983). In fact, one writer (Smith, 1981) has argued that sloppy conceptual and definitional work has impeded research into the very question of concern to us here: the motivation of volunteers. Accordingly, an appreciation of voluntary work behavior from the perspective of current theory and research in organizational psychology requires a careful understanding of the scientific meaning of needs and judicious use of the term. Therefore, all of the nuances in the foregoing discussion will be implied in subsequent reference to needs throughout the rest of this chapter.[1]

TYPES OF NEEDS

There have been a variety of attempts over the years to identify and list the most important human needs. Some theorists, such as Murray (1938), have generated lists containing as many as twenty or more such needs, while others, such as Maslow (1954) and Alderfer (1972), have proposed theories that feature fewer needs than found in Murray's lists but that also suggest that certain needs are more prepotent (more basic and urgent) than others. A complete description of these "hierarchical" theories can be found elsewhere in this volume, so only a limited treatment is necessary here.

---

[1] *Before we proceed, it should be noted that not all schools of thought in psychology and organizational behavior recognize needs or refer to them for the sake of understanding behavior. Nevertheless, since so much theory and research to date have focussed on the nature of needs and on their role in work behavior, this chapter adopts a need-oriented perspective. Alternative perspectives and the controversies associated with them are presented elsewhere (e.g., Pinder, 1984).*

Existence and Relatedness Needs: Extrinsic Motivation

As discussed by Maslow (1943, 1954) and others, human behavior is a consequence of the force associated with a number of innate and learned needs. Behavior instigated by these needs is intended to nourish, protect, and generally provide for the continued existence, health, and adjustment of the individual.

Existence Needs. Some of these have been referred to as "existence" needs by Alderfer (1972): these needs are responsible for the pursuit of food, water, sleep, sex, warmth, and safety. They are largely biological and/or physiological in nature and, for the most part, are not necessarily acquired through maturation. The goals or outcomes sought to satisfy existence needs are generally tangible (such as food and water) and zero-sum in nature, such that the more of them that are attained by one person, the less of them there are available for others. Most important, however, is that existence needs are more prepotent than other needs; that is, since they are the most fundamental for the ongoing survival of the person, their fulfillment is more urgent than is the fulfillment of other needs. The adjective "extrinsic" is often applied to motivated energy associated with existence needs because that energy is directed toward the acquisition of goods, commodities, possessions, and resources external to the person; these extrinsic "outcomes" are instrumental for meeting these needs.

Do existence needs manifest themselves in voluntary work activity? On the surface (and almost by traditional definition), it would appear that existence needs have little to do with voluntarism. On the other hand, a recent study of voluntary action in Canada reveals that a significant proportion of volunteer workers openly admit that non-altruistic goals account for many of their reasons for volunteering, and that existence needs can clearly be served by such "selfish" intentions (see the Report of the National Advisory Council on Voluntary Action, 1977).

For example, many young people engage in volunteer work as a means of gaining insight into prospective occupations and careers. Thus, a young woman may volunteer to visit with old and chronically disabled persons to help her determine whether she is suited for a career in medicine or clinical psychology. Likewise, a man who volunteers to assist in the management or administration of his trade union is motivated, at least in part, by a concern for meeting his long-term existence needs. Finally (although this list is far from exhaustive), the housewife who performs voluntary work for a social service agency as a way of "simply getting out of the house" is driven in large measure by a concern for her own mental health. The point is that a careful second look at voluntary work activity reveals that it holds the potential — at least for certain people engaging in certain specific types of work for particular types of voluntary organizations (Smith, 1972) — to contribute to the fulfillment of important existence needs, even though, on balance, other categories of human needs may be at least as or more important. Remember — most intentional human behavior serves more than single needs, one at a time.

Relatedness Needs. A second category of needs associated with extrinsic motivation are the so-called "relatedness" needs (Alderfer, 1972). These needs are concerned with the social side of human behavior. They instigate gregariousness and affiliation, and account for much of the human tendency to seek out and interact with other people. Therefore, the goals pursued to satisfy these needs are not zero-sum in nature; rather, increased social interaction by one person will raise the net level experienced by others. Nevertheless, there is still a dependency on sources outside the individual for relatedness needs to be satisfied, so in this sense they are often viewed as sources of "extrinsic" motivation.

Quite clearly, the desire to satisfy relatedness needs accounts for a certain amount of voluntary activity, although the relative importance of these needs in voluntarism vis-a-vis other needs seems to vary from one person to another. For example, the goals of companionship and meeting other people were ranked in seventh and tenth place, respectively, among ten of the most commonly cited reasons for voluntarism in one large study (Anderson and Moore, 1978). Other goals, such as "to help others," "to feel useful and needed," and "self-fulfillment" were mentioned far more frequently as explanations for why the people in that study engaged in voluntary work activity. However, it is important to reiterate that most behavior is determined by the force of more than one need, so that even if interacting with other people is not the primary incentive for a person to serve in a volunteer job, it may be one of many outcomes that such work serves.

Finally, it is important to remember the possibility that social interaction may either increase or decrease in importance over time as an explanation for a person's voluntary work activity, depending upon the length of time he has been engaged in that activity, the amount of affiliation he gains or loses elsewhere in his lifespace, and the emergence and decline of other consequences of his voluntarism. For example, Katz (1980) has shown that relatedness needs can be primary motivators during the early stages of a person's tenure in a work role, then diminish in comparative importance as the person proceeds to grow into and master the role. The same process likely occurs in the context of voluntary work behavior.

Growth Needs and Intrinsic Motivation

In contrast to extrinsic motivation, *intrinsic motivation* is reflected in effort which constitutes its own rewards. In simple terms, it is reflected in behavior that is activity for its own sake, rather than for the sake of attaining or avoiding some external consequence. But because recent research and theory has provided more and better understanding of the essence of intrinsic motivation than is reflected in this simplistic definition, and because of its importance in voluntary work behavior, we turn now toward a more careful answer to the question: what is intrinsic motivation?

According to Edward Deci (1975), a psychologist who has devoted most of his career to the topic, there are at least three ways of conceptualizing intrinsic motivation. Although each of these three approaches relies on a different set of assumptions regarding the essence of human nature (cf. Pinder, 1984; Walter and Marks, 1981), they are consistent with one another and collectively provide a coherent understanding of the phenomenon.

One approach to intrinsic motivation posits that human beings seek preferred or "optimal" levels of arousal. Arousal consists of stimulation of the brain and central nervous system by the individual's environment. If the level of stimulation a person experiences at a particular time deviates too much from his preferred level, the person is motivated either to increase it (if it is too low) or reduce it (if it is too high), bringing the amount experienced into line with the preferred level. From this perspective, intrinsically motivated behavior is behavior that is intended to increase or decrease the level of physiological stimulation the individual experiences.

A second conceptualization of intrinsic motivation holds that people desire and behave to attain an optimum degree of uncertainty or "incongruity" among their thoughts, beliefs, values, perceptions, and behaviors. The idea is that people differ in the degree to which they can tolerate inconsistencies, exceptions to general rules, and logical contradictions: some people are uncomfortable unless everything "adds up" or "makes sense," while other people seem to prefer varying levels of inconsistency. Under this view, motivated behavior is that which is designed either to increase or reduce the level of psychological consistency in the individual's mind, such that it is in line with whatever level the person desires and prefers.

A third approach to intrinsic motivation relies on needs — it is believed to be associated with behavior designed to satisfy the "growth" needs for self-actualization, self-esteem, competence, and achievement. Passing mention has been made of some of these needs earlier in this chapter; now we can examine each of them in a bit more detail. In the discussion that follows, keep in mind the multifaceted nature of human needs as it was presented earlier.

Self-Actualization. Our understanding of the need for self-actualization is most frequently attributed to the writings of Maslow (1943, 1954, 1968). Although his portrayal of this need varies slightly from one book and paper to another, the most widely adopted view is that it initiates behavior intended to permit the individual to fulfill her innate potential, to become all that she is capable of becoming. The amateur athlete who holds all of the world records, who enjoys widespread recognition as the best in her sport, and who is well endowed with friends and family, but who continues to train and push herself for the sake of continuing to improve her performance is an example of a person motivated by the need for self-actualization. Naturally, different people self-actualize in different ways, through the pursuit of different types of goals. Being a better father, a better supervisor, a more altruistic citizen, or simply a better overall person are examples of the infinite number of ways of self-actualizing.

The important point here is that some volunteer activities may be ideally suited to self-actualization experiences for some people but not to those of others: managers of volunteers must be careful not to assume that everyone working for them will be motivated to satisfy this need by engaging in any particular voluntary activity. Nevertheless, studies of voluntarism such as the one mentioned earlier (Anderson and Moore, 1978) consistently show that "self-fulfillment" and "personal development" are important consequences of the voluntary behavior of many people and may, for many others, comprise important a priori reasons for engaging in voluntarism.

Self-Esteem. Maslow also described the need for self-esteem in his writings (e.g., 1954). Generally, this need is responsible for acts designed to increase the person's regard for himself, to increase his assessment of his own worth. To quote Maslow (1954: 45), this need consists of "... the desire for strength, for achievement, for adequacy, for mastery and competence, for confidence in the face of the world, and for independence and freedom." When this need is fulfilled, the individual feels self-confident, worthy, strong, capable and adequate, useful, and necessary in the world. When it is unfulfilled or frustrated, the person feels inferior, incompetent, and helpless.

As in the case of self-actualization and virtually all of the other needs discussed here, the means by which people satisfy their needs for esteem vary from person to person, and from time to time for any particular individual. Nevertheless, it is quite plausible that many people find voluntary work behavior to be quite instrumental in fulfilling this particular need.

For example, Smith (1981) has argued that the concept of "altruism" that is often associated with (and invoked to explain) voluntary action is seldom, if ever, pure and unrelated to some degree of selfishness. According to Smith, the selfish outcome from helping others frequently consists of feelings of personal worth, of "being somebody," of being important. Smith (1981: 23) writes:

> ... there is literally no evidence to justify a belief in some 'absolute' form of human altruism, in which the motivation for an action is utterly without some form of selfishness .... No matter how altruistic an act appears, there is invariably ... some important degree of psychic reward or intrinsic satisfaction derived for one's self .... Altruism makes one, at least those who practice it, 'feel good' — receive psychic rewards for their selves, contribute to a positive self-image, induce ego enhancement, etc.

It is not surprising, therefore, that the second most cited "motive" for voluntarism in Anderson and Moore's (1978) study was "to feel useful and needed." The point is that common sense, everyday experience, and some empirical evidence show that the human need for self-esteem may be one of the most potent activators of a desire to engage in voluntary work activity: helping others can make a person feel good about herself.

Competence. Robert White (1959) has described a third need that is central to understanding intrinsic motivation. Referred to as the need for competence or efficacy, this need is related to a person's desire to interact effectively with his environment. For White, the capacity to be efficacious is neither innate nor developed through simple maturation. Rather, it is learned as a consequence of exploratory behavior, inquiry, and general experimentation with one's environment. Much of a child's curiosity and play behavior can be accounted for by this need, as can many forms of adult behavior such as reading, studying foreign languages, and generally seeking to learn new things. The parallel between White's need for competence and certain aspects of Maslow's need for self-esteem is apparent: both are concerned with achieving mastery of the environment, of being in control of things.

Achievement. A fourth need that is seen as accounting for intrinsically motivated behavior is the need for achievement. Henry Murray (1938: 164) defined this need as a desire to:

> ... accomplish something difficult. To master, manipulate, or organize physical objects, human beings, or ideas. To do this as rapidly and as independently as possible. To overcome obstacles and attain a high standard. To excel oneself. To rival and surpass others. To increase self-regard by the successful exercise of talent.

Again, there is considerable overlap between this need and the others we have discussed so far. Yet the important aspect of achievement motivation that makes it somewhat different from the others is that it consists, in part at least, of efforts to excel against one's personal standards of excellence, as opposed to acquiring mastery over elements external to one's self. Clearly, however, the similarities among the needs for achievement, self-actualization, self-esteem, and competence are more significant than are their unique differences.

How much opportunity does voluntary work activity provide for the satisfaction of the needs for competence and self-actualization? The answer to this question depends upon the person being considered because, as we have noted before, various needs express themselves in different ways for different people. So, for example, volunteering to simply sit and visit with convalescing patients may be a boring and mundane task for some volunteers while, for others who are naturally less skilled at making conversation or who possess relatively low levels of interpersonal competence, such a task could be a potent source of satisfaction for competence and self-actualization needs.

Competence and Self-Determination

According to Deci (1975), the essence of intrinsic motivation is the individual's desire to feel competent and self-determining. For Deci, intrinsically motivated behaviors are intended to find or create challenge and then to conquer or master it. He writes:

> Only when a person is able to reduce incongruity ... and only when a person is able to conquer the challenges which he encounters or creates will he feel competent and self-determining. He will feel satisfied when he is able to seek out pleasurable stimulation and deal effectively with overstimulation. In short, people seem to be engaged in the general process of seeking and conquering challenges which are optimal.

Notice the parallel between the building and reduction of challenge and incongruity in explaining intrinsic motivation on the one hand and the more general notion of increasing and reducing need-related tension (as we mentioned earlier) on the other hand.

In summary, we have seen three different approaches to intrinsic motivation: one based on a physiological model of human functioning; one based on a cognitive model; and one that is based on the assumption that human needs explain human behavior. Although they make different fundamental assumptions about human nature, it is easy to see that the three views complement one another and provide a convergent view of intrinsically motivated behavior. For the most part, this is behavior which is undertaken for its own sake rather than for the purpose of attaining material outcomes.

As an example of intrinsically motivated behavior, consider a person who dismantles a complex machine simply to learn how it works, and then reassembles it. The dismantling entails an increase in the physiological stimulation and psychological complexity experienced by the individual and creates a degree of challenge that will have to be met in order to put it back together again. The learning that takes place throughout the activity contributes to feelings of competence and, if he is successful, enhanced self-esteem and perhaps a modicum of self-actualization. If the machine is complicated enough, mastery of its design and operation should also bring feelings of achievement. Then, after it has been totally disassembled, the process of reassembly consists of reducing the complexity and stimulation created by having taken the machine apart.

In short, each of the three views casts some light on intrinsic motivation, each contributes some insight into what we might crudely refer to as behavior for its own sake, and each reveals a bit of understanding of the motivation to volunteer.

The Need for Power

Another need that seems to account for at least some voluntary work behavior is the need for power. Comparatively little research has been done on the role of this need in work activity, so its relationship with intrinsic and extrinsic motivation is not yet fully understood. Nevertheless, it would appear that the need for power is related to voluntarism, so we will examine it here.

As defined by McClelland (1970, 1975), the need for power compels people to have *impact*, particularly impact over and in relation to other people. Moreover, according to McClelland (1970), there are two types of power-related motivation. The first type is concerned with seeking to win over "active adversaries" (McClelland, 1970: 312). Life is viewed as a zero-sum game in which — as we noticed earlier — it is believed that "if I win, you lose" or "if you win, I lose." This form of power motivation is acquired in childhood, according to McClelland, before more subtle forms of influence are learned. People in whom this form of the need for power is strong are typically aggressive interpersonally, and are driven to seek and acquire symbols of status and authority. These individuals attempt to dominate others, using them as pawns for achieving their own goals.

The second variety of power motivation is:

> ... characterized by a concern for group goals, for finding those goals that will move men, for helping the group to formulate them, for taking some initiative in providing members of the group with the means for achieving such goals, and for giving group members the feeling of strength and competence they need to work hard for such goals. (McClelland, 1970: 317)

This form of power is directed toward exercising influence for other people, rather than *over* other people; it is aimed at inspiring other individuals to achieve their own goals.

People who possess a strong need for power have been found to express that need in a variety of ways. As mentioned earlier, for example, a strong need for power often manifests itself in the collection of prestigious possessions — symbols of power and status. Likewise, these individuals are more likely to engage in group activities, join organizations, and seek leadership roles in them, making it possible to exert authority and influence over other people. Moreover, such people are particularly likely to engage in sports activities; situations in which head-to-head competition and the potential for the domination of other people is possible. (By contrast, the need for power is less associated with sports such as track and field, swimming, and golf, where the competition involved is more with nature or a time clock rather than with a human opponent.)

Overall, based on the nature of the need for power and what is known from research about the way it is manifested in social behavior, it seems clear that a considerable amount of voluntary work activity can be attributed to power motives. Many voluntary activities provide the volunteer with opportunities to influence, direct, or control the lives of other people (such as the sick, the young, or the elderly). Other voluntary activities (such as serving on governing boards of social service agencies, universities, hospitals, and the like) also provide opportunities for volunteers to have impact through the design of policy and the implementation of executive-level control.

In many ways, power motivation seems less socially desirable and less noble than motivation attributable to most of the other needs we have discussed here. Whether or not this is so, our purpose here is merely to explore in an unbiased manner the possible range of human needs that might account for voluntary work activity. Finally, it is important to reiterate that most conscious behavior is determined by more than single needs, such that power motives, when they are responsible for voluntary work behavior, are usually accompanied by the motivating force of other needs as well.

RECAPITULATION AND A GLANCE AHEAD

A complete analysis of work motivation in general and of voluntary work motivation in particular must concern itself with the intensity, duration, and direction of the force associated with motivated effort, in addition to the origins of the force itself (cf. Katerberg and Blau, 1983). In the foregoing sections of this chapter, need theory has been offered as a means of understanding the *origins* of motivated work effort, and — to a lesser extent — as a way of understanding the *intensity* and *duration* of such effort. However, need theory, by itself, provides insufficient grounds for understanding the *directions* motivated energy may take; that is, for predicting and explaining the particular goals toward which motivated energy will be directed. In terms of the mission of this chapter, we are saying that need theory provides an insufficient basis (1) for predicting and explaining whether a person's need-related energy will be directed toward voluntary work activity, or, if the decision has been made to volunteer, (2) for predicting the specific voluntary activities that are likely to be pursued. Accordingly, Chapter 4 will examine a popular theory of work motivation that sheds some light on the processes associated with the particular *direction(s)* voluntary work behavior may take.

PART TWO:

NEED, FRUSTRATION AND MOTIVATION

To this point, we have ignored the fact that a considerable proportion of human behavior fails to achieve whatever goals it is intended to achieve. In other words, people are not always able to attain the goals in their lives that are necessary for them to fulfill their needs. The situation in which an individual's behavior is not successful in achieving need fulfilling goals is defined as frustration. In this section we will examine some common causes and consequences of frustration in general terms and discuss some major implications of the analysis for understanding the motivation to engage in and perform voluntary work. Much of what follows comes from the work of Norman Maier (1973) and his colleagues.

Before we begin, however, it is necessary to reiterate the distinction made earlier in the chapter between needs and goals. Recall that needs are hypothetical constructs that represent the fundamental forces that instigate behavior. They are characteristics of individuals and are relatively fixed in the short run. By contrast, goals are commodities, outcomes, and end-states that people strive to attain for the sake of fulfilling their needs. Failure to recognize the distinction between needs and goals in the analysis of frustration situations makes it difficult to diagnose and ameliorate such situations.

WHAT IS FRUSTRATION?

People tend to associate certain goals with the satisfaction of their particular needs, although, as was stressed earlier, there are few one-to-one connections between needs and goals that apply to all people. To some extent, that is, need-goal relationships are idiosyncratic. Nevertheless, individuals do tend to learn that particular goals are instrumental for satisfying their needs and, over a period of time, heavily reinforce the need-goal associations that work for them. Going to the refrigerator for a cold beer or soft drink, for example, can become a familiar and reliable means of sating one's thirst. In this example, of course, the need is thirst and the cold beverage is the goal. A less obvious example involving non-physiological needs would be the case of a person who finds that volunteering to work for public service agencies serves to satisfy her needs for affiliation, competence, and power.

But what happens when previously learned behaviors fail to reach the goal(s) being sought? What happens when the learned behavior is either not possible or, even if it is possible, fails to be successful? Further, what happens when a familiar behavior — one that has been learned and reinforced over a period of time — makes the attainment of a person's goals more difficult, rather than easier?

Situations such as these are common in life in general and especially ubiquitous in work settings. However, whereas they can be particularly troublesome when they occur in the context of a person's work, they have at least two important implications for the management of volunteer activity. First, unfulfilled needs in a person's work life and/or leisure life can generate a desire to engage in voluntary activity, at least to the extent that the individual perceives that voluntary work might provide goals that, when attained, are instrumental for satisfying his otherwise frustrated needs. A second implication of need frustration for an analysis of the motivation of volunteers is that people often find that, for any of a number of reasons (some of which will be discussed below), the voluntary activities they engage in fail to be as fulfilling as they had hoped. Therefore, people who manage volunteer labor forces frequently (and sometimes without knowing it) capitalize on the frustrations people encounter in their jobs and in their lives in general. On the other hand, volunteer managers must strive to prevent the frustration of volunteer workers once they have been recruited because, as will be discussed shortly, a common reaction to need frustration in any setting is withdrawal, either in the form of quitting, being tardy or absent, or simply losing interest.

Causes of Frustration

What sorts of things prevent a person's behavior from attaining his goals? In other words, what causes frustration? For the sake of discussion, we can identify two general categories of frustrating agents. The first category consists of factors that are external to the person in question; the second category consists of characteristics of the person himself.

Examples of the first category of frustrators that are common in work settings include things such as organizational structures that are pyramidal in shape, organizational rules and procedures that prevent freedom and spontaneity, co-workers who are incompetent, subordinates who are uncooperative, and superiors who don't listen. Other examples are inventory systems that frequently result in shortages of supplies, government regulations, and the acts of one's competitors. The point is that there are countless potential and real factors in any job setting that can block a person's attempts to behave in ways that lead to the goals that satisfy his needs. A second point is that some of these barriers are more obvious and more easily detected than others. A final key point related to external barriers such as the ones mentioned is that many (if not most of them) can be found in volunteer organizations at least as easily as they can be found in other work and non-work settings. However, although the list of such potential barriers is endless, careful management can either prevent them from occurring, minimize the frequency of their occurrence, and/or detect and remove them when they do occur.

The second category of frustrators is generally more difficult than the first to manage, for a number of reasons. The most important reason, of course, is that they consist of characteristics of the individual herself — characteristics that are frequently tough to identify and, more frequently, very difficult to alter. Examples of such factors are a person's personality, her interests and abilities, her experiences, her sex, race, social status, and so on. Another common source of frustration related to the person herself is her behavior: people frequently behave in ways that either erect barriers to the attainment of their goals or that exacerbate barriers that already exist. For example, people who cry in response to frustration can worsen the very barriers that cause them to cry in the first place if those around them belittle them or discount them for being so "insecure" or so "immature" that crying is the way they behave.

In short, there are countless characteristics of people and contexts faced by people that can cause them to be frustrated. Moreover, the factors that lead to frustration for one person may not cause frustration for other people, and a particularly frustrating agent may or may not function for a given individual, depending upon the circumstances. These subtleties make the detection and management of frustration difficult, although not impossible. Before we examine the problems of detection and amelioration of frustration, let's take a look at the consequences of frustration in order to gain an appreciation for the importance of the phenomenon.

Consequences of Frustration

Need frustration results in any of a variety of typical reactions, although different people display these types of reactions in idiosyncratic ways.

The most constructive reaction to frustration is problem solving — the person sets about to diagnose the causes of the frustration (identifying whatever internal or external barriers are responsible) and then attempts to deal with them. For example, a person who is unsuccessful at finding a high-paying job may recognize that her qualifications are too low and seek further education or training. Equally constructive are strategies in which the frustrated person pursues alternative goals rather than the one that has been unobtainable. Thus the woman in our previous example may change her pay expectations and seek employment in a lower-paying job that is more in line with the credentials she does have.

Aside from problem solving and selecting new goals, however, there are many other responses typically associated with frustration — some of them less constructive and acceptable than the first two. Two of the most common of these are aggression and regression. Aggression is some form of attack that is accompanied by anger (Maier, 1973). Sometimes it is overt and obvious; at other times it is concealed or disguised. Examples of open aggression include the use of physical force and violence, whereas gossiping behind a person's back or voting against a co-worker's project proposal illustrate less obvious forms of aggressive behavior. Sometimes the target of the aggression is the cause of the frustration; at other times the aggression is displaced onto other people or objects, particularly when it is safer or easier to direct it elsewhere.

Regression consists of the use of behaviors that the person has used and found effective in earlier stages of development. Pouting, crying and/or cursing are three examples of regressive acts often resorted to by frustrated people — acts that are less advanced or mature than one might otherwise expect from an adult. (To the extent that a person employed aggression when frustrated as a child, its continued use later in life constitutes regression as well.)

One often troublesome consequence of regressive acts is that they can worsen the frustration that triggers them. A boorish lout who is discounted by his co-workers may resort to further obnoxious language and conduct as a way of expressing his frustration, causing his colleagues to further ignore and discount him.

Fixation involves the repeated use of the same goal-seeking behaviors, *in spite of* the fact that they have proven unsuccessful. Rut thinking and obsessive-compulsive behavior are examples.

Finally (although this list is not exhaustive), resignation and withdrawal are common responses to need frustration. In this case, the person loses interest for the problem he faces, becomes nonchalant, and abandons all attempts to engage in problem solving, to find alternative goals, and/or to be aggressive or regressive. In work settings, this pattern expresses itself in uninspired job performance, low creativity, absenteeism, tardiness, and even turnover. In short, the person simply quits trying.

FRUSTRATION IN THE VOLUNTEER SETTING

We noted earlier that the frustration of a person's needs in the context of his personal life and/or his work life can provide an impetus for him to engage in voluntary work activities. But we also noted that frustration can occur in volunteer work as easily as it can in other contexts, resulting in any or all of the consequences we discussed. It becomes important, therefore, for the manager of volunteers to capitalize on the benefits of need frustration for the sake of attracting volunteers while, at the same time, assuring that unnecessary frustration does not adversely affect the performance of those who are already on board. In short, managing frustration involves both of these goals for the volunteer manager.

However, although managing a voluntary workforce involves successfully pursuing each of these objectives, simultaneously accomplishing them can be difficult, for a number of reasons. Let's look at them, one at a time.

First of all, many volunteer jobs require minimal skills and offer only limited opportunities for the satisfaction of many human needs — particularly the growth needs we discussed earlier. While it is important to reiterate that different people seek to satisfy particular needs in idiosyncratic ways, the fact remains that volunteer work often requires people to perform mundane tasks for extended periods of time, seldom leading to any hope of self-actualization, the exercise of power, or the development of competence.

Secondly, it is often the case that the same factors that are responsible for the frustration of a person's salient needs in her vocational and personal life can frustrate her attempts to satisfy these needs through voluntary work activity. This is particularly the case when the major frustrating agents are characteristics of the person herself (such as her sex, age, appearance, or her aptitudes and abilities). For example, poor technical qualifications and a general lack of interpersonal competence may inhibit a woman's upward mobility in the managerial-technical-professional hierarchy of her work organization, causing her to seek leadership influence on the board of directors of a service association. But the same personal and skill-related deficiencies that drive her to seek satisfaction through voluntary leadership activities may function to prevent her from achieving a leadership role with such an association, or — even if she managed to find herself in such a role — thwart her efforts to have impact once she is elected. The fact is that voluntary organizations are constituted of human beings with mixed and often incompatible goals, leading to the same general types of social and political dynamics that are found in other arenas of human activity. In short, voluntary organizations can be very political places that can dash the aspirations of well-intending individuals.

There is at least one other dynamic that can make it difficult to simultaneously achieve both of the goals related to frustration mentioned above. This third factor has to do with the difficulties that can arise when volunteers manage to work themselves into positions for which they are not suited. Low professional or managerial qualifications in the work setting can be just as detrimental to the successful accomplishment of the objective of a volunteer organization as they can be to the accomplishment of the objectives of profit-oriented organizations. We know that both motivation and ability are required for effective job performance, regardless of the setting. So, while a person might be highly motivated to engage in voluntary work (because of the frustrations she encounters in her vocational life), she may be no more qualified to achieve the types of goals that elude her in her career through voluntary work activity than she is on her regular job.

In summary, the frustrations associated with life in general and with vocations in particular can be responsible for much of the motivation of many people to pursue voluntary work activity. On the other hand, the very factors that are responsible for a person's frustration in other arenas of her life can also make it difficult for her to be effective in voluntary work roles, such that the effective placement of scarce voluntary resources into jobs is as important for the manager of volunteers as it is for managers of people who work for pay.

Preventing and Managing Frustration in Voluntary Work Settings

The analysis of the nature and causes of frustration presented in the foregoing section suggests a number of insights for the volunteer manager who wishes either to prevent (or at least minimize) the frustration experienced by her volunteer workers. Some of these insights suggest preventive measures such a manager may take; others suggest ameliorative steps that may be undertaken either to reduce or remove the frustration of the staff under her command.

Preventive measures suggested by the foregoing analysis include the careful recruitment, screening, and placement of prospective volunteer workers. Although many voluntary organizations are not in a position to pick and choose among applicants, realistic recruitment appeals outlining the true nature of the work that is available may prevent many people from seeking work that will be frustrating and dissatisfying for them (cf. Wanous, 1980). A second step at the recruitment stage would be to conduct careful interviews with prospective volunteer workers, probing as much as is possible into the needs and values applicants are seeking to fulfill through volunteer work, and trying to assess (again, as much as possible) the degree to which the specific tasks to be done can be expected to provide the types of outcomes the person desires. There is no doubt that some degree of this assessment of "goodness of fit" is conducted in many or most volunteer employment settings. However, a more systematic, deliberate attempt — made in the face of the requirement to fill slots when not many applicants are available — may pay off in the long run as a consequence of the reduction of frustration and turnover it could yield.

There are a number of other steps a manager of volunteers may take in order to reduce the overall levels of frustration among volunteer employees who are already engaged. The first and most obvious of these is to become more attentive to the signs and symptoms of need frustration; in order to ease it, frustration must first be identified. Flagging attendance (increased absenteeism), tardiness, declining enthusiasm, and reduced quality of work are symptoms of need frustration that are commonly manifested in work settings (Pinder, 1984). Many volunteer work settings are limited, of course, in their flexibility to rotate workers through voluntary positions, but attempts to make such rotations may be possible in some settings, forestalling or removing some of the repetition and tedium that often characterizes volunteer jobs — especially low-level volunteer jobs. Another approach worth considering is assessing the skill-related strengths and weaknesses of frustrated volunteers with a view to providing them with the sorts of training and development that are necessary to enable them to undertake other volunteer duties that entail more challenge, more responsibility, or more autonomy — three factors that contribute to the inherent interest value of many jobs (Hackman and Oldham, 1980).

In short, it is recognized that many of the jobs occupied by the volunteer workforce are, by their very nature, limited in scope and intrinsic interest value, and limited in their potential to be made interesting. And, to repeat, it is also recognized that volunteer organizations are often (usually, in many cases) faced with a dearth of attractive volunteer human resources, requiring them to "take whomever they can get." To the extent that these circumstances exist in a particular volunteer work setting, the application of many of the preceding practices for managing the frustration of volunteers will be difficult — perhaps even unfeasible. Nevertheless, simple solutions are rarely available for complex managerial problems; this appears particularly true in the case of the management of volunteers.

CONCLUSIONS

The primary purpose of this chapter has been to examine the motivation to engage in and perform voluntary work activity from the perspective of the need theory approach to work motivation. It must be emphasized that this theoretic approach does not exhaust all that are available; it is merely representative of the types of analyses that recent work in organizational psychology can offer. Other chapters in this volume will approach voluntarism from other perspectives, and a comprehensive overview of most of the viable theories of work motivation (in non-voluntary settings) has been provided elsewhere (e.g., Pinder, 1984; Steers and Porter, 1983).

Future theory in volunteer work motivation may progress most quickly via perspectives that combine concepts and techniques from a variety of extant approaches. For example, models of the motivation to volunteer may benefit from the use of cognitive behavior modification and social learning theory (see Mahoney, 1974; and Bandura, 1977 for examples). In fact, some work on the learning of altruism has already been conducted (cf. Bar-Tal, 1976; Rushton, 1980), showing how it may be possible to avoid reliance on "block box" intrapsychic constructs such as needs while maintaining respect for the importance of cognition, modelling, and vicarious conditioning. In the meantime, current theoretic models do offer some insight into the complex problem of the motivation of volunteers. This chapter has attempted to provide such insight.

REFERENCES

Alderfer, C.
1972 *Existence, Relatedness, and Growth*. New York: The Free Press.
Anderson, J.C. and L.F. Moore
1978 "The Motivation to Volunteer," *Journal of Voluntary Action Research* 7: 120-129.
Atkinson, J.W.
1964 *An Introduction to Motivation*. Princeton, NJ: Van Nostrand.
Bandura, A.
1977 *Social Learning Theory*. Englewood Cliffs, NJ: Prentice-Hall.
Bar-Tal, D.
1976 *Prosocial Behavior*. New York: Wiley.
Briggs, D.L.
1982 "On Satisfying the Volunteer and the Paid Employee: Any Differences?" *Volunteer Administration* 14: 1-14.
Cofer, C.N. and M.M. Appley
1964 *Motivation: Theory and Research*. New York: Wiley.
Deci, E.L.
1975 *Intrinsic Motivation*. New York: Plenum.
Hackman, J.R. and G. Oldham
1980 *Work Redesign*. Reading, MA: Addison-Wesley.
Katerberg, R. and G.J. Blau
1983 "An Examination of Level and Direction of Effort and Job Performance," *Academy of Management Journal* 26: 249-257.

Katz, R.
1980 "Time and Work," in B.M. Staw and L.L. Cummings, eds. *Research in Organizational Behavior*. Vol. 2. Greenwich, CT: JAI Press.

Lawler, E.E.
1973 *Motivation in Work Organizations*. Belmont, CA: Brooks-Cole.

Locke, E.A.
1973 "Job Satisfaction," in M.D. Dunnette, ed. *Handbook of Industrial and Organizational Psychology*. Chicago: Rand McNally.

Mahoney, M.J.
1974 *Cognition and Behavior Modification*. Cambridge, MA: Ballinger.

Maier, N.R.F.
973 *Psychology in Industrial Organizations*. Boston: Houghton Mifflin.

Maslow, A.H.
1943 "A Theory of Human Motivation," *Psychological Review* 50: 370-396.
1954 *Motivation and Personality*. New York: Harper and Row.
1968 *Toward a Psychology of Being*. New York: Van Nostrand Reinhold.

McClelland, David C.
1970 "The Two Faces of Power," *Journal of International Affairs* 24: 29-47.
1975 *Power: The Inner Experience*. New York: Irvington.

Murray, H.
1938 *Experience in Personality*. New York: Oxford University Press.

National Advisory Council on Voluntary Action
1977 *People in Action*. Ottawa: Secretary of State.

Pearce, J.L.
1983 "Job Attitude and Motivation Differences Between Volunteers and Employees from Comparable Organizations," *Journal of Applied Psychology* 68: 646-652.

Pinder, C.C.
1984 *Work Motivation: Theory, Issues and Applications*. Glenview, IL: Scott, Foresman and Co.

Pinder, C.C. and V.W. Bourgeois
  1982 "Controlling Tropes in Administrative Science," *Administrative Science Quarterly* 27: 641-652.
Rushton, J.P.
  1980 *Altruism, Socialization, and Society*. Englewood Cliffs, NJ: Prentice-Hall.
Smith, D.H.
  1972 "Types of Volunteers and Voluntarism," *Volunteer Administration* 6: 3-10.
  1981 "Altruism, Volunteers, and Volunteerism," *Journal of Voluntary Action Research* 10: 21-26.
Steers, R.M. and L.W. Porter, eds.
  1983 *Motivation and Work Behavior*. 3rd ed. New York: McGraw-Hill.
Vroom, V.
  1964 *Work and Motivation*. New York: Wiley.
Walter, G.A. and S.E. Marks
  1981 *Experiential Learning and Change*. New York: Wiley.
Wanous, John P.
  1980 *Organizational Entry*. Reading, MA: Addison-Wesley.
White, R.
  1959 "Motivation Reconsidered: The Concept of Competence," *Psychological Review* 66: 297-333.

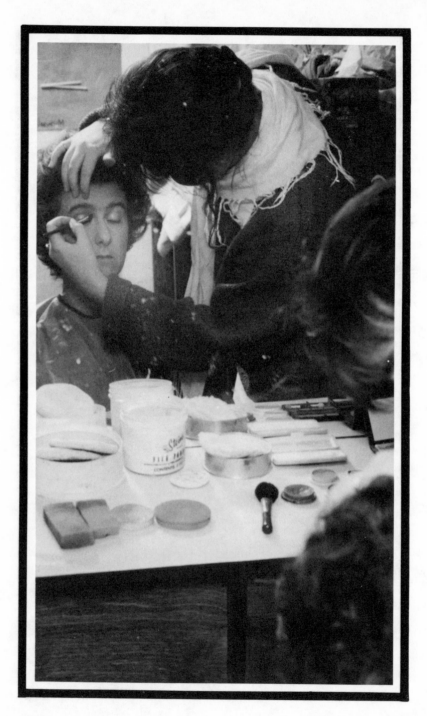

Chapter 4

BELIEFS, EXPECTED VALUES, AND VOLUNTEER WORK BEHAVIOR

Craig C. Pinder

The theoretic approach to work motivation that has attracted the most attention from organizational psychologists and stimulated the most research over the past two decades is, without doubt, that which was first proposed by Victor Vroom (1964). Variously referred to as "Valence-Instrumentality-Expectancy Theory," "Expectancy Theory," and even "Instrumentality Theory," Vroom's statement of this approach for understanding work motivation was actually a specific adaptation of the ideas of a number of earlier psychologists. For all intents and purposes, however, we can credit Vroom with formalizing this approach and pointing out its value for understanding the motivation to work.

Vroom's theory (and those which have evolved from it) assumes that people's behavior results from conscious choices among alternatives, and that these choices (i.e., behaviors) are based on their beliefs and attitudes. The purpose of these choices, generally, is to maximize the individual's pleasure and to minimize her pain. Hence, hedonism, combined with awareness and mental deliberation, provide the necessary ingredients for understanding behavior.

To understand why this theory is named as it is and to gain a better understanding of how the choice processes work, we need to examine four fundamental elements of the model: psychological force, valence, instrumentality, and expectancy.

The Concept of Force

For Vroom, a person's behavior is ". . . the result of a field of forces each of which has a direction and a magnitude." The "direction" of a force represents the nature of a particular act or deed (such as whether or not to engage in voluntary work behavior or, alternatively, which of several agencies to work for, while the "magnitude" represents the strength of commitment, degree of intensity, and/or the duration of each act or deed being considered. People constantly consider a variety of behaviors and choose to engage in those which are associated with the greatest force. So if the net psychological force associated with joining a volunteer agency is greater than that associated with not joining, and/or greater than that associated with pursuing other ways of occupying his time, an individual will likely try to join such an agency. Further, once such a decision is made, the comparative magnitude of the forces associated with each of a variety of agencies being considered will determine which particular one the person attempts to join. Finally, once the individual has begun to work in a particular voluntary role, the magnitude of the forces associated with various levels of work effort (e.g., high, moderate, or low) will determine how hard he elects to work while in that role. In short, Vroom's theory can be used to understand both a person's motivation to participate in a volunteer organization as well as his motivation to perform at whatever level he chooses (see March & Simon, 1958).

Two features of the force concept require elaboration at this point. First, it is important to recognize that these forces are useful only for predicting which ways an individual *intends* to behave. Everyone has experienced instances in which their clearest, most preferred choices have failed to result in the types of behaviors they have desired and/or in the types of consequences they have expected. (See my discussion of frustration in the previous chapter of this book.)

Second, notice that this theory implies that people are capable of somehow determining (or, at least, experiencing) a net level of psychological force related to a range or variety of behavioral alternatives. In the hypothetical example above, this would imply that a level of force would be associated for the person with each and every agency she is considering, and — once she is employed — with every possible level of performance possible in her role.

Notice that this force-driven intention model of human behavior, by itself, is insufficient for totally understanding behavior; we still need to know the origins of these forces, or psychological intentions to act. Here is where the three factors called "valence," "instrumentality," and "expectancy" (V, I, and E) become relevant — they are the three variables that combine to determine the psychological force associated with each choice alternative — with each prospective behavior. Therefore, let's look at these factors, one at a time.

The Concept of Valence

The theory assumes that people hold preferences among various outcomes or states of nature. For example, most people prefer, other things equal, clean working conditions rather than dirty ones. Here, working conditions are the "outcome" in question, and the preference for clean over dirty reflects the strength of the reader's basic underlying need state (see Chapter 3). The point is that most people have more-or-less clearly defined preferences among the various consequences that might result from their acts, and that these preferences constitute one of the three key determinants of the force associated with each act being contemplated.

The term "valence" refers to the emotional orientations people hold toward outcomes. Accordingly, an outcome (such as, for example, making a new friend) is said to be *positively valent* if the person considering it would rather have it than not have it. On the other hand, we might assume that most people place *negative valence* — negative expected value - on working long hours and being away from their families for extended periods of time. Finally, a person is said to be *indifferent* toward an outcome that holds neither positive nor negative valence for him.

The most important aspect of the valence concept is that it pertains to the degree of satisfaction or dissatisfaction a person *expects* to derive from an outcome. So, for example, a man may train to become a Boy Scout leader, expecting that he will derive fulfillment from the experience but learns, once he has witnessed the responsibility of leading a troup of other people's adolescent boys on their first cross-country hike, that the net satisfaction actually derived is far less than what he had hoped for! Of course, the comparative strengths of an individual's needs and values play the major role in determining the valence the person places on outcomes of various sorts, but people also develop and refine their beliefs and expected values of outcomes vicariously — by observing and identifying with the experiences of others (cf. Bandura, 1977). In short, valence refers to the satisfaction a person expects to achieve from an outcome rather than to the actual value of that outcome, as assessed after attaining it.

The Concept of Instrumentality

The second major determinant of the strength of the force associated with a behavioral act is referred to as "instrumentality." Instrumentality is a belief in the mind of the person — a belief concerning the strength of the connection between one event and another. The most important type of belief for our present purposes is that linking an act (such as joining a volunteer organization or expending extra effort for one to which a person already belongs) to an outcome (such as the satisfaction of helping others, or, on the negative side, the dissatisfaction of being away from one's family on weekends).

Instrumentality beliefs can be thought of as probabilities in the individual's mind, probabilities concerning whether an act (such as either of the two mentioned above) will result in an outcome. For example, a young man who considers helping old people shop on weekends may believe that the odds are 90 to 100 percent that he will make a number of friends among people of his grandparents' generation if he were to become so involved, whereas he may be less certain about the likelihood that volunteer work of this sort will provide him with opportunities to expand his technical skills. In such a case we would say that the man believes helping the old people would be highly instrumental (or useful) for making elderly friends but less instrumental for developing professional skills.

Notice that these beliefs are merely beliefs, based on the individual's own experiences as well as upon his perceptions of the experiences of others. As such, instrumentality beliefs may be overestimates or underestimates of the true association between one event and another; but it is the subjective probability linking events — not the true probability — that determines whether or not a person will be inclined to act a particular way. For example, if a person has observed that high levels of job performance are rewarded with high levels of recognition and praise, these experiences will strengthen his instrumentality beliefs linking performance and these particular outcomes. It is important to remember that both personal and vicarious experiences can influence a person's instrumentality beliefs — people learn from observing others.

The Concept of Expectancy

The third major determinant of the forces associated with alternative acts is referred to as "expectancy." Similar to the way valence is the person's *anticipated* level of satisfaction, and similar to the way instrumentality is the individual's *belief* concerning the strength of the connection between acts and outcomes, the expectancy component relates to the person's *beliefs* about the likelihood of whether, if he tries, he will be able to act or behave in the way intended. For example, a woman may desire to become the president of a neighborhood group, expecting that if she does, such a position will be instrumental for bringing her good times and influence in her community. But whether or not she attempts to become president of the group will depend upon the strength of her beliefs about whether it is possible for her to do so.

Vroom (1964) spoke of expectancy beliefs as "action-outcome" associations people make, representing the strength of their beliefs whether, if they try to accomplish something, they will be able to accomplish it. Conceptually, these beliefs range from zero ("There's no way I can do it!") to 1.0 ("Of course I can do it. It's easy!"). In practice, of course, a person's expectancy perceptions range between these two extremes, as subjective probability estimates that are subject to constant change while the individual acquires new skills, has new experiences, observes the successes and failures of other people, and so on.

In fact, a variety of factors influence the strength of a person's expectancy beliefs — that is, her beliefs concerning whether she is capable of doing what she wishes to do (Lawler, 1973). For example, her assessment of her own skills and abilities and her general level of self-confidence are especially important. Her level of personal experience at the task she is considering and the impressions she gleans from others about the difficulty of accomplishing the task are also important in shaping expectancy beliefs.

In summary, the expectancy component of VIE Theory deals with an individual's beliefs about whether it will be possible for her to accomplish a particular task or goal. If the person believes, for whatever set of reasons, that she will not be able to accomplish a particular task, it is said that her expectancy is low. If the task appears easy and/or routine, expectancy is said to be high. According to VIE Theory, the higher the person's expectancy concerning a particular event, the stronger is the force motivating her to try it.

The Determination of Choices: Combining the Three Factors

It is now possible to bring our understanding of each of the various components of VIE Theory together to see how they interact to determine work-related decisions. Before beginning, it is critical to stress that this theory assumes that it is people's subjective beliefs about themselves and about the behavioral alternatives they consider that determine the psychological force associated with each alternative, that these beliefs are frequently in a state of flux, and that they can be more-or-less accurate reflections of reality. Having repeated this important caveat, let's see how the components relate to decision making, the choice among alternatives, and the motivation to volunteer.

According to Vroom and most other VIE theorists, the total force associated with a behavioral alternative (such as whether to canvass for the Salvation Army or to join a bridge club) is the result of a combination of all three of the elements discussed above. Moreover, these elements are seen as combining in a *multiplicative* manner, such that if the answer to any of the following three questions is not favorable or positive, there will be no force compelling a person to opt for the alternative in question. The three questions are:

1) "If I try, can I do it?" (the expectancy component);
2) "If I succeed in doing it, what will it lead to for me?" (the instrumentality component); and
3) "How much satisfaction or dissatisfaction will I derive from the consequences?" (the valence component).

Thus, if a person doesn't believe that she can accomplish a goal (such as becoming president of a local volunteer association), or if she doesn't believe that being the president will lead to things she desires, or if she believes that being president will lead to outcomes that she dislikes, the total force compelling her to seek the presidency of the association will be low, perhaps non-existent. If the decision she is making is merely whether or not to join and if one of these considerations was sufficiently unfavorable in her mind, she may simply elect not to pursue the presidency. On the other hand, if the decision situation entailed a choice between seeking the presidency of the club and some other prospective use of her time, she would compare the net attractiveness (the net force or "subjective expected utility") of the presidency with what she associates with the other possibilities she has in mind, and consequently form the intention to behave in accordance with the comparative strength of these forces.

A Hypothetical Example

To illustrate how VIE Theory can be used to understand the motivation to participate in volunteer work *and* the motivation to perform well at it, consider the hypothetical example of Margaret Smith. Assume that Margaret is the wife of a college graduate who works as a clerk in a local department store. Margaret is also a college graduate, but her full-time job consists of raising her three children.

A friend of Margaret's asks whether she would be willing to canvass her neighborhood to raise funds for a local charity. Margaret learns that there is a shortage of volunteers to cover the neighborhood, and that a lot of help is needed for the charity to reach its fund-raising goal. She also knows that the bulk of the canvassing must be done during the evening, when people in the neighborhood are most likely to be at home.

How does VIE Theory explain Margaret's decision whether or not to volunteer? Moreover, how does this theory help us understand how hard Margaret will work once she has volunteered? Let's take these two questions in order.

First, the decision to volunteer. The expectancy component ("If I try, will I be able to join the fund-raising drive?") presents no problem. The shortage of volunteers suggests that if she elects to join the crusade, she merely has to sign up.

The issues related to the instrumentality and valence components are somewhat more complex. Margaret would consider a number of consequences (or outcomes) that may be related to joining the drive. Being away from her husband and children for several evenings, and being exposed to the cold and rain that are inevitable during winter (in Vancouver, B.C., at least) are examples of the types of outcomes she might consider. She may also think of the possibility of being threatened by troublemakers and thieves who could realize that she is gathering money from door to door, considerably vulnerable and unable to protect herself. Each of these outcomes are negatively valent to Margaret, of course. How instrumental would the fund-raising work be for each of these outcomes? The separation from her family would be a certainty. On the other hand, the ravages of the weather would be less certain because, after all, it doesn't rain *every* winter evening in Vancouver! Finally, the chances of being mugged may seem slight to Margaret because she knows that the crime rate is low in her neighborhood. In short, the main negative factor in her mind would appear to be the separation from her family.

But Margaret realizes that there are also some *positive* outcomes that could result from joining the campaign. For example, she would get a chance to help the friend who asked her to volunteer. She believes that the affection and camaraderie that would result would be highly valuable to her (high positive valence) and she has no doubt that it would be forthcoming (high instrumentality). Likewise, Margaret may believe that other positive outcomes are *bound* to result from joining the campaign: she would get some physical exercise, she would have a chance to meet her neighbors, and she would derive considerable personal satisfaction from helping the charity. Some of these consequences are more valent to Margaret than others, but each of them seems certain to result if she were to agree to volunteer. In balance, the combined weight of the positive valences of these outcomes, each "multiplied" by the strength of their respective probabilities of occurrence, would be considered in comparison with the combined weight of the negative outcomes Margaret considers, each multiplied somehow with the probability in her mind that each of them would result from volunteering.

Notice that Margaret's beliefs and expected values may or may not be accurate. She might underestimate the odds of being mugged and overestimate the pleasure of meeting her neighbors. If so, the net *actual* value of her participation may turn out to be considerably lower than what she expects it to be when she decides to join the fund-raising appeal. On the other hand, she might also underestimate the net value of becoming involved, and may, accordingly, decide not to become involved when in fact she should have. The point is that it is her perceptions and beliefs about the valences and instrumentalities that determine her decision whether or not to volunteer.

A second point is this: the net psychological force that Margaret feels in connection with joining the campaign (as a result of her assessment of all the valences and instrumentalities) will be considered in light of the forces she feels in connection with alternative ways for her to spend her time and energy. She may, for example, be entertaining the possibility of taking on a part-time job as a waitress in a local bistro, or she may be considering becoming involved in the parent/teacher association of her son's school. Each of these and other activities will have expectancies, valences, and outcomes associated with them in Margaret's mind, and each of these may be more or less accurate. Which of the various alternatives Margaret chooses (including merely staying home at night) will be determined by the comparative strengths of the net psychological forces associated in Margaret's mind with each one.

In order to illustrate how VIE Theory helps us predict and understand how hard a person works at a job, we must assume that the decision to participate has been made. In this case, we need to assume that Margaret has decided to accept her friend's request to join the fund-raising drive (the rain and muggers notwithstanding). The theory holds that Margaret will consider a wide range of performance levels, ranging from very low to very high, and that she will choose that level which holds the greatest positive (or least negative) psychological force for her. For the sake of the discussion that follows, assume that performance is defined as total dollars raised over a one-month period.

The expectancy factor plays a more significant role in understanding Margaret's performance decision than it did in examining her participation decision. In this case, it is likely that the strength of her expectancy beliefs ("Can I reach X dollars?") will be inversely related to each level of performance she considers. For example, she may estimate her chances of raising ten thousand dollars for the charity to be slight — say only five percent. On the other hand, she may believe that it would be quite easy to raise three thousand dollars — she may feel her chances are eighty percent of reaching such a figure. Other things (such as valences and instrumentalities) equal, the higher the performance goal, the lower the expectancy, and the lower the force associated with striving for it.

But these other factors are not equal, of course. Each performance level will be more or less instrumental in Margaret's mind for the attainment of outcomes that are more or less valent for her (positively and negatively). For instance, she may believe that high performance (reaching the ten thousand dollar figure) will *definitely* require (be highly instrumental for) her to be away from her family many evenings -an outcome that is strongly negatively valent for Margaret. On the other hand, she realizes that she will feel greater levels of pride (a positively valent outcome) if she were to succeed at reaching the ten thousand dollar goal. Similarly, the theory holds, each level of performance will be associated in Margaret's mind with different combinations of valences and instrumentalities, which, when combined with their respective levels of expectancy, will determine the net psychological force related to it. Margaret will strive to achieve that level that maximizes her expected subjective utility — that is, she will choose to strive for the level of performance that has the greatest net level of psychological force associated with it.

Before leaving our example, it is important to reiterate once again the subjective/perceptual nature of all this. Margaret's estimates of her own abilities may be inaccurate, such that she either overestimates or underestimates the probability of reaching particular performance levels. Likewise, she may overestimate or underestimate the strength of the probability that particular levels of performance will take her away from her family. Finally, she may overestimate or underestimate the actual value to herself of the feelings of pride and accomplishment that actually result from different performance levels. Again — it is Margaret's estimates of the probabilities of various outcomes and her estimates of the degree of satisfaction or dissatisfaction that will result from each that ultimately determine the performance level she strives to achieve.

Effort and Performance

Notice that the foregoing discussion of Margaret's motivation to perform spoke of the various levels of performance *she would consider striving to achieve*. Our everyday experience tells us that it is one thing to attempt to reach a goal; it is another thing to actually achieve it. VIE theory helps explain the amount of motivated effort a person will expend on a job, but by itself, it does not explain the actual performance levels people achieve. The reason of course is that effort is only one ingredient — albeit an important ingredient — in the determination of job performance. We have all known people who have tried hard to reach certain performance goals in work settings but who, due to a host of reasons, have seen their highly motivated effort fall short of those goals. In addition to effort, at least two other factors must be taken into account: ability and role clarity. Let's examine each of these two factors briefly.

The Role of Ability. Perhaps the most common reason that motivated effort fails to result in performance is a lack of ability on the part of the person. A man may be highly motivated to become an actuary, for example, but repeatedly fail because of a lack of mathematical aptitude and skill. Notice that an individual's ability to perform a task is a result of both his native aptitude and the degree of training and experience the person has undertaken to develop that aptitude. The point is that a person must be both *willing* and *able* to perform a task in order for it to be accomplished.

One important implication of the distinction between effort and performance is that a manager of volunteers must not equate low work performance with low work motivation; many performance deficiencies are the result of a lack of requisite ability on the part of the individual(s) involved. Therefore, a manager who responds to poor performance with tactics aimed at increasing a volunteer's desire to work will be ineffective. In fact, such a response may exacerbate the problem; the added pressure to perform can often worsen the feelings of frustration that result from failure. The only solution in such situations is to recognize the performance problem as an ability problem and to take the necessary steps, such as training, that are required to provide the volunteer with the skill(s) that have been deficient. The reader will find considerably more detail concerning the meaning and significance of ability in job performance elsewhere (Pinder, 1984).

Role Clarity. In addition to motivation and ability, at least one other factor influences employee job performance — the degree of clarity in the person's mind about what constitutes the job in question. In fact, this factor consists of two elements: (1) the degree of clarity in connection with what the individual is supposed to do; and (2) the clarity of understanding in regard to how his performance will be evaluated. In brief, the point can be made as follows: a highly motivated and highly able person is bound to be ineffective at a task unless he knows precisely what the goals of the task are! Many people waste their time, energy, and talent pursuing jobs that are not well defined in their minds. They don't understand what, exactly, they are supposed to be doing, so their motivation and ability are misdirected and the performance of work goals is not possible.

In addition to insufficient or inappropriate ability and lack of clarity on the part of a volunteer worker about what he is supposed to do, there are countless other practical factors that can prevent the volunteer from converting motivated effort into effective performance. Lack of budget, restricted access to facilities, low cooperation by other people — the list is endless. The critical point being made here is that astute management of volunteer work performance requires the volunteer manager to diagnose performance deficiencies carefully. It is often too easy to assume that poor performance results from a lack of desire when, in fact, ability, role ambiguity, and/or a host of other factors external to the individual may be responsible for his poor performance.

Some Implications for Volunteer Work Motivation

Now that we have discussed the various components of VIE Theory in somewhat general terms, we can briefly explore some of the most important implications this theory has for understanding the motivation of volunteers.

First, we note quickly again the importance of interindividual differences as well as intra-individual differences, especially in connection with the valence and expectancy components of the model. As argued at length in Chapter 3, different people's behavior is aroused and directed by different sets of needs, so different volunteers will find different outcomes valent. It can be very difficult to predict in advance or explain after the fact why certain people find the consequences of particular activities rewarding. For example, a young forestry student spends several hours a week chatting with and reading to eighty-year-old, chronically bedridden patients because he never knew his own grandparents, and — in his words — "it helps [him] better appreciate the problems of being old and facing imminent death."

Likewise, individual differences in expectancy perceptions are important in the volunteer context. Whereas some people might be inclined to volunteer to perform a certain activity (such as bookkeeping, for example) *because* it is easy for them to do so, others may volunteer for particular types of work in order to learn more about them by the process of performing them. And, again, the things one person finds difficult can be easy for someone else. As hard as it may be, managers of volunteers must try to be aware of the abilities of their volunteer workers in order to attain any influence over the expectancy element of the motivation of these workers to perform well on the job.

A second important point about the motivation to volunteer from a VIE perspective concerns the high instrumentality beliefs that can accompany many tasks that are associated with the satisfaction of the growth needs. Another way of saying this is that the very accomplishment of many tasks (such as helping people) is its own reward; the connection between performance and the receipt of growth need satisfaction by the volunteer is very strong and quite direct. Performance is highly instrumental for attaining these types of rewards, in large part because the feedback informing the volunteer that he has performed successfully is often immediate. An example would be the feelings of achievement that result from instructing a young Boy Scout how to light a campfire.

But the connection between effective performance and feelings of growth are not *always* so direct in volunteer work. People who have worked as volunteer counsellors with delinquent children know that success is often very hard to come by and that, even when they do succeed, knowledge of the positive outcomes of their work sometimes never become known to them. The primary implication for the motivation of volunteer work, of course, is to try to provide volunteers with knowledge of the results of their efforts, especially when those results are positive.

Organizational psychology has developed a full-blown theory of leadership based on VIE Theory. Known as the "Path-Goal Theory" of leadership (cf. Evans, 1970, 1974; House, 1971; House and Mitchell, 1974), this theory suggests a number of general principles for influencing an employee's work motivation by influencing the person's valence, instrumentality, and expectancy beliefs. While a complete treatment of this theory is beyond the scope of this chapter, three of its major tenets with particular relevance to the management of volunteers deserve brief mention. The logical connection between each of these tenets (or prescriptions) and the elements of VIE Theory should be readily apparent.

First, the effective manager is one who maximizes employee expectancy beliefs by providing support and resources and by assuring that the people under her command possess the requisite skills and abilities to get the job done. In a sense, she "clears the path" to successful performance by removing barriers and impediments, and clarifying the nature of the goals of the job.

Second, such a manager influences motivation and performance by offering, as much as possible, individualized rewards for effective job performance. Not only must outcomes be tied to performance (thereby raising instrumentality perceptions), but the outcomes must be, as much as possible, those things that individual volunteers need and desire. In volunteer settings, money is not available as a reward, so other outcomes must be tailor-made and tied to successful task accomplishment — such things as recognition, status, feelings of accomplishment, and so on.

The third suggestion to follow from this theory is to make sure that effective performance does not result in aversive or dissatisfying outcomes for volunteers. Loss of pride, out-of-pocket financial losses, and unnecessary inconvenience are three examples of aversive outcomes that might be incurred by a volunteer in the act of executing her job. VIE Theory and the Path-Goal model of leadership would prescribe that the volunteer manager would do her best to prevent such aversive outcomes from being associated with effective task performance.

In conclusion, the VIE approach to the motivation of volunteers rests heavily on the cognitive-perceptual aspect of human nature (cf. Walter and Marks, 1981). It explicitly assumes that people observe events, and that they form and modify beliefs based on those events. And most importantly, the theory assumes that ultimately no two people are alike; rather, it openly acknowledges the individuality of the human being.

REFERENCES

Bandura, A.
   1977   *Social Learning Theory*. Englewood Cliffs, NJ: Prentice-Hall.
Evans, M.G.
   1970   "The Effects of Supervisory Behavior on the Path-Goal Relationship," *Organizational Behavior and Human Performance* 5: 277-298.
   1974   "Extensions of a Path-Goal Theory of Motivation," *Journal of Applied Psychology* 59: 172-178.
House, R.J.
   1971   "A Path-Goal Theory of Leadership," *Administrative Science Quarterly* 16: 321-338.
House, R.J. and T.R. Mitchell
   1974   "Path-Goal Theory of Leadership," *Journal of Contemporary Business* 3: 81-98.
Lawler, E.E.
   1973   *Motivation in Work Organizations*. Belmont, CA: Brooks-Cole.
March, J.G. and H.A. Simon
   1958   *Organizations*. New York: Wiley.
Pinder, C.C.
   1984   *Work Motivation: Theory, Issues, and Applications*. Glenview, IL: Scott, Foreman and Co.
Vroom, V.
   1964   *Work and Motivation*. New York: Wiley.
Walter, G.A. and S.E. Marks
   1981   *Experiential Learning and Change*. New York: Wiley.

Chapter 5

IMPROVING VOLUNTEER MOTIVATION THROUGH JOB DESIGN

Ivan H. Scheier

INTRODUCTION

This chapter describes certain methods of improving volunteer motivation through the way in which the work is designed. The significance of these methods is then considered briefly, in terms of broad alternatives possible in our approach to motivation.

THE METHODS

The methods are based on fifteen years *in situ* observation of volunteer program administrators — what they actually do in designing or redesigning work for greater motivational appeal to volunteers. The writer's only contribution has been to recast these approaches in more explicit, self-conscious and systematic form than they ordinarily occur in current field usage.

The methods selected for presentation here appear to have in common an expectation that manipulation of certain primarily physical features of task and surrounding situation, can increase a volunteer's willingness to perform the work. So far as this writer is aware, the basis for this belief is "common sense" and anecdotal rather than research-founded.

The same is apparently true of an earlier but parallel development oriented towards paid employment in business and industry. Thus, in his chapter on "Work Design: Job Design Factors in Motivation," Hackman (1983: 492) states as follows: "In sum, it appears that despite the abundance of writing on the topic, there is little definite information about why work redesign is effective when it is, what goes wrong when it is not, and how the strategy can be altered to improve its general usefulness. . ."

Hackman (1983) also clearly states the re-orientation in assumption on which job design approaches are based, in a way which applies equally well to our concern with volunteer job design.

> Why have behavioral scientists not been more successful in their attempts to remedy motivational problems in organizations and improve the quality of work life of employees? One reason is that psychologists (like managers and labor leaders) have traditionally assumed that *work itself was inviolate* — that the role of psychologists is simply to help select, train, and motivate people within the confines of jobs as they have been designed by others. Clearly, it is time to reject this assumption and seek ways to change both people and jobs in order to improve the fit between them (Hackman, 1983: 495).

Several such approaches, which have evolved from our observations of *volunteer* work, will now be reviewed.

APPROACH A

Instrumentation: The Equipment Factor

All of us are aware of the extent to which machines, especially when the intent is to automate, can shrink or deaden motivation for work. Thus, Studs Terkel's book *Working* (1972) is full of people's comments on the dehumanizing effects of machines in the workplace. There is some resentment, too, e.g., the frequent observation that managers take better care of the equipment than they do of the workers, or else essentially treat people like robots.

Less well understood or capitalized on is the opposite case in which a tool, not necessarily the most efficient one, can increase a person's motivation for a task.

Thus, an acquaintance of mine will wash dishes willingly only when issued rubber gloves colored green. My young nephew declined to help control houseflies with the usual equipment, a fly swatter, but participates avidly when provided with a popgun. I suspect many of us have definite equipment needs for motivational facilitation of writing, e.g., softness versus hardness of pencil, fineness of penpoint, lined paper or not, etc. Few seem immune to the equipment factor in some form or another. I was once stymied in getting a group of juvenile delinquent youths to talk anonymously about why they got in trouble; that is, I was stymied until I produced a microphone and tape recorder. Then the problem was to control the rapid verbal flow.

A volunteer leader told me she was having trouble getting a person motivated to tie bows on gifts for a nursing home. Then she discovered that a certain kind of dog currying brush provided as a bow-tying tool, greatly increased the person's enthusiasm and perseverance in this task.

The equipment factor principle can be stated as follows: motivation for a task can sometimes be enhanced by the equipment provided for accomplishing the task. The principle does *not* assume that *efficiency* will be increased comparably, or at all. Although in the long run it seems difficult to imagine absence of some overall positive correlation between motivation and performance, this relationship appears in need of further research.

The potential for application seems promising enough so that we should encourage more self-conscious awareness of the principle among leaders of volunteers. This self-consciousness should also include awareness of limitations in application. Obviously there is the matter of equipment expense, in some cases. A fleet of canary yellow Porsches might motivate more volunteer drivers, but the average people-helping organization can't afford such "incentives." Ordinarily, far less costly tools can motivate, but unfortunately for efficiency in applications, there is no formula for predicting individual differences in equipment preference. For every person who wants a fine point pen, another wants a broad point. For some potential dishwashing volunteers, the motivating machinery may be neither green, nor rubber, nor a glove; it could be instead a scented biodegradable soap. A practical approach here might be to offer a selection of affordable tool choices, based on knowledge of the range of likely individual preferences, but ultimately, there is probably no substitute for knowing each potential volunteer's individual preferences.

APPROACH B

Component Analysis: Division and Combination

Component analysis depends on the possibility of analyzing a job into relatively discrete task elements. The process then capitalizes on variation in motivational attractiveness over different task elements for a given individual. Component analysis can move in either or both of two directions: division and combination.

1. *Division.* Division begins with the proposition that an overall job or piece of work can include components which might have very different "motivational values" for people.

For example: *"Please Take Care of the Potluck for Volunteers"* can include subtasks such as:

— Decide who's to be invited
— Select date, time, place
— Design invitations
— Address and mail invitations
— Arrange food (who brings what)
— Plan and get equipment for games
— Etc.

Suppose a potential potluck volunteer is willing or even enthusiastic about all subtasks except "arrange food," to which he or she has a raging aversion. Therefore, that person might turn you down because the negative motivational sign "infects" perception of the whole job. For this reason, "splitting" or dividing a task into component parts will sometimes get you yes's where before you were getting no's, because you now allow people to choose parts that appeal to them. Thus, one volunteer can now avoid the food arranging and is more likely to say yes to some or all of the other parts, while other people who enjoy arranging food can be recruited for that component.

In the same way, division can be an excellent way to plan work for a committee or group. Once the overall work is divided, individuals are more able to sign on for things they each most like to do and can do best, while avoiding the rest. When this situation is maximized for the entire group, there's a better chance the overall task will be accomplished willingly and effectively.

There are, nevertheless, some cautions in the division process:

    a) Make the analysis as fine-grained as possible. You can always combine elements later.

    b) After division, each individual tends to have a smaller piece of the overall action. Therefore, we must be especially careful that individuals still understand how their piece fits in the overall picture.

    c) Once divided, a piece of work stands more in need of an overall coordination function.

    2. Combination. Division seeks to eliminate the possibility of a motivationally unattractive component pulling down an associated attractive task. Of equal logical probability is the opposite effect, in which a motivationally positive work element pulls up an associated negative one. The implied process then becomes combination, rather than division/separation of task elements.

In the potluck supper example, the expectation would be that when all the attractive elements are combined with arranging food, the aversion to that subtask would be dampened, or possibly even converted to modest enjoyment, "in context."

But combination may be more than the mirror image of division, because combination could add elements not strictly a part of the original job as defined. Thus, classical Americana would have us believe that a teenager's zest for polishing the family car is far greater when associated with anticipation of impressing a date that evening. Addressing envelopes in a fund-raising campaign can be more motivating when associated with a role in deciding how the money raised will be allocated. (Other examples are in following sections; see especially the principles of variety and completion.)

Finally, the task elements combined may have little or no interrelatedness as contributors to the same work purpose.

Thus, the Need Overlap Analysis process of volunteer job design (Scheier, 1981) produces an assortment of ordinarily unattractive "spinoff" tasks plus typically more attractive "dream" tasks; these have in common only their origin in the same job factoring process applied to a set of paid employees and/or volunteer leaders. It is then assumed that the more attractive tasks can in some way "sweeten" the more routine spinoffs for volunteers, when they are associated.

The choice is not either/or between the division and combination processes. Both can be worth trying in the same work situation, and either might enhance volunteer motivation depending on whether unattractive subtasks are dominating attractive ones, or vice versa.

APPROACH C

Work Building (The Architecture of Work)

Motivational enhancement occurs not just in the sheer fact of association or lack of it among task elements (combination and division); there are also motivationally significant variations due to the manner in which components are associated. Four types of principles are identified and described below, relying mainly on the following example: we want to motivate volunteers to wrap gifts for nursing home residents. Thus far, enthusiasm for this task has not been overwhelming.

1. *Main Sequence*. Link elements over time to show evolving purpose. Ordinarily it is best to avoid giving people only assembly line cross sections of the total work. Instead try to look back in time to planning or other earlier stages (e.g., help select gifts) and also forward in time closer to achievement of purpose (e.g., deliver gifts to nursing home).

2. *Variety*. At about the same time as one thing is being done, seize the opportunity to do something else for contrast, variety, a change of pace.

This other task is not directly or closely related to the same work purpose. Thus, while a person is wrapping gifts in an office, he can occasionally greet people who enter the office. While a little variety is good to break the monotony, too much variety can be distracting, disruptive, counter-productive. For a volunteer whose main job is proofing manuscripts, answering the phone occasionally may provide a freshening "break"; but more frequent phone interruptions will tend to destroy the concentration necessary for proof-reading.

3. *Completion*. At about the same time as one thing is being done, seize the opportunity to do something else which gives a fuller sense of total purpose achieved. As with the principle of variety, two different things are done during the same general time period, but, in the case of completion, both things are directly related to achievement of the same overall work purpose. For example, when the volunteer delivers gifts to the nursing home, let her know she's also welcome to stay and chat with the giftees. Similarly, it may help to motivate your volunteer driver to let him know he is more than just a chauffeur for institutionalized youth, driving to and from medical attention; he can also talk to the young people while they are in the car.

Sometimes, attempts to apply the principle of completion result in clarifying and enlarging the definition of work purpose. Thus, one neighborhood in a medium-sized city was having trouble recruiting and retaining enough volunteers to deliver the neighborhood newsletter, especially during severe winter months. This situation improved markedly when they asked paper delivery people also to check for dangerous amounts of snow or ice on the house roof, and report these to the resident or neighbor. In this

83

case, the enrichment of completion occurred because understanding of work purpose was broadened from delivery of newsletters to something more like "the safety and well-being of neighborhood residents."

4. *Feedback Loops*. The end of a work process feeds back into an *improved* repetition of the work cycle (more than sheer repetition). In other words, the job is designed to reflect respect for the volunteer, specifically for what she has learned in the process of earlier work cycles. In the Figure 1 example, the volunteer who talks to nursing home residents as they receive their gifts naturally sees that some gifts go over better than others with certain kinds of people. He also has good on-site opportunities to formulate hypotheses as to why this is so. Closing the feedback loop enables such guidance to be channeled back into improved future selection of gifts for this nursing home. Feedback loops are usually advisory only; they need not assume policy control of the work by volunteers. But, even so, feedback loops tend to motivate by conveying to the volunteer a sense of respect and ownership.

Figure 1 illustrates the simplest possible application of the four work-building principles. Obviously, the designs could be far more complicated and elaborate, and they usually are in practice.

But even the simplified Figure 1 diagram clearly illustrates how much larger the job becomes after application of some or all of the principles; what we ended up with was certainly much more than wrapping gifts.

The question frequently raised is whether the additional time and effort required for the larger job tends actually to de-motivate volunteers. Where this seems to be so, and particularly where the person is perfectly happy wrapping gifts — or whatever the originally defined task was — the work-building principles should, of course, not be applied.

On the other hand, application of the principles might not always require much more time of the volunteer. Thus, where one person might be separately engaged in each of the five task elements in Figure 1, all five people could do the entire job less frequently with approximately the same individual and total time involvement. Indeed, for reasons of efficiency, somewhat less time might be needed.

But even when the "organically enlarged" job does ask more time of an individual, the irony is that one often has a better chance of getting the expanded involvement because the total task is more meaningful. Where limits of available volunteer time are nevertheless reached, the individual can at least be offered organically related segments of the whole. Moreover, the total diagram can also be used to orient volunteers on how their work fits into overall achievement of work purposes.

The four work-building principles can be used in two main ways:

1. "Creating" new or expanded jobs by building more motivation into a task which is difficult to get people to do willingly, e.g., wrap gifts, filing, attending board meetings, and/or

---

Figure 1: The Architecture of Work

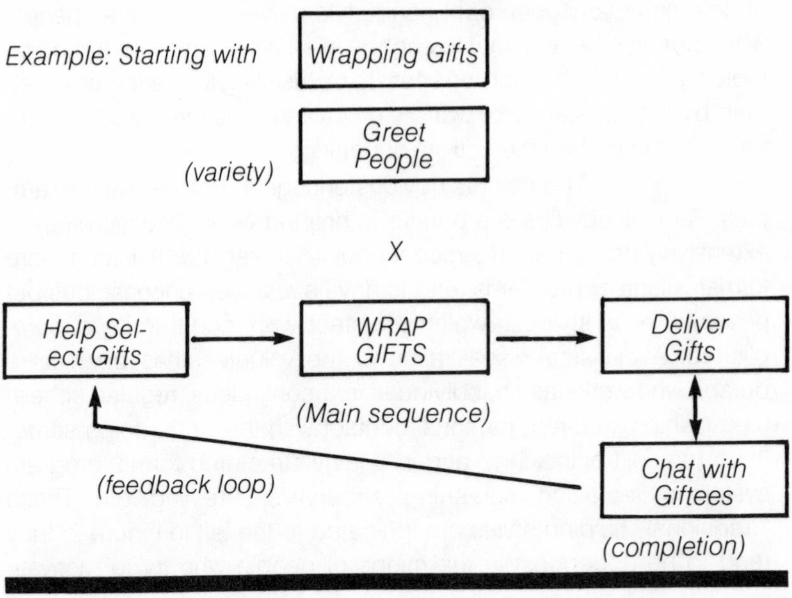

Example: Starting with   Wrapping Gifts

(variety)   Greet People

X

Help Select Gifts → WRAP GIFTS → Deliver Gifts

(Main sequence)

(feedback loop)   Chat with Giftees

(completion)

2. Applying the principles to volunteer jobs or roles already in existence, by drawing a map of such work as in the Figure 1 example. If, as diagrammed, an existing volunteer role seriously misses observance of most or all of the principles, you may be headed for motivational trouble with this volunteer job (or already be there).

APPROACH D
Style Profiling

A distinction can be made between a type of activity and the different ways in which this activity can be accomplished; between substance and style of work, if you will. Thus, hammering a nail remains essentially the same kind of activity whether the hammering is performed left-handed or right-handed; say the same for batting in baseball or serving in tennis. Just so, there are numerous different styles of walking, running, dancing, talking — though all these retain their identity as walking, etc., more or less regardless of variation in style.

Now, in recruiting volunteers for your softball team, you would probably not insist that everyone play left-handed; for fear of deterring many good right-hand-style players. In general, people who appear to be reluctant to engage in an activity may be turned off more by the style in which we seem to be insisting it be accomplished than by the substance of work, e.g., by the requirement to bat left-handed, rather than the activity of batting.

The point is obvious enough in most athletic examples. Far less obvious is a parallel in helping work. One hypothesis, extensively developed in a recent book (Scheier, 1980), is that more formal volunteer programs tend to have a relatively unconscious but powerful fix on styles in which volunteer work ought to be accomplished. A classical visualization of the volunteer has been as a person who works as an individual; in a continuous, regular, scheduled fashion; in direct personal contact with the work; doing something (not just onlooking); and in a fairly structured formal program system of recruiting, screening, supervision, training, etc. These "traditional" helping styles are indicated to the left in Figure 2; they tend to be uppermost in the minds of people who try to motivate volunteers, sometimes coming across as if they were the *only* ways in which the work purpose might be accomplished. Yet, as Figure 2 shows, each of these helping styles has an alternative (with many points in between the two poles as well) by which the same or a similar helping purpose might be achieved. Thus, a person who is unwilling to visit prisoners as an individual, may be more motivated to do so in an alternative style, that is, with his service club or church group. If a woman doesn't want to be tied down volunteering her graphic arts skills on a regular, scheduled basis, she might still be willing to do so in an occasional on-call style (skillsbank). Then, take the task of reminding people their charitable pledges are due. Some people, who would not volunteer to do that in person, might do it by phone, in the "at distance" style. The person who's disinclined to help the cause in an active service or "doing" role might still be persuaded to help as an observer, studier, thinker, advisor, on a committee or board. Finally, some people who appear apathetic to a program or organization are really more de-motivated by the formal, structured style, than the cause or purpose. Such people might well be willing to help in more informal ways.

Entire chapters have been devoted to each of the style alternatives indicated above, and other style dimensions as well (Scheier, 1980). One hopes only that enough has been said here to illustrate the potential for motivating volunteers by providing the job design and options in style of accomplishing a particular helping purpose. After division, combination and the four work-building principles have done everything possible to motivate volunteers by manipulating type or substance of work, these further manipulations of surrounding conditions have additional potential to motivate volunteers by offering a wider, more flexible array of stylistic alternatives.

One process for so doing has been called style profiling. The purpose, again, is to get more people involved more willingly in helping to achieve a work purpose. (More willing because we have effectively adapted the work to people's natural styles of helping.)

Step 1. Choose a volunteer job, actual or planned, which might be or is, in fact, difficult to recruit for. Example: "Friendly Visitor."

Step 2. For any set of style options, graph the central tendency of style *for this job as presently conceived*. Example: the line to the *left* in Figure 2 below.

Step 3. *Generalize* the job to an overall purpose of which it is a part.

Examples

Specific Job	General Purpose of Which It Is a Part
Friendly visitor	Companionship to the lonely
Tutor	Helping people learn
Grant-writer	Raising money
Board member	Helping us set policy

Step 4. Draw in another line to show the outer limit(s) of other styles by which this overreaching purpose could be achieved. In the example below, this is the line to the *right*.

Figure 2 illustrates application of the process for the job title: Friendly Visitor.

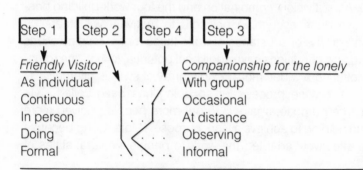

Figure 2: Steps in Style Profiling

The space between the two lines represents the increased scope of opportunity for involving people to achieve your purpose, because you've opened up more style options for them to choose from.

SIGNIFICANCE OF METHODS IN TERMS OF POSSIBLE APPROACHES TO MOTIVATION

The methods considered in this chapter are experimental, behavioral, and analytical in their approach to motivation.

The methods are not experimental in the strict sense of controlled laboratory experiment, but they do deserve the description in the broader sense of considering motivation as a dependent variable which can be influenced by manipulation of conditions external to the individual (independent variables).

As a dependent variable, the operational definition of motivation is behavioral. The behavioral outcome of consistently engaging in a piece of behavior (job, work) is considered sufficient evidence of motivation for that job or work. Little or no emphasis is placed on feelings per se, or any other factors "internal" to the person, unless or until they eventuate in defined work-behaviors, or clearly fail to do so.

Therefore, the approach is not analytical in the psychodynamic sense of probing the historical precursors of an individual's motivation or investigating that other non-present, the unconscious. But in the here and now the approach *is* analytical in a perhaps more literal sense, for it depends largely on the ability to break a total job down into task elements or components; the isolation or recombination of these components in various ways is a central feature in most of the methods.

Finally, a brief comparison may be worthwhile between the Hackman (1983) job design model for paid employment and the present approach based on volunteers. So far as I am aware, these two models developed essentially independently of one another. Yet there is substantial overlap, notably in the principles of "main sequence," "variety," and "completion" (using the present terminology), with partial overlap occurring in the principles of "combination" and "feedback loops." At the same time, Hackman does not appear to deal significantly with the volunteer job design principles here called "division," "style profiling," and "the equipment factor"; he also deals with several aspects not in the present volunteer model.

The two developments might have much to learn from one another, on the assumption that quality of work life is governed by essentially similar considerations, whether one happens to be paid for that work or not. Such a comparison could also help us begin to identify any fundamental differences which might exist between paid and unpaid work.

REFERENCES

Hackman, J. Richard
    1983 "Work Design: Job Design Factors in Motivation," in R.M. Steers and L.W. Porter, eds., *Motivation and Work Behavior* (3rd ed.). New York: McGraw-Hill, 492-495.

Scheier, Ivan
    1980 *Exploring Volunteer Space: The Recruiting of a Nation*. Boulder, CO: Yellowfire Press.
    1981 *The New People Approach Handbook*. Boulder, CO: Yellowfire Press.

Terkel, Studs
    1972 *Working*. New York: Pantheon Books.

91

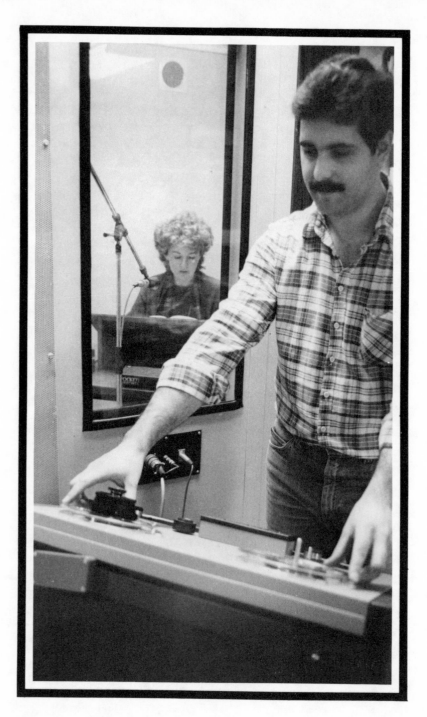

Chapter 6

MOTIVATION AND GOAL SETTING

Ronald J. Burke and Lary Lindsay

INTRODUCTION

Motivation and goal setting are two closely related concepts. This chapter will demonstrate how the use of a formal goal-setting process can be useful to the voluntary sector manager as a tool to increase and maintain the motivation levels of the volunteer work force. Before discussing the practical applications of goal setting, however, it may be helpful to have a basic understanding of the concept of motivation, the theory of and research into goàl setting, and what the volunteer experience really is. Once these basics are grasped, it will be possible to look at how goal setting can be put into practice on a day-to-day basis within a voluntary organization.

Any theory of motivation could be described as an attempt to explain why people engage in the behaviors that they do. To be more specific, motivation theory tries to explain what *initiates* behavior and what determines the *direction* and *persistence* of behavior (Lawler, 1973). Most voluntary behavior is goal oriented. People engage and persist in behaviors directed towards the achievements of some goal. The question that arises from this observation is what causes them to choose a particular goal and engage in activities that they expect to lead to its achievement. There are two models at the basis of most theories on how and why people choose goals that motivate them to engage in goal-directed behaviors.

The first model is based on the concept of man having basic instincts or drives that lead him to pursue specific goals. These instincts or drives are inherited and unconscious. These theories suggest that a basic need or drive is responsible for initiating goal-directed behavior, the direction and nature of which may be influenced by the environment. Drive is the energizing mechanism, and behavior is directed towards achieving a goal that will reduce the drive and re-establish a balance. Hull (1943) was a major proponent of this theory. He divided the concept of drives into primary and secondary, secondary drives being learned through association with the primary drives. While drive theory may be helpful in accounting for the initiation, persistence, and direction of behavior in some instances, it is unable to account for the variety and complexity of goals that people pursue even when they have no direct relation to the primary physiological drives and, on occasion, may even run counter to them.

The other model of motivation theory suggests that goals are chosen in a more rational fashion, based on needs, wishes, or desires. The individual is aware of what goals are being pursued and acts in the manner that *he feels* will best facilitate the achievement of these goals, whether or not this is in fact the most effective way to achieve them. The method used in trying to attain the goal will depend on environmental factors and the learned associations and experience of the individual. How the individual chooses a particular goal or goals is a more complex question. Maslow's theory of a "hierarchy of needs" proposes that there are five categories of human needs: physiological, safety, love, esteem, and self-actualization (Maslow, 1943).

An individual will always choose to satisfy the lower needs first, and only when these needs have been satisfied will he be motivated to pursue needs higher up the scale. Other needs or motives that have been recognized include needs for achievement, affiliation, and power. These needs appear to be inherent to human psychological make-up, and while their strength may vary at different times and between individuals, they are not related to primary physiological needs.

Both of these theories suggest that individuals set goals, either consciously or unconsciously, in response to some combination of internal and external or environmental factors. The presence of these goals motivates them to engage in activities which have led or which they believe will lead them to the achievement of the goals. Achievement of goals provides satisfaction and frees the individual to again be motivated to pursue additional goals. Of course, this is a gross simplification, as people may pursue a variety of unrelated goals simultaneously. Furthermore, lack of success in achieving a goal by one method may motivate the individual to either change the method of reaching the goal, or perhaps to change the goal itself. Thus goal setting is ubiquitous and is recognized, explicitly or implicitly, in every theory of motivation (Locke, 1978).

The implications for a manager are profound. If the manager can participate in the goal-setting process of his staff, he may be able to provide satisfying rewards in association with the goals he has set and coordinate organizational goals with the personal goals of the workers in order to reduce conflicts that might adversely affect motivation. At the same time, he may educate his staff as to the most effective means of achieving organizational goals, and thus their personal goals. This sounds like an easy thing to do, but there are a variety of issues to be considered in applying a formal goal setting process within an organization. Before examining how goal setting can be put into practice as a motivational technique, it may be useful to understand some of the theory and research that have been done in this area.

Goal setting is the process of determining a specific objective to be attained through a course of action. It is something that we all do to some extent, consciously or unconsciously, in our daily lives. It is equally prevalent, and perhaps more easily recognizable, in the business world. This process forms the basis of, or is a component of, many management and employee motivation techniques (Latham and Baldes, 1975). These include incentive plans, management by objectives, and quality circles, among others. Incentive plans use rewards, frequently in the form of money, to motivate employees to set or accept organizational goals. Management by objectives is a technique that uses goal setting, usually based on financial or cost accounting, as a measure of managerial performance. Quality circles involve groups of workers together discussing the effectiveness of their work, searching for solutions to problems that may enable them to more easily reach existing goals or set new goals. While goal setting may form an integral part of each of these motivation techniques, they do not of themselves form the process of goal setting.

Despite the fact that the concept of goal setting is

well known, it is frequently not used in an effective manner. There are a variety of factors that influence the success or failure of any goal-setting program and, if these are not taken into account, it is unlikely that the program will be as successful as it could or should be. There is a considerable body of research that has developed a comprehensive theory of how and why goal setting works, and what the necessary components of the process are (Latham and Locke, 1979). These factors include goal clarity and challenge, the presence of a measure of goal achievement, and feedback on performance in achieving goals. Though most of the research into goal setting has been conducted in industrial or laboratory settings, the theory should be equally applicable to the voluntary organization. Goal setting is a very practical motivational technique that can easily be established, and it is flexible enough to be adaptable to almost any situation.

The Goal-Setting Concept

To understand the theory of goal setting we need to know how we define a goal or objective, why the process works, and what each of the above-mentioned factors of clarity, challenge, achievement measure, and feedback contribute to the process that makes them so necessary. We can learn this by examining each of the factors separately and what role they play in increasing motivation and performance. A look at some examples of supporting evidence for goal-setting theory will help to illustrate how the process works and the dramatic effect it can have in improving performance (Locke, Latham, Saari, and Shaw, 1981).

A goal may be described as a task, a time limit, a quota, a standard, an objective, or any combination of the above. A goal is a particular outcome that is sought for some reason, an outcome that is subject to some form of measurement or judgement to determine whether it has been reached. Goals may encompass the overall strategic objectives of an organization or may detail the day-to-day tasks necessary to achieve the strategic objectives. They may be quantitative or qualitative. Ideally, goals should be set for every level of an organization, and the goals for each level should be integrated with those of other departments on the same level, as well as those above and below, in order to ensure that goals are pursued as efficiently as possible without duplication or conflict in efforts. Good clear goals serve several useful purposes: they clarify the relationship of the desired accomplishments of different organizational units to ensure appropriate direction and minimize duplication of effort; they provide direction for the generation and comparison of alternative methods of achievement; and they provide a reference base against which to compare the actual results being achieved during implementation.

Why Goal Setting Works

There are many reasons why people who set specific and challenging goals perform better than those who do not have such goals (Ivancevich, 1976). The use of a formal goal-setting process helps to clarify exactly what is to be done and how it is to be done. A specific goal helps the worker to identify clearly exactly what expectations are held of him, thus enabling him to focus his efforts on actions that will lead to the fulfillment of these expectations. Employees in goal-setting experiments have frequently commented that they had previously never understood exactly what it was that their supervisors expected them to do. Studies have shown that specific goals are far more effective in increasing performance than vague goals because they are more effective in directing the efforts of those pursuing the goals. It is less likely that conflicts or misunderstandings of what is expected will arise. The more specific the definition of the goal, the more effective it is likely to be. A goal may specify a quantity, a quality, and a time limit. Each of these specifications helps to clarify what is expected and to direct effort towards the achievement of the specifications. Being specific in setting goals may also help identify problems in advance so that they can be remedied or so that the goal can be adjusted before time and energy are wasted in pursuit of an impossible objective. Problems that may be spotted by using specific goals may include factors in the external environment, conflicting internal goals, or lack of knowledge or available resources.

Setting difficult or challenging goals is more likely to improve performance than setting easy goals. People work harder to achieve a difficult goal if it appears within the realm of possibility to attain it, and they tend to sustain their efforts. A goal that is seen to be easy to achieve will not inspire the same effort and, once the goal has been achieved, efforts will likely fall off unless new goals are set. A difficult goal is more likely to encourage the worker to examine carefully the efficiency of his actions in striving for it and to be innovative and creative in finding ways to improve his efficiency. Challenging goals are more likely to foster an atmosphere of competition. This may be either an individual attempting to exceed his own past performance at achieving a particular goal or a friendly competition between workers who share the same goals, with each striving for the best performance of the group.

Though difficult goals are effective in improving performance, care must be taken in setting them to ensure that they do not have a negative impact on motivation. The goal should be challenging, but should also appear to be attainable. A goal that appears impossible may discourage any efforts to attempt it. However, if it appears possible and if partial success in achieving it will be meaningful and bring credit to the person, then even an unattainable goal will prove motivating. If a goal is particularly difficult or long term, it may be useful to break it down into smaller subgoals that may be more easily reached. This will help to create an ongoing feeling of accomplishment and motivate the worker to persist in his efforts towards the ultimate goal.

The third factor that has been identified as critical to the goal-setting process is the presence of achievement measures. We have already discussed the importance of being specific in defining goals. Being specific in setting goals makes it easier to measure what progress has been made towards achieving them. If the goal specified a quantity or a deadline, it is simple to determine whether this has been reached. The method by which achievement of a goal will be measured must be clearly spelled out before the goal is assigned. This is necessary to be certain that both the manager and the employee understand exactly the basis on which performance will be evaluated. Progress towards a goal may be subjected to the standard of measurement in order to determine if, or to what degree, the goal has been achieved. This measurement is important because it is used to provide feedback to both the employee and management.

It is important to give careful consideration to the kinds of achievement measures adopted. Some things are easier to measure than others, i.e., the quantity of widgets produced as opposed to an improvement in the quality of widgets produced. Achievement measures should not be conflicting and should be directly related to success in achieving the goal that is under the control of the individual whose work is being measured. There is no point in giving or withdrawing credit when the performance has resulted from external factors beyond the control of the employee, nor is it desirable to create a situation where performance may score high on the measure of achievement although very little, if any, real progress is made towards achieving the goal. Achievement measures may be based on time-motion studies, past performance, units produced, time deadlines, money, behaviors, or actions. How a particular measure is chosen requires judgement, but once it has been chosen, in association with the desired goal, an objective can be set that will identify if the goal has been reached.

Feedback

Feedback is an extremely important part of any goal-setting program (Ilgren, Fisher, and Taylor, 1979). It is not enough only to set specific goals and a standard for measuring progress towards their achievement. Those working towards the goals must be informed of how they are doing if the increase in motivation and performance levels is to be maintained. Feedback may come in various forms. It may be as simple as keeping a chart that shows how many or how much of something has been produced. It may be in the form of a smile or encouraging comment from a supervisor, or it may be a more concrete reward, such as a gift or a certificate of accomplishment. It can be informal or more formal, as in a performance review. Whatever form it takes, feedback should always be positive, constructive, consistent, and frequent.

Feedback should be positive because it is intended to help increase motivation. Criticism is one of the fastest ways to decrease motivation and self-esteem , and when these are lowered, performance levels usually follow. In a volunteer organization an unhappy worker may simply leave the organization. If a specified goal has not been reached, feedback should focus on the progress that has been made towards reaching the goal and not on any mistakes that may have prevented its achievement. It is helpful to show recognition of desired behaviors and actions, rather than criticizing undesirable ones. This reinforces the motivation to repeat those actions that are desirable and have been praised. If the method of setting the goals has been specific enough, these actions should be easy to identify and measure, thus making it easy for both the volunteer and supervisor to recognize when they have been successfully performed. Attaining goals results in the employee experiencing "psychological success" (Hall, 1979), an important element in both work motivation and commitment.

The process of giving feedback should also be constructive; it should lead to the setting of additional goals for future performance. There is no point in crying over spilled milk. If a goal has not been reached, the emphasis should be on what can be done differently or better in the future in order to reach it. Does the worker need more training? Is there a conflict between goals that means that priorities should be rearranged? If the goal is too difficult, perhaps it should be broken down into a series of more manageable subgoals. It may be necessary to reallocate resources within the organization to facilitate progress towards the goal. Constructive feedback is oriented towards identifying action that can be taken to improve performance. Before a performance review ends, both the supervisor and the volunteer should clearly understand exactly what actions are to be taken, how they are to be measured, and when the next review session will take place.

Volunteers should be kept aware of how often and in what manner their performance will be evaluated. Where feedback includes suggestions directed towards further improvement of performance these should be limited to one or two specific ideas at a time. Too many new things to work on at once are only likely to confuse people and lead to a diffusion of their efforts.

Some Research Findings

A study by White and Locke (1981) illustrates the conditions perceived by workers to increase or decrease productivity. The presence of specific, challenging goals and deadlines (one method of measuring achievement) contributed to more than half of the high productivity scenarios, while almost 60% of low productivity was perceived to be caused by the lack of these factors. Responsibility, promotion, recognition, and pleasant personal relationships could all be considered facets of good feedback, and also make a significant contribution to high productivity.

The results of other research studies in a business or industrial environment illustrate the simplicity and effectiveness of instituting a goal-setting program, as well as demonstrating how the components of clarity, challenge, achievement measures, and feedback work together to effect its success (Latham, Cummings, and Mitchell, 1981).

Goal Setting and the Voluntary Organization

Now that we have reached some understanding of motivation and the concept of goal setting as a formal motivational technique, what more should we know to apply this technique within the voluntary organization? Since goal setting usually is an attempt to persuade the workers to accept the organizational goals and work towards them in order to help satisfy their own personal goals, it would probably be useful to gain some understanding of the volunteer experience (Moyer, 1983). What motivates someone to do work for which there is no monetary reward? This is not the norm in our society, so they must be receiving some other form of satisfaction. What happens to volunteers once they join an organization? What do they expect of it and what does it expect of them? The volunteer administrator needs to have some understanding of all these issues as they apply to the volunteers within his organization if he wishes to use goal setting as a technique to improve their motivation, performance, and effectiveness (Wiehe and Isenhour, 1979).

Motivation and the Volunteer

Both the perception of what kind of activity volunteering is and the types of people who volunteer are in the process of undergoing a radical change due to changes in the environment in which voluntary organizations function (Jenner, 1981). It used to be that the typical volunteer was a middle-class housewife who had no other job and perceived her volunteer work as a leisure activity which might enable her to get out of the house, meet people, increase her self-esteem by making her feel that she was "doing good," or increase her social status. Today that middle-class housewife with time on her hands is a vanishing species. Volunteers must be enlisted from other groups of people who have more work, family, and other responsibilities placing demands on their time. At the same time, there are more voluntary organizations developing to meet different needs, i.e. charities, medical research, arts, political change. Volunteering is seen more as a job that pays off in non-monetary compensation. "Selfish" motives are more likely to prevail. This means that the voluntary agency has to compete in order to attract and keep a motivated volunteer (Henderson, 1981).

Anyone who becomes a volunteer is motivated by some form of private agenda which includes their own goals and expectations of what being a volunteer will mean for them. People may be motivated to volunteer for a wide variety of reasons. Factors underlying their reasons for volunteering may be a need for achievement, a need for affiliation, or a need for power. Some of these reasons may be described as altruistic or internally motivated, and some as selfish or externally motivated.

Some examples of motives referred to as altruistic could include a desire to help those less fortunate, the expression of personal values, and social affiliation. The perceived reward for engaging in behaviors such as these may be an enhanced sense of self-esteem. External or selfish motives usually have more concrete and easily apparent rewards. These may include gaining academic credit, developing social contacts, acquiring work experience, or exploring careers.

This change in attitudes towards volunteering from something that was perceived as a leisure activity or hobby to a job that pays off in non-monetary compensation has profound implications for the volunteer administrator. If they treat volunteers' efforts only as a hobby, to be pursued when and as they please, it is very difficult to expect much in the way of consistent performance or responsibility from the volunteers. This can create a vicious circle, as those volunteers who do not know what specifically is expected of them will have no incentive or motivation to improve their performance. They may tend to be inconsistent in how often or how long they work, or in how much they accomplish, and they may become unreliable as workers. At the same time, since the lack of knowledge of what is expected of them gives them no means by which they can measure their success in achieving the goals of the organization or their own personal goals, some of the intrinsic rewards of success are lost, and they may lose their motivation to volunteer, creating a high turnover in the organization.

On the other hand, there are some inherent difficulties in treating the volunteer as a worker, rather than a hobbyist

(Pierce, 1983). A worker generally has the advantage of an extrinsic reward that is easily measured, such as a paycheque, available to justify his efforts on the job. The rewards of a volunteer are not so easily identified. They tend to be the more intrinsic rewards of personal satisfaction derived from the successful accomplishment of a task or the feeling of having done some good or learned something new. In addition, some laboratory studies have found that when the perceived extrinsic rewards for a task are few or difficult to identify, people tend to believe that they like the task itself better, in an attempt to explain to themselves why they are doing it. These rewards provide the justification for engaging in a volunteer activity and the motivation for continuing it. However, rewards, whether intrinsic or extrinsic, are usually related to successful performance in achieving some objective. For the employee, what is expected of him is usually fairly clear. It is not always so for the volunteer. If volunteers are to feel the intrinsic rewards of successful performance, they need to be able to identify what successful performance is. This means that they will be more motivated if they are treated like employees and given clear expectations as to accomplishments, hours of work, tasks to be performed, deadlines to be met, etc. The motivated volunteer is likely to be a reliable volunteer, and the effectiveness of a volunteer organization can be greatly enhanced by the dependability of its workers.

Whatever the initial motivation for volunteering may have been, if the volunteer is to remain committed to the organization, there must be some perceived level of achievement or satisfaction. This may be in the form of education, recognition, social interaction, personal satisfaction, or an identifiable contribution to the purpose of the organization.

The formal use of goal setting can be an invaluable tool in a voluntary organization. Unlike most business organizations which tend to have quite explicit goals underlying their operations, i.e. increasing profits or productivity to specified levels, many voluntary organizations tend to have very vague objectives which cannot be easily measured. In addition, the employee in a business usually has a fairly specific job description and a fair understanding of what is expected of him. The volunteer, on the other hand, may not know exactly what commitment is expected or what duties should be performed, other than to "help." The employee likely receives frequent feedback and evaluation of his performance; the volunteer only an occasional thank you, if that. Many voluntary organizations persist in viewing the volunteer as a hobbyist, of whom little can be asked or expected.

Spending time defining the objectives of a voluntary organization in specific terms and how these goals are to be achieved can vastly improve the effectiveness of the organization in achieving those objectives. Goal setting will also help to clarify the psychological contract between the volunteer and the organization, leading to an improvement in the motivation, commitment, and effectiveness of the volunteer. This process will probably also pay off by improving the utilization of financial and other resources which tend to be scarce in many voluntary organizations.

Applying the Goal-Setting Concept

How can the voluntary sector manager take this theory on goal setting and apply it within a particular organization? What are the day-to-day techniques he should use to make the practical application of a goal-setting program effective?

Ideally, goal setting should be used at every level of the organization, from the strategic and long term to the mundane and day-to-day. This will not always be the case, but even if goal setting begins only in one area of the organization, it may be effective in improving performance in that area. When the performance improvement is noted in other areas, the technique may spread.

Any organization will usually have a variety of goals. The major goals of many include such things as performing a service or activity, fund raising, attracting and keeping motivated volunteers, etc. The major goals are interrelated, and each may be divided into a series of tasks necessary to achieve the desired objectives. It is important when subdividing goals into tasks that the tasks be coordinated in order to avoid duplication of effort and that priorities of different goals or tasks are identified.

The implementation of a goal-setting program requires three elements. The first step is to obtain the commitment of the workers to the program. The second step is the planning process. Finally, once the program has been accepted and begun, there must be an ongoing process of review and evaluation.

The first step in the implementation of goal setting is to obtain the commitment of those who will have to work with the goals. Where goal setting is a new technique in the organization this is more complex than dealing with people who are used to having goals assigned to them, although, even in the latter case, commitment is necessary if the goals are to be achieved.

As a general rule, it is not necessary to enlist the participation of workers in the process of setting goals in order to obtain their commitment to the goals that are set. Such participation can be useful in defining goals but does not seem to affect commitment to goals and only affects performance if it leads to higher goals being set than would otherwise have been the case. However, in a voluntary organization it may be a good idea to enlist the participation of the volunteers in defining goals. Since volunteers work by choice, they may be less likely to continue to work if they do not agree with the objectives of their work.

Some suggestions that may be useful in obtaining the commitment and cooperation of those involved in a goal-setting experiment are as follows:

(1) Explain the purposes of goal setting and how the goals were set, i.e. to increase efficiency and productivity.

(2) Stress that the participation in achieving the specified goals is voluntary.

(3) Indicate that there will be no penalty or sanction taken against anyone who fails to achieve the specified goals or objectives.

(4) Describe what rewards internal or external, may be received by those who participate, whether or not they achieve or exceed their goals.

Once a commitment to the principle of goal setting and acceptance of the goals that have been set is obtained, the implementation of the goal-setting program requires an action plan. An action plan should focus on the most effective and efficient methods of facilitating goal attainment. This may be by using the same methods that have been used previously, or it may be useful to be more creative and consider and evaluate alternative methods.

The action plan may be a means of testing whether objectives can be achieved as planned, or whether there are unanticipated stumbling blocks or problems that need to be resolved before putting it into effect.

The action plan stems from the initial setting of objectives and forms the basis for the interaction between the manager and the worker in striving to achieve the objectives. The initial goals are set by management, keeping in mind the importance of setting clear, specific, and measurable goals. From there, the manager and volunteer work together to determine on a day-to-day basis how the work should be done.

In establishing an action plan, it can be very valuable to enlist the participation of the workers affected by it. While participation in the act of setting goals has not been shown to be effective or necessary for goal acceptance, unless it leads to the setting of higher goals (though it may be necessary in voluntary organizations to ensure that the volunteers agree with the goals), it may be extremely useful in forming an action plan. Few are more likely to see a better, more efficient or creative way of performing a task than those who actually do that task.

In general, there are three basic principles that should be kept in mind when preparing an action plan. First, the volunteer needs to know what is expected of him. This reinforces the need for a clear, specific goal. Second, the volunteer needs to know how he is doing. This means he should thoroughly understand how the performance will be measured, as well as the review process for evaluating performance. Finally, the volunteer needs to be able to obtain assistance when necessary. He should know where and who to refer to for assistance, and this should be easily available. An example of one use of goal setting in an organization, termed Work Planning and Review, is shown in Appendix A.

In working with the volunteer to form an action plan, the manager should first outline to the volunteer what specific goals he is expected to achieve. It is useful to relate these goals to the goals of the department or section and indicate how they may contribute to the overall goals of the organization. It may also be helpful to have the volunteer prepare a list of suggested goals before the planning session. A comparison of what the manager and volunteer perceive as goals can facilitate the determination of tasks necessary to reach the goals. Once you have identified the basic subject matter for a goal, it is necessary to word it and write it down so it is clear and understandable. To really get at the "results desired," ask questions such as these:

— What end result is desired?
— What situation are you trying to create?
— What must the work in this area accomplish?
— What new conditions are to be created?
— What achievements are wanted?
— What returns are expected?

A well thought out goal usually specifies a single specific end result to be accomplished, specifies a target date for its accomplishment, specifies maximum cost factors (money or effort), is as specific and measurable as possible (or at least is observable and describable), and is realistic and attainable.

The next step is to define these tasks. This is the area in which the people actually doing the work can make the greatest contribution. If they appear capable or have experience in the job, it is worthwhile to have them develop the plan, indicating how they intend to go about the necessary tasks to achieve the goal, and what these tasks are. From here, the method by which achievement is measured can be developed.

It is vitally important that both the volunteer and the manager clearly understand how achievement is to be measured. This is the means by which the volunteer may judge his own progress and how his progress will be evaluated when it comes time for a review. The achievement measures must be specific and directly related to the work being done.

There are a number of things that should be considered in outlining achievement measures. They should be designed in such a way that they cover all of the tasks that will be done in pursuit of the goal. This may mean that several measures need to be developed on different scales or for different tasks. The measures should be as objective and specific as possible. Indicators that are too broad or too general can be easily misunderstood, and thus lose their effectiveness. They should be designed in a positive spirit, not as a means of trapping or hindering the worker. Do not use time, quantity, or quality objectives alone. Measures of this nature usually need to be used in conjunction with each other to be effective.

Keep in mind the need for flexibility and common sense. Take a positive attitude in setting goals and achievement measures, and try to establish indicators that will improve job performance. Do not become too tied up with procedures that are nonproductive, such as filling out forms, to the extent that they interfere with the work being done. Be ready to adjust the goals or the measure of achievement if it proves necessary or if conditions change.

So far, then, we have had the manager and the volunteer draw up a list of goals and an action plan that outlines the steps that will be taken in pursuit of the goals and how progress will be measured. When the two sit down together to discuss the action plan, it is crucial that there is a mutual understanding and agreement on the goals and the measures of achievement. It is essential that this agreement be reached before the job is begun, in order to prevent misunderstandings later on. If difficulties arise in reaching agreement, this usually indicates that the goals are unrealistic for one reason or another. This is where the element of flexibility comes in.

It is preferable to identify and resolve problems at the planning stage than to wait and discover them later when it may be more difficult to find a solution. Problems may arise if the goals are too broad or general. In this case, they may have to be subdivided to make them more specific and easier to measure. Dividing a goal into subgoals may also be appropriate if the goal is long term. It is easier to keep a short-term goal in sight, which may help to sustain motivation.

A thorough planning process can identify other obstacles. Occasionally some goals may be in conflict with or duplicate others. Duplication of efforts can easily be eliminated early. When goals are in conflict with each other, it may be necessary to adjust the goals themselves, or to set priorities between the goals. Priority among goals is an important item to be resolved in the planning session. There are usually some goals that should be accomplished before others, or that should be given more effort than others. These should be clearly identified and understood by the participants in the planning session.

The goal-setting process is also useful in terms of the factor of control. Control can be thought of in the sense of a driver steering a car — keeping things headed where you want to go. To keep headed in the right direction you need to know two things: where you want to go (the goal) and where you are heading now (the results to date). For the job of controlling, people look at the goals and existing plans as their major tools. They will have a better basis for keeping track of progress if they know what it is they want to achieve and how they plan to achieve it. When something does go wrong, they can quickly spot the difficulty before it becomes crucial.

There are three basic activities involved in control: (1) measuring results to date, (2) comparing actual results to the goals and analyzing deviations, and (3) providing feedback for corrective or adaptive action. A critical step in the control system is measuring or monitoring the progress to date and getting that data fed back in useful form at the right time. Some useful questions to ask are: How will I know when this job or plan is being satisfactorily performed? How will I identify and measure the level of performance achievement against this goal? What are some specific and timely mileposts to track the progress of the plan? What will trigger the contingent action plans? Then it is time to work with the available sources of the required information to arrange for the necessary feedback of progress towards the goals. Sometimes the data is not readily available in the form requested but will prove satisfactory if a relatively minor change is made to the wording of the goal. When the individual knows what results he is supposed to accomplish and has the measures available to track his own progress, he does not have to wait for his supervisor to let him know how he is doing; he will know already. The emphasis will be on self-control.

Another item that may be identified in the planning session is the need for further training of the volunteers. Training may be time consuming initially, but will almost invariably pay off in higher productivity. This increases satisfaction all around. We have noted that many volunteers are seeking to increase their experience. Learning a new skill can help them to achieve that goal and, in combination with the increased productivity of their efforts, will enhance their satisfaction. The satisfied volunteer will remain more committed to the organization. The manager, though initially providing close supervision, will ultimately need to provide less supervision.

At this point it may be useful to consider a model organization in the voluntary sector. By looking at a composite of typical goals in voluntary organizations, we can follow the goal-setting and work-planning process.

Most voluntary organizations exist to provide some form of service. Providing this service is usually the primary goal of the organization. However, in order to achieve this goal, there are several things that must be done. The facilities to provide the service must be obtained, the recipients of the service must be identified, funds must be raised to finance the effort, and volunteers must be recruited to perform all of the functions required to keep the organization running. All of these things are subgoals that are necessary to achieve the primary goal.

The first step that should be taken is for the management of the organization to sit down and work out specific definitions of each goal. These are the longer term, strategic goals. If the object is to provide a service, this process should define exactly what the service is. For our purposes, we will consider the service to be offered as providing food to the needy. Will the food be provided as prepared meals from a soup kitchen or as grocery supplies? How many people will be served each year? Will they be served on a regular or an emergency basis? How frequently will the food be supplied? How will the recipients of the food be identified? Will they have to apply for the food and be subject to a means test or will they be located through social service agencies? They may be restricted by geographical location or through some other classification which should be strictly defined.

The facilities necessary to provide the service must be identified and obtained. If the food is to be provided as prepared meals, a kitchen and dining hall will be needed. If a grocery service is contemplated, some form of warehousing and perhaps provisions for delivery are necessary. The location and size of the facilities may be determined by the number and location of the clients to be served. Funding requirements will be affected by the decision to buy or lease.

The funding requirements to operate the organization must be determined and a budget prepared. An average cost per meal or package of groceries can be set and multiplied by the number of recipients the organization plans on serving. Administrative costs must be added in, including the cost of facilities, paid staff, if necessary, and office costs. The budget should be broken down to indicate weekly or monthly costs, as well as annual costs. This helps ensure better control of costs, as well as providing a means of identifying when adjustments should be made to the budget.

How are these funds going to be acquired? Will fund raising be conducted on an ongoing basis, or in one or more campaigns during the year? Fund raising may provide the cash to buy food and meet expenses, or donations of food and supplies may be sought. Donations may be sought through government or corporate financing, or appeals may be made to individual donors.

Volunteers will be needed to perform the functions identified. They may be available from a particular source, such as a church, service club, or university, or it may be necessary to recruit them from the general public. What level of commitment will they be required to make? It may be possible to have fewer volunteers if they are willing to put in more hours per week. The expectations of the organization should be made clear to volunteers at the start, in terms of time or hours worked and duties performed.

Once the above goals are specifically defined, work planning can be done on a more functional, task-oriented basis between the manager and the individual volunteers. Let us examine the types of tasks and measures that might be applicable to the fund-raising process.

When the funding requirements were determined, a budget was drawn up. This budget provides the target or goal that must be reached in dollar figures for the year. This can be broken down to provide goals for the amount to be raised in shorter periods, whether fund raising is ongoing or limited to a particular campaign period. We now have a dollar figure and a deadline, two measures of whether or to what extent the goal has been reached.

There are many methods of raising money. Personal appeals, mail or telephone solicitation, and advertising are a few. These may be used alone or in combination. Estimates or past experience may be used to determine how much activity in each task will be necessary to meet the goal. This level of activity then becomes a subgoal. The volunteer may be expected to send out so many letters, or make a certain number of phone calls, or knock on a specific number of doors each week or day. If this level of activity is adhered to, the level of donations should be as expected. The point is that the type and quantity of effort expected from an individual can be very sharply defined and measured at this level. The manager and volunteer can come to a clear agreement and understanding of what the volunteer will accomplish and what resources or training may be necessary. This means that the psychological contract between the volunteer and the organization is well defined, so expectations may be more easily filled, leading to greater satisfaction on both sides.

Successfully completing the planning process is not

the end of the story. Progress towards the achievement of goals must be constantly and carefully monitored and a comprehensive review system established. The review system serves both as a vehicle for evaluating progress and as a means of facilitating additional planning and adjustment of goals or tasks. It also provides an occasion for reinforcing the motivation and satisfaction of the volunteer. This is where the volunteer can learn how he or she is doing.

Review sessions should be conducted as often as necessary. In some cases, this may mean that they are scheduled at a regular time interval. Sometimes they may be set at the completion of a particular task or goal. Even if the usual timing of review sessions is based on one of the above, it is important to be flexible. If a review time comes up and does not seem necessary, do not waste too much time on it. On the other hand, if a review seems appropriate but is not yet scheduled, do not hesitate to sit down and go over things.

A review session provides the opportunity for the manager to give the volunteer feedback on what progress has been made. If the planning process has been well organized and if the manager and volunteer reached a good understanding and agreement on goals and achievement measures before the work was started, the review session should be easy for both parties. The volunteer will already have a good idea of how he is doing and where he measures up according to the standards that were set. If the goals or achievement measures have been poorly laid out, the review sessions cannot be as productive or serve to increase motivation and improve performance.

The emphasis in a review session should always be on positive, constructive ideas. The direction taken should be on what will improve performance in the future and not on taking a judgemental attitude towards past performance. The review session provides the manager with a chance to assess the level of contribution the volunteer is making. This is the time when efforts can be made to improve the contributions of volunteers who are falling below expectations or to encourage those who are meeting or exceeding what is expected.

There are a number of factors or types of behavior which have been found to either increase the motivation and satisfaction of workers, or to decrease these feelings. Some of the positive factors include:

(1) providing recognition and praise;
(2) assigning tasks of increasing challenge, responsibility, and freedom;
(3) supporting and encouraging creative ideas;
(4) involving workers in joint problem-solving;
(5) helping the worker develop skills;
(6) indicating how the job or function contributed to unit or organizational goals;
(7) mediating conflicts that hampered job performance.

Some of the negative factors include:
(1) strongly criticizing job performance;
(2) providing too close or not enough supervision;
(3) not providing or obtaining answers to workers' questions;
(4) unilateral decision-making by the supervisor;
(5) lacking openness to new ideas and approaches;
(6) lack of trust in workers;
(7) lack of praise for job performance;
(8) assigning boring or tedious tasks.

Some of the positive and negative factors are opposites, while others are unique. The positive factors seem to have a direct bearing on job performance, while the negative factors impact first on motivation and indirectly from there to decreasing performance. All of these factors should be remembered both in day-to-day management and during review sessions.

Before conducting a review session, both the manager and the volunteer should go over the goals and measures of achievement. While doing this they should keep in mind for discussion the progress that was made, problems or obstacles and how they might be solved, and ideas or new goals to be considered for future planning. The review session should be a time to discuss and agree on how far we have come, and where we go from here. By the end of the review session both parties should have reached agreement on new goals and what tasks will be done next, just as in the planning session.

An important part of providing feedback and holding

review sessions is the opportunity to provide recognition or rewards. These help to provide the volunteer with a sense of achievement, which increases personal satisfaction and helps to maintain or enhance the motivation to continue as a volunteer. The value of this should not be underestimated. Many voluntary organizations have a high turnover of volunteers. If turnover can be reduced, the efficiency and effectiveness of the organization will be improved. Fewer resources will need to be spent on recruiting and training volunteers. Existing volunteers are likely to be more productive as well.

Although volunteers do not receive monetary rewards as compensation for their efforts, there are many other options that can provide them with recognition. Day-to-day supportive responses such as a smile, congratulations, or a few encouraging words are one way of providing recognition. Increasing responsibilities or providing more challenging tasks also indicate that the volunteer is performing well. A social get-together to celebrate success in some endeavour will be appreciated by volunteers who have an affiliation motive as part of their reason for volunteering. These may also be occasions for the presentation of awards in recognition of particular accomplishments.

Many organizations have some system of certificates to recognize the contribution a volunteer has made. Blood donors have a card to carry. When the volunteers come from a group whose motivation is to acquire experience or skills, particularly students, these may be extremely useful in reducing turnover. Providing a certificate that indicates hours of service or skill levels attained may help to reduce or eliminate those who sign up in order to list the organization on a resume and then do little if any real work. This type of reward also serves to clarify the expectations and psychological contract between the volunteer and the organization.

Managing Day-To-Day Job Performance

The concept of goal setting is also relevant to one other important area of staff motivation and performance. This area deals with the way supervisors manage the day-to-day job performance of their staff. Managers have their own "theories" about how they can influence the motivation level of their staff through their own actions. Oldham (1976), building on available motivational theories, proposed a set of leader activities predicted to have a significant impact on work effectiveness indicators (motivation and job performance). He hypothesized that the more frequently supervisors applied these motivational strategies, (a) the more effective they would be rated in motivating their subordinates, and (b) the greater would be their subordinates' rated productivity.

Nine motivational strategies were identified by Oldham:

(1) Personally Rewarding — interpersonal rewards distributed to subordinates in response to subordinates' behaviors (congratulations, pats on the back, a nod or smile indicating a job well done, similar supportive activities).

(2) Personally Punishing — interpersonal punishments distributed to subordinates in response to subordinate behaviors (yelling at, ignoring, acting unpleasant towards).

(3) Setting Goals — the setting of specific performance quotas, goals, or standards for subordinates to achieve. This motivational strategy requires slightly more supervisory control than (1) or (2).

(4) Designing Information Feedback Systems — providing subordinates with more complete information about previous performance levels (giving information more frequently, adding data to the report).

(5) Placing Personnel — assigning or allocating subordinates to existing jobs or tasks that challenge their operational and/or interpersonal skill. The superior evaluates the salient characteristics of the jobs under his control while also assessing the needs and skills of his immediate subordinates. He then attempts to place individuals on jobs that he feels are sufficiently complex to prove challenging or demanding to them.

(6) Designing Job Systems — designing, changing, or developing subordinates' existing jobs so

that the job becomes more challenging (giving more or different duties, giving more responsibility, independence, etc.).

(7) Materially Rewarding — material rewards are distributed to subordinates in response to subordinate behavior (monetary bonus, afternoon off with pay).

(8) Materially Punishing — material rewards are withheld from subordinates in response to subordinate behavior (downward adjustment in salary, sending subordinates home for a day without pay).

(9) Designing Reward System — altering the reward system under which one's subordinates work, designing the reward system so that more meaningful incentives are obtained by individuals for better performance (putting some subordinates on piece rate).

The last three motivational strategies are not relevant to volunteers.

These motivational strategies suggest that supervision can have a large impact on the motivational level of their staff, and hence on staff performance. These motivational strategies cost nothing to the organization. All supervisors have the opportunity to exercise each of them. Two of them, Setting Goals and Providing Feedback, are consistent with the thrust of this chapter.

The use of goal setting on a daily basis is a simple process. It involves saying, "I would like you to have this report typed and ready for my examination by Friday afternoon" instead of "I'd like you to do this report for me." The former statement includes a goal with a specified time frame. The evidence suggests that the supervisor will receive the completed typed report in the first instance but perhaps not in the second.

We have come to believe that supervisors have countless ways of influencing the level of motivation and performance of their staff in their daily interactions with them. We also are convinced that goal setting works. It is an element in every theory of work motivation. Finally, goal-setting processes may be the most powerful motivational tool we know about.

116

Summary

The purpose of this chapter has been to provide a discussion of goal setting as a motivational techique. More specifically, it has attempted to provide background information on these concepts and to provide practical suggestions on the application of this technique in a voluntary organization.

The concept of motivation attempts to explain what causes the initiation, direction, and persistence of behavior. There are two basic theories to account for this. One attributes motivation to be caused by inherent, unconscious drives; the other to conscious needs, wishes, or desires. In both cases, behavior is motivated by the presence of some goal that will alleviate the drive, or satisfy the need. Satisfaction of a particular goal will lead the individual to pursue additional goals that may have been lower in priority.

Motivation and goal setting are intimately related. We have defined goal setting as the process of determining a specific objective to be attained through a course of action. Our concern has been to show how this process can enhance motivation and improve performance. What factors should the voluntary sector manager consider if this process is to prove of value? It sounds like a simple enough process, but it still requires some care in implementation.

If a goal-setting program is to be established, there are four factors that must be present if the program is to be a success. Goals must be specific and they should be clearly defined. Progress towards a goal must be subject to achievement measures that can be easily measured and understood. Finally, there must be frequent and useful feedback between the manager and volunteer on how efforts are progressing towards achievement of the goal.

There is a reasonable body of research available that substantiates the evidence that goal setting can be a very effective method of increasing motivation and improving performance. The research indicates that goal setting can often be implemented at very little cost without affecting the results. The important point is that the goals must be specific, clear, measurable, and that feedback be available.

The implementation of a goal-setting program in a voluntary organization requires three stages. First, there has to be an acceptance of and commitment to the program on the part of the volunteers. This may be helped by encouraging the volunteers to participate in the design of the program. Second, there must be an action plan. This is devised by the manager and the volunteer together. It outlines in specific terms the goals that are sought and the measures to be used to follow progress towards obtaining them. The action plan should be clearly understood and agreed upon by the manager and volunteer before the job or task is begun.

Finally, there should be a review process. This type of session provides the opportunity to give feedback, to recycle the planning stage, to evaluate the goals and progress measures, and to adjust them as conditions warrant. The review process also offers the chance to provide recognition or rewards in some form, which help to increase the satisfaction and sense of achievement of the volunteer. Review and feedback are crucial to the success of goal setting, as they are extremely motivating if done properly.

The typical volunteer has changed. That person can no longer be defined as a socially conscious, middle-class housewife. With volunteers coming from all walks of life for many different reasons and with more and more voluntary organizations springing up, recruitment of volunteers has become more competitive. It has become important for the manager to understand who volunteers for his organization and why, if he wants to keep the volunteers he has and if he wants to attract more. One method of reducing volunteer turnover is to fit the goal-setting program to the motivation of the volunteers within the organization.

Many voluntary organizations have traditionally been very vague in all aspects of goal setting. Organizational and strategic goals were rarely specific or well defined. The psychological contract between the organization and the volunteer was vague and did not really indicate what expectations were held of the volunteer. The implementation of a goal-setting program can improve these deficiencies. It may be the key to improving productivity and the use of resources within the organization, and thus to remaining viable in today's competitive environment.

ACKNOWLEDGEMENTS

Preparation of this manuscript was supported in part by the Faculty of Administrative Studies, York University. We would like to thank Tony Cunliffe and Mel Moyer for their help in collecting relevant literature and Lynn Welsh for preparing the manuscript.

REFERENCES

Hall, D.T.
  1976 *Careers in Organizations*. Pacific Pallisades, CA: Goodyear.
Henderson, K.A.
  1981 "Motivations and Perceptions of Volunteerism as a Leisure Activity," *Journal of Leisure Research* 13: 208-218.
Hull, C.L.
  1943 *Principles of Behavior*. New York: Appleton-Century-Crofts.
Ilgen, D.R., C.D. Fisher, and S.M. Taylor
  1979 "Consequences of Individual Feedback on Behavior in Organizations," *Journal of Applied Psychology* 64: 349-371.
Ivancevich, J.M.
  1976 "Effects of Goal Setting on Performance and Job Satisfaction," *Journal of Applied Psychology* 61: 605-612.
Jenner, J.R.
  1981 "Volunteerism as an Aspect of Women's Work Lives," *Journal of Vocational Behavior* 19: 302-314.
Latham, G.P. and J.J. Baldes
  1975 "The 'Practical Significance' of Locke's Theory of Goal Setting," *Journal of Applied Psychology* 60: 122-124.
Latham, G.P. and S.B. Kinne III
  1974 "Improving Performance Through Training in Goal Setting," *Journal of Applied Psychology* 59: 187-191.
Latham, G.P. and E.A. Locke
  1979 "Goal Setting: A Motivational Technique That Works," *Organizational Dynamics* 8: 68-80.
Latham, G.P., L.L. Cummings, and T.R. Mitchell
  1981 "Behavioral Strategies to Improve Productivity," *Organizational Dynamics* 10: 5-23.
Lawler, E.E.
  1973 *Motivation in Work Organizations*. Monterey, CA: Wadesworth.
Locke, E.A.
  1978 "The Ubiquity of the Technique of Goal Setting in Theories of and Approaches to Employee Motivation," *Academy of Management Review* 3: 594-601.
Locke, E.A. and G.P. Latham
  1984 *Goal Setting: A Motivational Technique That Works!* Englewood Cliffs, NJ: Prentice-Hall.

Locke, E.A., G.P. Latham, L.M. Saari, and K.N. Shaw
   1981 "Goal Setting and Task Performance: 1969-1980," *Psychological Bulletin* 90: 125-152.
Maslow, A.H.
   1943 "A Theory of Human Motivation," *Psychological Review* 50: 370-396.
Moyer, M.S., ed.
   1983 *Managing Voluntary Organizations*. Toronto: York University.
Oldham, G.
   1976 "The Motivational Strategies Used By Supervisors: Relationships to Effectiveness Indicators," *Organizational Behavior and Human Performance* 15: 150-163.
Pearce, J.L.
   1983 "Job Attitudes and Motivation Differences Between Volunteers and Employees from Comparable Organizations," *Journal of Applied Psychology* 68: 646-652.
White, F.M. and E.A. Locke
   1981 "Perceived Determinants of High and Low Productivity in Three Occupational Groups: A Critical Incident Study," *Journal of Management Studies* 18: 375-387.
Wiehe, V.R. and L. Isenhour
   1977 "Motivation of Volunteers," *Journal of Social Welfare* 19: 73-79.

APPENDIX A

A. WHAT IS WORK PLANNING AND REVIEW?

A flexible way of getting the job done and, at the same time, increasing work motivation, performance, and job satisfaction.

The sessions themselves are meetings between the volunteer and the manager, oriented toward the daily work. This should result in mutual agreement as to the job to be done, achievement measures to determine the extent to which the job has been done well, a review of progress, and mutual solving of problems which arise in the course of getting the job done.

B. WHY HAVE IT?

Actually, work planning is nothing new. Managers do this every time they lay out an assignment for a subordinate. However, there are many different ways to plan and lay out the work. Some result in increased work performance; some do not.

In general, three basic principles are important in getting more mileage from the planning you are already doing. To improve job performance:

(1) A volunteer needs to know what is expected of him.

(2) A volunteer needs to know how he is doing.

(3) A volunteer needs to be able to obtain assistance when and as needed.

Work Planning and Review was designed to implement and utilize these three principles. The work planning and review diagram shows how this is done.

C. HOW DO YOU DO WORK PLANNING?

As the diagram illustrates, the first motivational principle requires developing mutual agreement between the volunteer and the manager as to what is expected. It consists of two closely related parts, (1) outlining the job to be done and (2) outlining achievement measures or yardsticks to determine when a job has been done well.

1. Job To Be Done

The job to be done stems from two different but related sources, the position guide and the Department needs. The guide remains relatively unchanged. It gives the overall level and types of responsibility of the individual. On the other hand, the Department needs are constantly changing. This is reflected in the changing tasks that individuals must do.

The manager has a two-fold responsibility in defining the job to be done. He must ensure that specific tasks and projects contribute to the Department needs. He must also make certain that he and his subordinate are in agreement on the job to be done.

121

A good method of increasing agreement between volunteer and manager is to have the subordinate prepare a list of suggested goals and commitments prior to the planning session. During the session, the two discuss the goals and make any changes necessary to reflect the manager's ideas.

Here are some specific do's and don't's in outlining the job to be done:

Do

* Ensure that you and your subordinate agree on major plans and tasks.
* Make the plans specific rather than general.
* Relate work plans to Department and Section milestones.
* Change work plans to conform with the needs of the business.
* Have the volunteer develop his own work plans when you feel he is capable.
* Remain as informal as possible. Jot down work plans, rather than having six carbons.

Don't

* Try to set work goals too far in advance.
* Make activities, responsibilities, or tasks too broad.
* Become over-involved in completing forms, rather than concentrating on mutual understanding.
* Be inflexible about changing work plans as the need arises.

2. *Job Well Done*

Identification of the specific goals, tasks, or activities is only part of implementing the first principle of "Knowledge of what is expected." The second part is to develop achievement measures.

These assist volunteer and manager in determining when a job is done well and/or in outlining areas for improvement in work per-

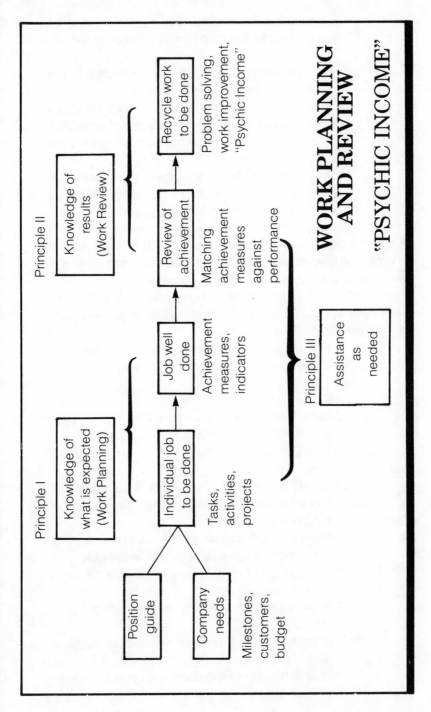

formance. For best results, these must be outlined so that both participants can agree with them.

Developing achievement measures is not easy. These are the yardsticks by which the results are to be measured. They are designed to answer the question for both volunteer and manager: "How will we both know whether or not the job is done well?"

The yardsticks, or achievement measures, should be specific to the task. They should be measured as objectively as possible.

However, good judgmental, subjective measurements are preferable to poor objective measures. Time deadlines are, of course, one type of measurement, but should be used alone only when these are the *only* factor of job success.

If you have the subordinate develop his own work plans for your review, you will want to have him develop the result measures at the same time.

Here are some specific do's and don't's in developing and outlining the achievement measures:

Do

* Make certain these are laid out as well as possible before the volunteer starts the task or project.
* Make certain the measures cover the whole project.
* Ensure that you and your subordinate agree that these are yardsticks that will determine whether or not the job was well done.
* Make the measures as specific as possible.
* Make the measures as objective as possible.
* Get agreement on the measures before the job is started.
* Be willing to change measures if the task or conditions change.
* Approach from a positive rather than negative direction.
* Establish indicators that can be used to improve job performance.

124

Don't

* Use time deadlines only. This is only part of a job well done.
* Develop the measures as a way of "trapping" your subordinate.
* Make the indicators too broad and general.
* Become over involved in completing forms rather than concentrating on mutual understanding of what is expected.
* Use indicators that are "go/no go" or "yes/no." These are of little help in improving performance.

In summary, the steps in work planning are:

* Have the employee develop a set of work goals and measurements on a work planning sheet. (You may omit this step if you wish to do this yourself.)

* Schedule a planning session.
* During the discussion, ensure that you and your subordinate come to a mutual agreement on tasks, due dates, and measures of achievement.
* After the planning session, transfer the finally agreed upon goals and yardsticks to the work plan. Keep one copy for yourself and give one to the employee.

D. HOW DO YOU DO WORK REVIEW?

As the diagram illustrates, work review involves implementing the second principle, "Knowledge of results." It is an *integral part* of the job cycle. Here, after the project is finished, volunteer and manager go over their previously agreed upon goals, measuring performance against the yardsticks established in the Work Planning session.

To the extent that the work planning was done well, work review is easy. The secret is in developing good achievement measures. When these are done well, the review process follows almost automatically. In fact, the volunteer knows, before the review, how the manager will feel about his work. When the achievement measures are not good, or consist only of time deadlines, the review stage is slipped over or ignored. This, of course, does not contribute to increased motivation or improved performance.

It is highly important that the work review session *not* become a judging session. Instead, the emphasis should be placed on an objective, job-centred discussion of the extent to which the goals have or have not been met, and the reasons and causes. Overemphasis on rigid measurement and goal attainment will destroy the mutual problem-solving situation. *The manager must act as a helper, not a judge.*

On the basis of the review, corrective action can be taken, goals can be reset, and new goals established. This completes the job cycle.

In brief, the steps are:
* Several days in advance of the review session, ask the volunteer to review the goals and measures of achievement and to be prepared to discuss progress, problems, solutions, new goals, etc. Also, be prepared to do this yourself.
* In the discussion with the volunteer, encourage him to summarize his progress, status, problems, and solutions. Introduce your own comments as appropriate. Encourage a discussion of both points of view so that there is complete mutual understanding of progress and next steps. Summarize the review sessions.
* If the discussion uncovers major problems or development needs, these should be stated in the form of goals and listed in the work plan.
* At this meeting, update and add new goals as necessary.
* Remember, the review session is not a performance appraisal. Rather, it is a review of progress with an emphasis on the joint solution of problems involved in getting the job done.

Here are some specific do's and don't's in doing Work Review:
Do
* Use review to improve performance.
* Review work when appropriate rather than at fixed periods, e.g. at the completion of a project or specific sub-project.

* Use review time to discuss achievement on the performance measures.
* Use review time to recycle and replan work.
* Use an informal rather than formal approach.
* Use review to encourage rather than to criticize.
* Use review to provide assistance in improving performance.
* Establish a climate in which you and your subordinate can mutually agree on results accomplished, problem areas, and future accomplishments.
* Remember that the purpose of a review is to obtain mutual knowledge of results for the purpose of improved performance.
* Ask subordinates to initiate their own reviews if they feel confident in this role.

Don't
* Approach in a punitive rather than an encouraging manner.
* Put off review to fixed dates. Review as necessary and appropriate.
* Always try to review the whole job at a time. Try reviewing specific projects or activities instead.
* Talk about personalities. Concentrate on the job and ways you can help improve job performance.
* Conduct reviews in a formal, stilted manner. Your object is to help improve performance, not to punish.

E. WHAT IS THE TIMING?

The exact timing of work planning and review sessions is up to you. Work planning should be done often enough to ensure that you and your subordinate mutually understand what is expected. Reviews should be done often enough to ensure that both of you agree on the results. In addition, you will probably want to talk about specific projects or tasks rather than the total job.

Chapter 7

MOTIVATING VOLUNTEERS THROUGH ENHANCING THEIR COMPETENCE

Eva Schindler-Rainman

Volunteer motivation is a complex and changing dynamic. Volunteers give and get as a result of giving. And so it should be. Therefore this chapter will deal with ways to enhance the competence of volunteers so that they give even better service, and also so that they continue to feel motivated to volunteer.

Competence means skill, capability, and a feeling of confidence and comfortableness with what one is and does. It is important for persons to feel good about themselves and their activities regardless of age or stage in life. A competent self-image energizes people to act, and to become involved with others, and increases the possibilities for desire to learn more, and to contribute and expand as a person.

Among the motivations to volunteer are: the wish to learn; the hope to succeed; the eagerness for new experiences; the desire to help and give of self; the need to exert power and influence and to participate in problem solving and decision making; the possibilities of having fun; the demand to advocate chosen causes; the need to feel needed; the longing to make a difference; the chance to add experiences to one's resume; the aspiration to meet new people and make new friends; opportunities to be creative; the ambition to become more visible and perhaps socially more mobile; and the desire to become more skillful, more knowledgeable, more useful, and more competent.

People who volunteer do a great variety of jobs that might fall into these categories: administration and policy making, direct service, connecting providers and consumers of services, research, social action, fund raising, and human kindness jobs. Today's volunteers are persons from three to one hundred and three, male or female, from all racial, ethnic, national, and religious groups, from all life style and economic backgrounds, employed as well as unemployed, professional and blue collar, home executives and corporate executives, as well as healthy and at risk persons. In other words anyone can be and is a volunteer. The possibility of increasing their motivation through enhancing their competence applies to each and every present and potential volunteer.

PROGRAMMING FOR COMPETENCE

How then can competence, achievement and improvement be part of volunteer management systems?

1. There must be a *diagnosis of a volunteer's motivations, needs, and skills*. This can be done through one-on-one placement conversations, or group interviews. In some instances pen and pencil instruments are used. Or it is possible to give potential volunteers an opportunity to explore and experiment to see what they can do in any given volunteer job. Self-evaluation can also be utilized.
2. It is helpful to have *clear delineation of each volunteer job*, and the qualifications needed. However, this must be a flexible description, whenever possible, so that prospective volunteers are challenged and excited rather than feeling overwhelmed and incompetent.
3. *Supportive and careful placement* with appropriate (to the job and to the volunteer) training is part of any humane volunteer management program and progress. Placement may include a trial period so that both the volunteer and the volunteer manager can see if the job is suitable and satisfying both ways.
4. Clear definition of and agreement on service and/or product outcomes are absolutely essential. Volunteer service must be measurable. Persons who volunteer want to know what is expected of them, and why it is a necessary task. Administrators and boards need clear accounting of volunteer contributions to a service.

5. They need *regular feedback sessions* on how things are going. These sessions should give opportunities to volunteers and professionals to give reciprocal feedback so that competence is increased both in terms of task and process.

6. *Opportunities for growth and change* can be included to motivate volunteers as they become familiar with the volunteer job, the system, the mission of the system, and as they become more comfortable and more competent. For instance, experienced volunteers can help train new persons.

7. Ongoing *learning opportunities are important*. These may be formal seminars and workshops, or informal on-the-job conferences. They may be chances to participate in sessions in-house, or in conferences and classes in the community, or even, if possible, outside of the community. Not only is the need to learn an important motivation, but also competence is increased through learning new or additional skills, or increasing knowledge in particular areas.

8. *Opportunities to influence the system* can also be made available. Often volunteers in a particular program or service have useful ideas for improvements. For example, volunteers in the intake service of a large welfare agency suggested ways to simplify the application blanks clients had to fill out. They also suggested that these forms be translated into several other languages.

POSSIBLE TRAPS

1. When volunteers become both competent and confident they may provide some anxiety and *stress for paid staff*. In an era of economic restraint, paid personnel are worried about keeping their jobs, and they may perceive a threat to their job security when volunteers do a fine, useful, dependable and skillful job. Therefore it is essential to develop volunteer jobs that extend and enhance the work of paid persons. It must be made clear that volunteers are there to humanize and individualize services, and are *not* there to replace or displace the staff.

2. Another trap is *unclear definition of volunteer job(s), role(s) and relationships*. It is helpful for volunteers to have a defined support system including a staff consultant, colleague relationships, and an understood place in the structure and function of the system.

3. *Lack of feeling part of a team* is another trap because it may lead a

person to do his/her thing unrelated to the important others. Team building and maintenance is a motivator and enhancer of volunteer performance.

4. Trap number four may be that as volunteers become more competent they try to get *involved inappropriately in the management and operations of the system*. It helps to clarify appropriate ways to make suggestions, ask questions, and share ideas.

5. Competent *volunteers may get restless* unless they are given opportunities to participate in meaningful ways in influencing the system. For example, volunteer participation in all or selected staff meetings may be equally useful for the volunteer and the staff.

6. *Lack of clear communication lines and methods* is often a frustration for volunteers who care and who want to do a good job. Each volunteer must know who is her/his immediate listening ear.

7. *Lack of explicit recognition* of the volunteer's contributions and presence. Often between the official recognition events the important "we missed you" — "thank you" — "that is a splendid idea" are forgotten, or at least not expressed in meaningful ways.

SOME PAYOFFS OF HIGHLY MOTIVATED VOLUNTEER PARTICIPATION
For the System

Satisfied, competent, and motivated volunteers enrich a system in innumerable ways. They serve as *public and community relators* to enhance the visibility of the organization. They add resources of skill, knowledge, loyalty, service, and sometimes money.

Volunteers can *increase the quantity and quality* of the services of the system. For instance, a teacher can give just so much attention to 25 students, no matter how high the quality of that service. If one or two volunteer educational aides are also present in the classroom more students can get more individual attention. Teachers can then work with those students they feel need them most at any given point in time.

Confident, competent *volunteers can make life easier for staff*. Staff persons then have a support system on which they can depend. Also, paid personnel can safely delegate appropriate tasks to volunteers. This should decrease staff overwork load and the resultant stress. Also, good volunteers are important colleagues for the paid workers, and often become part of a *human service team*. This team, made up of persons with a varied menu of talents, skills, resources and experiences, can decide together how and when to deliver needed services.

Often competent service volunteers can be recruited to become *knowledgeable decision makers* as members of boards of directors and committees. Indeed it is helpful to have some enthusiastic, committed, knowledgeable insiders on today's decision and policy-making bodies.

For the Volunteer

1. *Enhanced self-image* as a result of good volunteer experiences motivate the volunteer and contribute to her/his personhood.
2. *New and/or increased skills* that can be utilized in other parts of the volunteer's life will keep the person's loyalty and increase interest and commitment.
3. *Knowledge, new or more*, about given areas such as health maintenance, mental retardation, youth leadership, is usually a welcome addition to a person's repertoire.
4. Often volunteers develop *increased human relations and communication skills*, which are transferable to home and other interactions.
5. *Meeting new people and making new friends* is *the* important motivator. When volunteers maintain such relationships it makes them feel competent as a friend and a colleague. On-the-job volunteer relationships may well be integrated into the volunteer's personal and social life.
6. Another pay-off for the volunteer is the fact that volunteer experiences and references can *become part of a person's resume* and useful in job and/or educational pursuits.
7. Volunteering may help people *to transit* from work to retirement; from paid work to volunteer work; from being married to being single; from many family responsibilities to fewer responsibilities; or in moving from one community to another.

SOME WAYS TO MEASURE COMPETENCE

As discussed at length in Chapter 6, if a volunteer job is well defined in terms of purpose, scope, and product(s), it should not be too hard to analyze its components and then measure the effectiveness of the efforts. There are a variety of tools available, including paper and pencil tests and check sheets, self-analysis and evaluation, videotaping of services being rendered with analysis by the consumer of the services, the volunteers, and the staff.

Group interviews, conducted at given intervals during the year are also useful measurement tools.

And it is possible to calculate in dollar terms how much time and effort volunteers are contributing to the system. Just determine a reasonable hourly or daily rate for volunteer services. These may vary depending on the service given.

Structured interviews with consumers of services can also be useful.

WAYS TO HELP VOLUNTEERS GROW

Daily on-the-job support and training are probably the most useful ways to help volunteers learn, grow, and change. Individual and group conferences; group seminars, workshops, classes, and meetings are all possible ways to help people learn. To these methods can be added observation, internship, seeing and analyzing videotaped or written case presentations, exploratory participation, audiotapes, and behavioral skill practice (Schindler-Rainman and Lippitt, 1977).

In order to grow and change, many people need to practice new behaviors, and behavioral skill practice is designed to help increase human relations skills. Volunteers also appreciate learning meeting design skills, influencing skills, communication skills, and collaboration skills. There is much that can be learned right on the job through skillful consultation with and supervision of the volunteer.

A real growth and development opportunity is for experienced volunteers to help new volunteers as orientors, trainers, co-workers, consultants and supporters.

Volunteers are also motivated or re-motivated when they can represent the system on community-wide committees, or as representatives to "outside the system" events.

Participation in staff meetings is another way to help volunteers learn more about the system. Also, such participation gives them an opportunity to share ideas, and for staff and volunteers to get better acquainted.

There are many, many ways to encourage growth of volunteers. It is important to remember that most people want to learn, to grow, and to develop to their fullest potential.

RECOGNITION

To be seen as a valuable "making a difference" person is important to all people. Recognition may be a smile, or the hand on the shoulder by another person. It may be a warmly said thank you, a handwritten note, or a supportive glance. Pins, plaques, and scrolls are often the more tangible awards given at special occasions (Schindler-Rainman, 1979).

New jobs or new and additional responsibilities are also ways to recognize the competence of a volunteer. It is possible that such acknowledgment in itself increases a volunteer's motivation to continue to work as a volunteer in the system.

Opportunities for additional training and education are perceived as a communication of the worth of a volunteer's contribution. It is important to individualize the ways in which awards, rewards, and other acknowledgments are delivered. Both informal and formal occasions are appropriate, and for many people some visibility is gratifying. This may be with pictures in the in-house or community paper, or being called on at a meeting attended by colleagues, family and friends, and having one's name on a program.

Volunteer personnel files are a rather recent form of recognition of the value of volunteer service, and of individual volunteers. Also, volunteer personnel policies are being developed as part of a volunteer human resource development trend.

Whatever vehicle is utilized, visibility and success are key motivators for most human beings. Also, volunteers feel recognized when they see that they are an integral and important part of a success oriented system.

It is clear from the foregoing comments that volunteers can, as part of lifelong learning, increase their competence and therefore their confidence. As this occurs they will become more turned on, more motivated to contribute their best to the services of the system or systems in which they find themselves. It is a challenge for administrators of volunteer services to ensure that the keys to motivation are always turned, and to realize that helping volunteers learn and become increasingly competent is a constant and rewarding task.

REFERENCES

Miller, F. W.
  1982 "Measuring the Value of Volunteer Efforts," *Association Management* (November).
Schindler-Rainman, Eva
  1979 "Recognition — Who Needs It? We All Do!" *Volunteer Hawaii 4(1)*.
  1981 *Transitioning: Strategies for the Volunteer World*. Vancouver, BC: Voluntary Action Resource Centre.
  1982 "Voluntarism in a World Turned Upside Down," Occasional Paper No. 10. University of Victoria: School of Social Work.
  1983 "Voluntarism in Transition — Challenges and Choices." Keynote address at Catherine McAuley Health Center Symposium on Voluntarism, Ann Arbor, Michigan, 1982. *National Association of Hospital Development Journal*.
Schindler-Rainman, Eva and Ronald Lippitt
  1972 *Team Training for Community Change: Concepts, Goals, Strategies and Skills*. Riverside: University of California.
  1975 *The Volunteer Community: Creative Use of Human Resources* (2nd ed.) San Diego: University Associates.
  1981 *The Group Interview: A Tool for Organization Diagnosis and Action Research*. Washington, DC: Development Publications.
  1981 *The Group Interview Tool Kit*. Washington, DC: Development Publications.
Schindler-Rainman, Eva and Ronald Lippitt in collaboration with Jack Cole
  1977 *Taking Your Meetings Out of the Doldrums*. San Diego: University Associates.

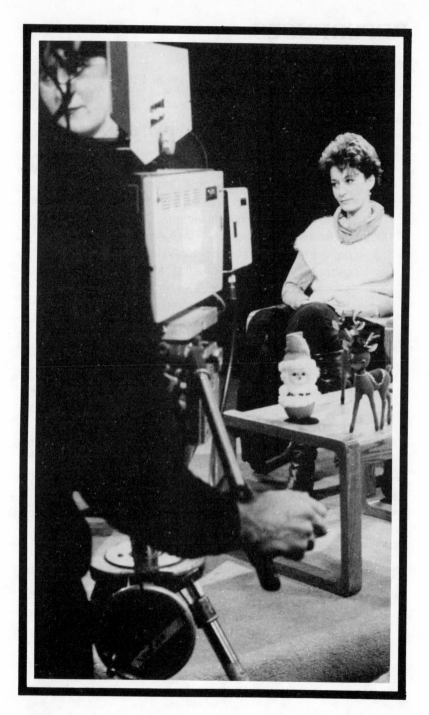

Chapter 8

FUTURE IMPLICATIONS FOR VOLUNTEERISM

Valerie A. Ahwee

Futurists are forecasting significant changes in several spheres: continued increase in the 65 and over population; transition in the work force; society's concept of leisure, community involvement, and lifelong learning. In this chapter, we will look at some of the new directions, as forecasted by futurists, among them John Naisbitt, author of *Megatrends*. Coverage in this chapter is by no means exhaustive. While we will be focusing *only* on those trends or some symptoms of those trends which are likely to have the greatest impact on the voluntary sector and the motivation to volunteer, the speculations we draw from them are just that — speculations — and not definite conclusions. What we hope to offer are some considerations which anyone working with volunteers can bear in mind in the years ahead. The changes discussed in this chapter can be placed in two broad categories: 1) changes shaping society as a whole, and 2) changes in attitudes and values. (See Table 1.)

CHANGES SHAPING SOCIETY AS A WHOLE
DEMOGRAPHIC
Increase in the 65 and Over Population

The face of the North American population is altering. According to Statistics Canada, the 65 and over population will make up 17% of the total population in 2001 (as compared to 8% in 1951), while a similar trend will take place in the United States. The U.S. Bureau of the

Census predicts that the same age group will make up 12% of the population in the year 2000 (as compared to 8.2% in 1950). For retired persons, withdrawal from the work force can mean leisure and a chance to pursue interests for which they previously had no time. Yet for others, retirement can mean the shutting of doors to familiar life patterns rather than the opening of doors to new experiences, or the loss of an occupational role which was so much a part of self-identity.

TABLE 1

CHANGES SHAPING SOCIETY AS A WHOLE

DEMOGRAPHIC: — continuing increase in 65 and over

ECONOMIC: — shrinking industrial sector in developed countries
— continuing increase in women's labor force participation rate
— escalating development and use of high tech in the workplace

CHANGES IN ATTITUDES AND VALUES

COMMUNITY: — decentralization of services: increasing sense of community self-reliance and responsibility in dealing with local issues or concerns

INDIVIDUAL: — leisure: concept of leisure is redefined to include constructive, productive usage of time
— lifelong learning: concept of education is broadened to include continual self-development

Status and identity are closely tied to occupation and raising a family. With the working years behind them and the family dispersed, retired persons may find themselves role-less for the first time. Some adapt to retirement by becoming involved in more activities, while others who find the change unsettling may withdraw and become less active.

For those who find the transition to retirement difficult, community involvement can mean the difference between activity versus inactivity; feeling needed versus feeling superfluous; or socialization versus isolation. Volunteer work offers the opportunity to add to and/or maintain self-identity and to participate in the community.

Some Motivations of the Older Volunteer

Some motivations driving the older volunteer might be the desire for affiliation, the need to know that one's contributions are valued, the need for self-esteem and a socially-valued role in the absence of a paid occupation.

Retirees have experience-honed talents — and enough leisure time to put them to use. However, it is up to the agency to involve this group in its recruitment efforts, to make them aware that volunteer work is a viable retirement activity, to find out what the volunteer would like to derive from the involvement, and to ensure that assignments continue to be interesting and beneficial in some way to the person. With their working years behind them, retirees, unlike career-explorers or career-changers, do not "have to" volunteer to gain work experience. For them, volunteer activity is one of many ways they can spend their time. It is the agency's responsibility to perpetuate the volunteer's interest and to find out if that interest in involvement is driven by the desire to add to self-identity, the desire for affiliation with a cause or organization, the need for socialization, or something else.

What the Agency Can Offer

The agency will need to consider some questions when involving the retired volunteer in programs. Does the retired volunteer require more support from staff than a younger volunteer? Will special recruitment and training strategies need to be developed for the older volunteer?

Does the volunteer want the involvement as a form of recreation and relaxation, or is the person looking for volunteer work to build a second career which will demand a large proportion of his or her time and energy?

Whatever the retired volunteer is expecting to gain from an assignment, the agency is more likely to keep the person interested by ensuring that they take the time to offer and, if necessary, tailor assignments so that the volunteer's needs and expectations will be met. Not to be overlooked are economic and capability considerations. Because retirees are often under financial limitations, agencies need to keep in mind that reimbursement for any out-of-pocket expenses should always be available. Also, some older volunteers may prefer work that is closer to home, assignments which are not physically demanding, or daytime (as opposed to evening) assignments.

For those who are looking for affiliation, a role, or a niche, agencies can provide assignments which have a clear connection with the goals of the organization and which are recognized as an important part of an integrated whole. They can offer a social network to provide positive interaction and to foster a sense of teamwork. Agencies can also offer retired persons the opportunity to share or teach their skills, an idea which the business community has developed with success. In Canada, the Counselling Assistance to Small Enterprises (C.A.S.E.) connects small businesses which need the benefit of hands-on counselling with retired business persons who are knowledgeable about everything from payroll to profits, inventory to cash flow. The same concept could be adapted for non-profit organizations, to the benefit of agency and volunteer.

ECONOMIC
Shrinking Industrial Sector; Increase of Women in Labor Force

Naisbitt (1982) observes that it is "too late to recapture our industrial supremacy because we are no longer an industrial economy." We are moving from an industrial to an information society in which information has become the mass-produced product. It is estimated that manufacturing will provide only 11% of the jobs in the year 2000, down from 28% in 1980, displacing a large number of blue-collar workers (Cetron, 1983: 15).

142

The second economic shift is the rise in two-income families as an increasing number of women join the work force. According to a report entitled "The Nation's Families 1960-1990," issued by the Joint Center for Urban Studies of MIT and Harvard, husband-wife households with only one working spouse will dwindle to 14% of all households in 1990, as compared with 43% in 1960. Furthermore, wives will contribute about 40% of family income in 1990, as compared to 25% in 1982. The continuing increase of women in the work force is precipitated by the reality, for many, that two incomes in a family are no longer a luxury but a necessity.

Some Motivations of Volunteers in Transition in the Work Force: Displaced Workers and Career-Explorers

As the manufacturing sector shrinks and as computers, robotics, and the electronic brain systematically take over functions formerly performed by people, displaced workers and people who are re-entering the work force, either for the first time or after a long absence, obviously will view the need for work experience as a top priority. However, agencies will need to identify the specific purpose behind the volunteer's search for work experience. If the volunteer is a displaced worker, does he or she require an assignment which will facilitate the development of new marketable, transferable skills which will prepare the volunteer for the transition to a new career field? If the volunteer is entering the work force for the first time (or returning after an absence), will she be searching for varied assignments which offer a wide range of experiences for the purposes of career exploration? It is important that the agency make the distinction between work experience for skill development versus work experience for career exploration, as the type and duration of assignments will, of necessity, vary with each.

What the Agency Can Offer

For those who are interested in skill development, the agency can suggest assignments which require a certain amount of commitment while yielding in-depth experience and the opportunity to develop expertise in a particular area. For those searching for career-exploration opportunities, the agency might suggest a series of short-term assignments which will provide the volunteer with a wide sampling of experiences so that the person can investigate and narrow down some potential career areas.

In a tight job market, volunteer activity becomes an even more attractive option if volunteers can be assured that the time they invest will reap dividends: basic entry-level skill development for those who need it; opportunities for career-explorers to compare and contrast some very different jobs; opportunities to make new contacts in a job search; a chance to build self-confidence and to demonstrate talents. It is up to the agency to make certain these expectations are met by developing a businesslike relationship with the volunteer, including orientation and training, job descriptions, performance standards, evaluations, records of training undertaken and skills acquired, and references. Perhaps the best summary, although directed to the business sector by Peters and Waterman (1982: 239), is the following observation, which also has notable application to the volunteer community regarding respect for the individual worker:

> These [organizations] give people control over their destinies; they make meaning for people. They turn the average Joe and the average Jane into winners. . . . . They accentuate the positive. . . . . . We are talking about tough-minded respect for the individual and the willingness to train him, to set reasonable and clear expectations for him, and to grant him practical autonomy to step out and contribute directly to his job.

This vote of confidence in the worker can be the most effective motivator of all for those in transition between jobs or careers, particularly since unemployment and job hunting are often accompanied by depression and the need to validate self-worth.

WORKPLACE

The Brave New World of High Tech in the Workplace

The escalation in high tech has transformed the workplace which, in turn, has brought forth what Naisbitt (1982: 36) calls a "highly personal value system" to compensate for the impersonal nature of technology. This brave new world of high tech has intensified the mindlessness of routine jobs in which workers become mere extensions of machines, as Toffler (1981: 186) observes in *The Third Wave*:

> . . . the growth of the white-collar work force can be better understood as an extension of industrialism [rather] than as a leap to a new system. While it is true that work has grown more abstract and less concrete, the actual offices in which this work is being done are modeled directly after Second Wave factories, with the work itself fragmented, repetitive, dull, and dehumanizing. Even today, much of the office reorganization is little more than an attempt to make the office more closely resemble a factory.

As the flow of information becomes faster, the routine of work more monotonous, and the contact with people more limited, we must, says Naisbitt (1982: 36), "learn to balance the material wonders of technology with the spiritual demands of our human nature." The message is that the video terminal is no substitute for human interaction: the more technology is introduced into the workplace, the greater the need workers will have to be with people, presumably in that part of their lives spent *outside* the workplace.

Humanistic Counter-Revolution

Those who spend their days in 9 to 5 jobs which are largely mechanical, repetitive, and isolated may naturally gravitate toward counterbalancing activities, those which are more sociable and interactive. This growing interest in what Naisbitt (1982) refers to as the "self-help or personal growth movement" is a reaffirmation of our own humanness in the midst of what is rapidly becoming a dehumanizing and impersonal society. There is that need, now greater than before, to focus on individuality rather than impersonality, socialization rather than isolation, and creativity rather than mechanization. What Naisbitt (1982) calls "personal growth," Yankelovich (1981) terms "self-fulfillment." It is perhaps expressed most succinctly by Yankelovich (1981: 39) in this observation:

> Seekers of self-fulfillment . . . are eager to give more meaning to their lives, find fuller self-expression and . . . impose new demands for intangibles — creativity, leisure, autonomy, pleasure, participation, community, adventure, vitality, stimulation, tender loving care. To the efficiency of technological society they wish to add joy of living. Why, they argue, should we accept as inevitable the view that a resourceful,

highly educated people has to choose between the efficiency of technological society and quality of life? Why can we not have both? Are we to serve the machine, they ask, or is the machine to serve us?

What the Agency Can Offer

Why indeed can people not have a measure of meaningful activities and interaction to balance the impersonality of technology? Community involvement opens possibilities for latent talents or skills which may not be used advantageously in the workplace.

For workers who work in technological wastelands, agencies might make extra efforts to provide placements which have a degree of autonomy, self-direction, and creativity — characteristics which are often lacking in their paid occupations. Team jobs or one-on-one assignments can meet these needs for socialization.

CHANGES IN ATTITUDES AND VALUES

COMMUNITY

Decentralization and Increased Need for Community Self-Reliance

Government cutbacks, reduced social services, and increased community needs are becoming an all too familiar and doleful tune. The reins of responsibility for community services are being handed back to the community as government funding runs dry, and as citizens become disenchanted with the ineffectiveness of large institutions and higher levels of government in handling local issues (Naisbitt, 1982).

Many of the issues that will dominate public concern — be they improved services for seniors, energy conservation, urban renewal, or other — will be best dealt with by people doing more to help themselves at the local level. Since the consequences of local problems are the most obvious at the community level, the motivation to solve them there will be the most direct, and the benefits from action will be the most immediate.

The trend toward decentralization has come about

partly out of a desire to avoid the bureaucratic process which tends to bog things down rather than make things happen. By returning responsibility to the grassroots level, individuals will become more important, work groups will be smaller, and each person will be expected to contribute a wider variety of skills to the organizational pool. This will provide abundant opportunity for volunteers who want to learn, develop, brush up, or broaden skills.

Self-Starters and Community Catalysts

The decentralization trend has many implications for volunteers and the motivations prompting their involvement. As society places more emphasis on individual and community self-reliance, the volunteer role will become more critical. Local grassroots action will be necessary to advocate, raise funds, and implement needed community services. Self-starters and community catalysts will need to have a wide range of entrepreneurial skills in everything from research and planning to resource development, from public relations to evaluation. Furthermore, they will need the foresight to envision the program and be capable of taking a leadership role in implementing it.

How the Agency Can Help

The agency can play a major role in helping to "make things happen" by giving volunteer self-starters a free rein. These are people who perceive themselves as activators, organizers, and catalysts in energizing others toward action. The agency or volunteer program can attract and retain the interest of this type of volunteer by encouraging a sense of "esprit de corps" in working toward a common cause, by giving autonomy and opportunity for creative problem solving, by recognizing that such volunteers are attracted by challenge, the desire to take hold of a difficult situation and make something worthwhile happen. Flexible structure, the opportunity to work out ideas, and the challenge of the task will only stimulate these volunteers to involve themselves more avidly.

INDIVIDUAL
Changing Concept of Leisure and Lifelong Learning

As the community undergoes a change in attitude, so too do individuals, specifically in the concept of leisure and lifelong learning. The traditional definition of leisure as relaxation will take on a new dimension to include opportunities for self-development or self-fulfillment, so that it will be not merely leisure but *productive* leisure. Gerald McCready (1977: 143) predicts that:

> . . . an increasingly better educated populace with greater leisure time at its disposal will not only seek out a broad spectrum of involvements, but will choose those which maximize opportunity for personal development . . . . To a greater degree than ever before, people will adopt a multiplicity of roles as leisure time expands. The 1980s will bring about fundamental changes in people's attitudes toward how free time should be spent. Productive leisure will be seen as positively contributing to the society in which one lives, whereas idle leisure will be viewed as the reverse.

This change in attitude is the result of a trend toward reduced formal work hours, longer vacations, and an increase in opportunities for leave of absence for personal development.

McCready (1977: 143) believes that a "greater number of people will be seeking to improve their self-esteem and broaden their skills by improvement in fields totally unrelated to their normal occupational endeavours." Needs for personal growth and lifelong learning will reshape our concepts of education. Naisbitt (1982: 98) observes that:

> In education we are moving from the short-term considerations of completing our training at the end of high school or college to lifelong education and retraining. The whole idea of what education is will be reconceptualized during the next decade.

In the context of volunteerism, productive leisure and lifelong learning may become intertwined when community involvement is perceived as offering two distinct but related advantages: 1) the chance to

148

spend free time constructively, and 2) the chance for self-improvement by learning new skills.

Sabbaticals, Public Service Leaves, and Self-Improvement

McCready (1977) notes that the increase in productive leisure time will come about largely through sabbaticals (during which employees are permitted to take time off from their jobs to take on a meaningful self-study project), and through public service leaves (during which employees are released from regular responsibilities to pursue some experience unrelated to the job, usually by working for a non-profit organization).

For corporate volunteers, the chance to spend their released (leisure) time constructively and the chance for self-improvement (lifelong learning) together yield the attractive possibility of gaining recognition or a higher profile within their own organizations by performing community service.

The idea of self-improvement through lifelong learning would appeal not only to corporate volunteers but to a cross-section of ages and occupations — housewives, students, young adults, established professionals — anyone who perceives volunteerism as a door to education in the broadest sense. What is "learned" need not be limited to marketable skills, but may include philosophies, self-awareness, hidden talents, or something else which lies in the realm of personal discovery.

What the Agency Can Offer

Positions with a high profile, status, recognition, extensive responsibility, and the chance to "make a mark" will appeal to corporate volunteers who are interested in making an impression on their employers and possibly giving their own careers a boost. The idea is to enable those who are volunteering on a productive leisure basis (be it a sabbatical, public service leave, or other) to represent their employers while performing community service. This would have a three-fold advantage: 1) the community would benefit, 2) the corporate volunteer would gain recognition within his own organization, and 3) the employer would gain a favorable image by granting a leave to enable the employee to work on behalf of the community.

To encourage the idea of self-improvement or self-development through volunteering, the agency can develop creative jobs, offer specialized training, or allow the volunteer to develop his own job within a specified parameter. Viewed from the perspective of the volunteer who perceives community involvement as a learning experience, variety and a chance for self-discovery would be the most attractive.

SUMMARY

In order to meet the challenge of the changes shaping society and attitudes and their effect on volunteer motivation, coordinators of volunteer programs should keep in mind the need to:

- develop more creative placements
- be prepared for higher turnover as more volunteers seek variety through short-term jobs
- make an extra effort to develop skill training and personal development opportunities
- expect a greater diversity in volunteer background, experience, expectations, and make an extra effort to tailor the job to each individual in order to maximize its attractiveness to the volunteer

As changes shape society and attitudes, so too will they affect the needs and expectations of volunteers. What motivated a volunteer at the onset of an assignment may not necessarily be the same impetus for involvement three months, six months, or a year down the road. Volunteers who are involved in a planning process will be in a better position to relate their own jobs to the overall purpose of the organization. A sense of control over one's activities, an awareness of how one's job relates to the organization's mandate, and an agency which is sensitive and alert to one's changing needs will help to perpetuate a volunteer's long-term interest. Volunteers have every right to expect a return on their investment of time, and it is the agency's responsibility to ensure that the experience is mutually profitable. Now more than ever before, it is important to remember that community involvement is not merely an end in itself, but a means to an end.

REFERENCES

Cetron, Marvin J.
  1983 "Getting Ready for the Jobs of the Future," *The Futurist*, Vol. XVII, No. 3, June.
McCready, Gerald B.
  1977 *Profile Canada: Social and Economic Projections*. Georgetown, ON: Irwin-Dorsey.
Naisbitt, John
  1982 *Megatrends*. New York: Warner Books.
Peters, Thomas J. and Robert H. Waterman, Jr.
  1982 *In Search of Excellence*. New York: Warner Books.
Statistics Canada
  1979 *Population Projections for Canada and the Provinces*. Ottawa: Statistics Canada.
Toffler, Alvin
  1980 *The Third Wave*. New York: Bantam Books.
U.S. Bureau of the Census
  1983 *Statistical Abstract of the United States, 1984*. 104th ed. Washington, DC.
  1977 Current Population Reports, Series P-25, No. 704, *Projections of the Population of the U.S.* Washington, DC: Government Printing Office.
Yankelovich, Daniel
  1981 "New Rules in American Life: Searching for Self-Fulfillment in a World Turned Upside Down," *Psychology Today* 15: 35-91.

Part Two
SELECTED PAPERS

154

Selected Paper 1
ALTRUISM IS NOT DEAD:

A Specific Analysis of Volunteer Motivation

Robert Flashman and Sam Quick

At a recent conference of educational and human services professionals, the highlighted speaker authoritatively stated, "Altruism is dead." He followed this statement with comments such as: an individual participates in an activity for what he or she personally gets out of it; and, if people don't pay money for something, they think it has no value.

Based upon the quiet acceptance and head nods of approval, the audience (with few exceptions) seemed to wholeheartedly agree that, practically speaking, altruism is indeed dead. This idea, incidentally, is supported by most major theories of motivation (Bolles, 1975). In fact, judging from what has been written about the psychology of motivation, one could conclude not only that altruism is dead, but that altruistic motivation — with rare exceptions — probably never existed.

The vast majority of motivation theory and research is built upon the assumption that everything we do is directed toward benefiting ourselves. Even when we actively reach out to assist others, it is assumed that our desire to help is motivated by a desire to increase our own welfare or to reduce guilt and shame.

While this line of thinking does have some value and certainly contains a measure of truth, we believe that such reasoning is limited, partially inaccurate, and destructive. It is our conviction that altruism has not been adequately recognized as an actual and potential motivating factor. Moreover, we believe that altruism is a central, and potentially *the* central, impetus for volunteer activity. In the course of this paper we will expand upon the reasoning behind these convictions. Specifically, we will:

— Define altruism
— Cite a variety of sources that support the existence and importance of altruism
— Using the Altruism Double Bar Continuum, propose that altruism and self-interest are mutually reinforcing rather than being antagonistic
— Introduce SOS Learning Networks as an example of voluntary action rich both in selflessness and self-care
— Summarize specific research on SOS Learning Networks as evidence that altruism is alive and kicking
— Present a provocative model of altruism
— Offer a concluding set of propositions concerning the nature, importance, and expansion of altruistic behavior

Altruism Defined

Webster (1975) defines altruism as "the unselfish regard for or devotion to the welfare of others." The opposite of altruism is self-centeredness. Self-centeredness refers to a selfish concern for one's own welfare and a general disregard for the well-being of others.

Support for Altruistic Motivation

Although altruism is assigned little importance in most traditional theories of motivation, its value has not gone unrecognized elsewhere.

Desire to Help Others. In a report entitled *Americans Volunteer — 1974* (Wilson, 1979), the Census Bureau reports the results of a survey of volunteers designed to determine reasons for volunteering. Respondents were allowed to check one or more of a short series of possible motivations for volunteering. The most common reason given (53%) was "Wanted to help others." Other common responses included, "Enjoy volunteer work itself" (36%), and "Had sense of duty" (32%). The fact that 53% of the respondents indicated that their motivation was at least, in part, to help others suggests that altruism is alive and well. Of course, this type of survey has obvious shortcomings in that respondents were only given a limited number of categories to choose from, and they may have withheld or rationalized socially unacceptable responses.

Emerging Research Studies. As pointed out previously, few of the predominant psychological theories of motivation allow for the possibility of truly altruistic motivation. However, during the last decade a small number of researchers (Batson and Coke, 1978; Krebs, 1975; and others) have been hypothesizing that some behavior may indeed be truly altruistic, that is, directed toward the end-state goal of reducing another's distress. For example, Batson et al (1981), in an experiment that raises possible ethical questions, presented female college students with a female confederate who was ostensibly receiving moderate electric shocks. Students who felt a high degree of empathy wanted to help the confederate by taking the shocks for her, even when it was possible to leave the experiment and not observe the "shocks," thus preventing personal distress. These were altruistic responses, according to the researchers, because the students did not leave the experiment when they could have; their concern lay with the confederate, not themselves.

Examples of Altruism Abound. Although lacking the scientific rigor of the just-mentioned research study, evidence in support of the existence of altruism is visible all around us in the many ways people are reaching out, giving of themselves, and sharing with one another. For example, throughout the country volunteer drivers are lending a helping hand to the elderly and handicapped by providing transportation for medical appointments, grocery shopping, and other essential trips (Cyra, 1982). In 1981 over 16,000 volunteers assisted the National Forest Service by doing work valued at 8.3 million dollars (U.S. Department of Agriculture, 1982). The self-help movement has been expanding rapidly (New York City Self-Help Clearinghouse, 1982; Gartner and Riessman, 1980). A book recently published by the U.S. Office of Consumer Affairs entitled *People Power* (1980) is abundant with examples of creative voluntary action projects that communities have undertaken to help counter economic hard times. Volumes could be written simply enumerating the ubiquitous examples of voluntary activity that appear to be at least partially motivated by altruism.

Altruism As a Genetically Determined Behavior. Lewis Thomas, M.D., in an article entitled "Altruism: Self-Sacrifice for

Others" (1981), discusses the existence of altruism in the animal kingdom. According to Thomas:

> Altruism is not restricted to the social insects, in any case. Birds risk their lives, and sometimes lose them, in efforts to distract the attention of predators from the nest. Among baboons, zebras, moose, wildebeests and wild dogs there are always stubborn, doomed guardians, prepared to be done in first in order to buy time for the herd to escape.... It is genetically determined behavior, no doubt about it. Animals have genes for altruism.... We get along together in human society because we are genetically designed to be social animals, and we are obliged by instructions from our genes to be useful to each other.... I maintain, despite the moment's evidence against the claim, that we are born and grow up with a fondness for each other and that we have genes for that. We can be talked out of that fondness, for the genetic message is like a distant music and some of us are hard of hearing. Societies are noisy affairs, drowning out the sound of ourselves and our connection. Hard of hearing, we go to war. Stone deaf, we make thermonuclear missiles. Nonetheless, the music is there, waiting for more listeners.

Altruism Double Bar Continuum

It generally would be inaccurate to describe an individual as absolutely self-centered or totally altruistic; rather, a given individual (or group) might best be described as fitting somewhere on a continuum from self-centered to altruistic.

Selflessness and Self-Care Go Hand-in-Hand. Selflessness means a concern for others that leaves little or no room for oneself or one's own interests. The opposite of selflessness is selfishness. The dimension of selfishness-selflessness is the primary dimensional component of altruistic behavior. However, to say that altruism is only a matter of selfless service to others is incomplete and, probably to most people, somewhat unappealing. There is a secondary aspect of altruism: self-care. Self-care means, within reason, keeping oneself in an optimal state of physical, mental, and spiritual well-being. The opposite of self-care is self-neglect, or the failure to properly care for one's basic needs. This failure to care for oneself often manifests as a lack of self-discipline and in overindulgence. The secondary dimensional component of altruism is the

158

self-neglect-self-care dimension.

The primary and secondary dimensions of altruism are depicted graphically in Diagram 1, the Altruism Double Bar Continuum. In this diagram selfishness and self-neglect are seen as complementary components of self-centeredness, with self-centeredness resulting in both individual and collective self-destruction. On the more positive side, selflessness and self-care are depicted as mutually reinforcing components of altruism, with altruism resulting in what might be called enlightened self-interest.

Intelligent self-care enables an individual to be at his or her best, to function at a high level of general well-being. When an individual is functioning at a high level of well-being, he or she is in an optimal position to be aware of and contribute to the welfare of others. Similarly, as we intelligently and selflessly contribute to the well-being of others, we tend to enhance our own well-being in that we feel a sense of satisfaction, and others in turn tend to care for us. Referring

DIAGRAM 1
ALTRUISM DOUBLE BAR CONTINUUM

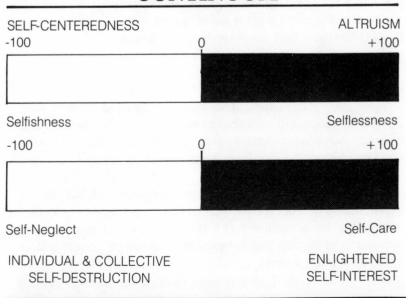

SELF-CENTEREDNESS   ALTRUISM
-100   0   +100

Selfishness   Selflessness
-100   0   +100

Self-Neglect   Self-Care

INDIVIDUAL & COLLECTIVE   ENLIGHTENED
SELF-DESTRUCTION   SELF-INTEREST

to the Altruism Double Bar Continuum, the most skillful forms of altruistic behavior would receive a rating of close to 200. In other words, altruism, at its best, is maximally beneficial to all parties involved.

This understanding of altruism can go a long way in transcending the longtime controversy over egoistic versus altruistic motivation. The Altruism Double Bar Continuum points out that altruism is not an all or none behavior; rather, it exists on a continuum — a continuum that unites self-concern and concern for others as mutually reinforcing rather than antagonistic. It essentially helps to eliminate the artificial division between self and others — a division that is at the root of so many of our individual and collective problems, a division that tends to melt away in the presence of love, a division that modern quantum physics has taught us is a mutually self-destructive illusion (Capra, 1977).

SOS Learning Networks: An Example of Altruism

An SOS Learning Network (Quick, et al, 1981 a and b) is a community-owned, volunteer-run, informal learning and development program. It is a model of community learning whose time has come. A Learning Network is based on the following simple concepts:
a. We are all learners and we are all teachers.
b. We often learn best when we share with others.
c. Sharing ourselves is one of the keys to creative community development.
d. We grow as we share ourselves.

SOS Learning Networks are also forums for meeting community needs and mechanisms for joining together persons who have common interests. Learning Networks involve ordinary people in decision making and give them a measure of control over their own lives.

SOS stands for Sharing Our Selves. An SOS Learning Network is built upon identified community needs and interests. It is based on the understanding that every individual, regardless of formal academic credentials, has skills, knowledge, talents, and/or experience worth sharing.

SOS Learning Network activities are built around almost any interest: home landscaping, cheesemaking, beginning guitar, CPR, creative writing, picture framing, getting drunk drivers off our roads, the Lauback method of teaching adults to read, tune-ups for sick cars, or a preschool parents social hour. Forums for examining issues and concerns facing community life such as zone changes, special needs of the elderly, and challenging drug abuse are encouraged. Learning Networks also help launch community ventures such as food cooperatives, farmers' markets, and day care cooperatives.

After community interests are identified and learning activities and volunteer sharers have been selected, a catalogue of activities is developed and distributed inviting everyone to register and participate. Teachers may or may not have degrees. Meetings are held in free space in churches, schools during "off hours," libraries, parks, homes, banks, and so forth. Then a simple evaluation is conducted and preparations are begun for the next semester's activities. There are usually two semesters of course activities each year.

Research Indicates That Volunteers Want to Share With Others

The results of an independently conducted statewide Kentucky telephone survey (n=661), carried out as part of the SOS Learning Network research project, indicates that 45% of the general population are willing to share their ideas, knowledge, talents, and hobbies with interested others in an informal educational setting. When this 45% was looked at more closely, it was found that race, home ownership, and geographic area did not affect people's willingness to share skills with others. Sex, age, and marital status significantly affected responses. Males (51%) were more interested in sharing skills than females (40%). Persons between ages 20-40 (61%) were most likely to be willing to share skills, and persons over 65 least likely (28%). Separated and single persons fall into the category of most likely (59%) to share skills with others, with widows and widowers (23%) being the least likely to share their skills.

When the 45% of the population who were willing to share their skills were asked if they would do it for free, 97% said yes. Taken as a whole, this research indicates that a large portion of the general population are willing to altruistically share of themselves in areas where they have both the interest and capability. However, even among this portion of the population, the willingness to share drops significantly when such sharing is perceived as being unfair. When the 97% of the sample who were willing to altruistically share were asked if they would still do it for free if others were getting paid, 20% said no.

An additional factor was studied that directly pertains to the motivational model of voluntarism described in the next section. It is the factor of empowerment, which refers to the generation of a positive sense of control over one's life. In a 1982 statewide evaluation of participants in existing SOS Learning Networks, approximately 45% said they had developed more control over their lives as a direct result of their participation in a Learning Network. This ability to create a feeling of empowerment has repeatedly emerged as an important ingredient in the success of Kentucky's system of Learning Networks.

Balance Model of Altruism

In Kentucky there are currently over 15 SOS Learning Networks in operation, actively involving 10,000 individuals annually in person-to-person educational exchanges. The first Learning Network was formed three years ago. Since that time the networks have proliferated and continue to do so. In analyzing the success of these Learning Networks, it became obvious that the operation of an altruistic motivational system was of prime importance. We attempted to isolate the variables that comprised this motivational system and which also seem to explain and activate other successful systems of individual and collective altruism.

What resulted was the Balance Model of Altruism which appears in Diagram 2. Table 1 outlines the components of self-centeredness versus the parallel components of altruism which together make up the Balance Model of Altruism. The core factors and spin-off factors are relatively self-explanatory. The specific factors are explained in Table 2. Referring to the Balance Model of Altruism, when self-centeredness outweighs altruism, the scale tips toward confusion and destruction. If altruism outweighs self-centeredness, the scale tips to the positive side and results in harmony and growth. Note that when the scale is balanced, that condition is represented at the zero mark on the Altruism Double Bar Continuum.

162

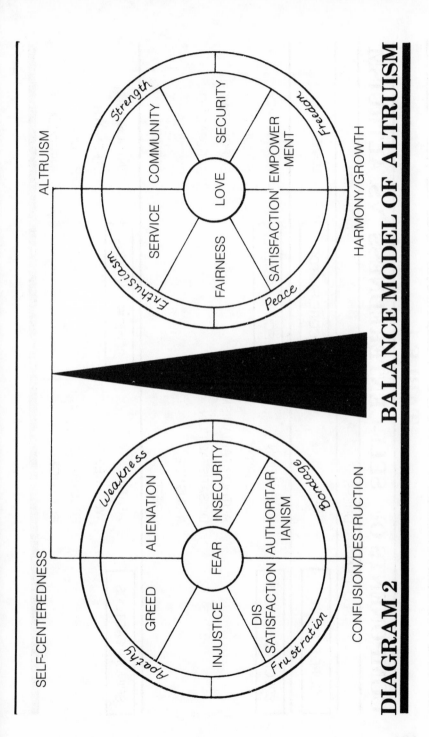

BALANCE MODEL OF ALTRUISM

DIAGRAM 2

ALTRUISM

HARMONY/GROWTH

Strength

COMMUNITY — SECURITY

Freedom

SERVICE — LOVE — EMPOWERMENT

Enthusiasm

FAIRNESS — SATISFACTION

Peace

SELF-CENTEREDNESS

CONFUSION/DESTRUCTION

Weakness

ALIENATION — INSECURITY

Bondage

GREED — FEAR — AUTHORITARIANISM

Apathy

INJUSTICE — DISSATISFACTION

Frustration

TABLE 1

COMPONENTS OF SELF-CENTEREDNESS VS. ALTRUISM

	SELF-CENTEREDNESS	ALTRUISM
CORE FACTOR	FEAR	LOVE
SPECIFIC FACTORS	ALIENATION INSECURITY AUTHORITARIANISM DISSATISFACTION INJUSTICE GREED	COMMUNITY SECURITY EMPOWERMENT SATISFACTION FAIRNESS SERVICE
SPINOFF FACTORS	APATHY WEAKNESS FRUSTRATION BONDAGE	ENTHUSIASM STRENGTH PEACE FREEDOM

TABLE 2

SPECIFIC FACTORS OF SELF-CENTEREDNESS VS. ALTRUISM

SELF-CENTEREDNESS	ALTRUISM
1. Factions divided against one another (alienation)	1. Sense of oneness (community)
2. Worry that one's own basic needs may not be met (insecurity)	2. Trust that one's own basic needs will be cared for (security)
3. Concentration of power (authoritarianism)	3. Self-control and self-reliance (empowerment)
4. Absence of joy of giving (dissatisfaction)	4. Visible benefits of giving (satisfaction)
5. A preference for letting the other person sacrifice (injustice)	5. A willingness to engage in mutual sharing and/or sacrifice (fairness)
6. Primary motivation is material and/or financial gain (greed)	6. Primary motivation is to help others (service)

Both the Altruism Double Bar Continuum and the Balance Model of Altruism apply at many levels; in other words, to a specific situation and/or time, to a specific individual at a particular time, to a marriage, a family, an organization, a community, and so on. These two models are offered as visual tools designed to enhance our practical understanding of the relatively neglected yet critical concept of altruism. Although altruism plays its central role in voluntary action, its importance generalizes to all forms of activity.

Propositions Concerning Altruism

What follows is a set of propositions designed to stimulate thinking and serve as a series of tentative conceptual guidelines for understanding and expanding altruistic behavior.

1. Altruism is a primary motivational factor in volunteer behavior; to perhaps a lesser degree, it also plays an important motivational role in behavior that could be classified as non-voluntary.
2. The artificial division between egoistic and altruistic motivation (self-concern versus concern for others) must be healed. We need to realize that we live in a unified system where the well-being of each of us affects the well-being of all of us.
3. We feed what we concentrate upon. If we concentrate on self-centeredness and attribute self-centered motivations to one another, we may well be feeding into a self-fulfilling prophecy of a destructive nature.
4. We feed what we idealize. If we hold a vision of altruism and help one another live up to this ideal, we will more easily express altruistic behavior and reap its advantages.
5. The more we can teach one another to feel for all people as we feel for ourselves and our loved ones, the more easily altruism will become a natural behavioral response.
6. The educational and material resources of the world are more than adequate; our problems lie in systems of manipulation that perpetuate unnec-

essary suffering. An expansion of altruism at both the grassroots and organizational levels can help solve this distribution imbalance and thereby eliminate a large measure of unnecessary suffering.

7. As a creative response to the many challenges facing the world, our entrance into the 21st century will be marked by a parallel rise in both altruism and voluntary activity.

REFERENCES

Batson, C. Daniel, Bruce D. Duncan, Paula Ackerman, Terese Buckley, and Kimberly Birch
    1981 "Is Empathetic Emotion a Source of Altruistic Motivation?" *Journal of Personality and Social Psychology* 40: 290-302.
Batson, C.D. and J.S. Coke
    1978 "Altruism and Human Kindness: Internal and External Determinants of Helping Behavior," *Perspectives in Interactional Psychology*. New York: Plenum Press.
Bolles, Robert C.
    1975 *Theory of Motivation*. New York: Harper & Row Publishers.
Capra, Fritjof
    1977 *The Tao of Physics* (Chapter 10) Boulder, CO: Bantam Books.
Cyra, David J.
    1982 "At the Wheel — Volunteer Drivers," *Extension Review*, 53: 38-39.
Gartner, Alan and Frank Riessman
    1980 *A Working Guide to Self-Help Groups*. New York: New Viewpoints/Vision Books.
Krebs, D.L.
    1975 "Empathy and Altruism," *Journal of Personality and Social Psychology* 32: 1134-1146.
Quick, Sam, Jim Killacky, Robert Flashman, and Arlene Gibeau
    1981a "SOS Learning Networks," *Journal of Extension* (January/February), 7-10.

Quick, Sam, Robert Flashman, and Arlene Gibeau
    1981b "SOS Learning Networks: A Model of Interorganizational
        Cooperation," *Journal of Voluntary Action Research* 10
        (July-December).
New York City Self-Help Clearinghouse
    1982 *1981-82 Directory Self-Help Groups*. New York: Graduate
        School University Center, City University of New York.
Thomas, Lewis
    1982 "Altruism: Self-Sacrifice for Others," *The Saturday Evening
        Post* 254: 42-45.
U.S. Department of Agriculture (Office of Governmental & Public
Affairs)
    1982 "These People Work For Free — On the U.S. Forest Lands."
        Report on U.S. Department of Agriculture Electronic Informa-
        tion Exchange and Dissemination (July).
U.S. Department of Consumer Affairs
    1980 *People Power*. Produced by Consumer Information Division.
Webster, A.M.
    1975 *Webster's New Collegiate Dictionary*. Springfield, MA.: G. &
        C. Merriam Co.
Wilson, Marlene
    1979 *The Effective Management of Volunteer Programs*. Boulder,
        CO: Volunteer Management Associates.

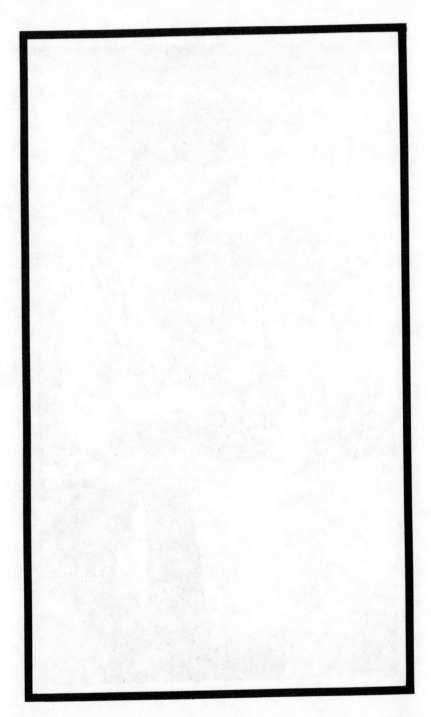

Selected Paper 2
THE MOTIVATION-NEEDS PROFILE

George Ray Francies

(Portions reprinted with permission from *The Journal of Volunteer Administration*, Vol. I, No. 3, Spring, 1983. Copyright 1983, Association for Volunteer Administration.)

INTRODUCTION

The problem addressed in this study is that of volunteer turnover. It is a common experience for volunteer coordinators to recruit, train, and place volunteers, only to find at the end of the year that the volunteer staff is no larger than at the beginning of the year. Why do volunteers leave, usually within the first three months (Gidron, 1976)? A clue to the answer may be found by considering another question. Why do people volunteer? A common answer is that people volunteer for altruistic reasons. However, a number of authorities on motivation do not accept this notion. (See for example, Walster et al., 1978; Kennett, 1980; Scheier, 1980; or Darley and Latané, 1970.)

The setting of this research was Brown County Department of Social Services in Wisconsin and the Voluntary Action Center of Brown County. Several assumptions were investigated: (a) Volunteers offer to work without pay because they have needs that can be met by volunteer work; (b) If their volunteer work meets their felt needs, the volunteers will experience satisfaction; and (c) If a volunteer feels satisfied, he or she will remain in the assigned task. Thus it is assumed that volunteers whose needs are well matched to the task will not drop out of volunteer work as quickly as those not well matched. Space will not permit a complete discussion of the empirical studies that support these assumptions. The reader is referred to the work of the author in Francies (1982) for a fuller report.

We began this study by asking our volunteers, by way of their monthly report form, "What benefits have you received from your volunteer work this month?" Over several years a large number of responses were collected. These benefits reported by the volunteers seemed to fall into seven categories of met needs. Empirical support for each need-benefit relationship was obtained from the literature. A brief description of each motivation-need is given next.

NEEDS SPECIFIC TO VOLUNTEERING IN A SOCIAL SERVICE SETTING

The Need for Experience

To break into job market, try out different skills, a new learning experience, to do something not possible with daily work, to get in touch with a different part of ourselves (eg., "young people keep me feeling young"), promote personal growth.

Feelings of Social Responsibility

Concern for others, feelings of "ought" and "should," the need to do something about social problems, caring, wanting to get involved, relieving feelings of guilt about one's good life as compared to others.

Need for Social Contact

To make new friends, to "get out of the house," to justify our existence and feel needed ("I'm important to someone"), alleviate loneliness, a sense of belonging, of being included, a part of something, to test out values and norms.

Responding to the Expectations of Others

Required by High School Class, Club, or employers, pressured by a spouse, friend, or peer, expected by church or pastor, responding to "all my friends are doing it" type peer pressure.

Need for Social Approval

Want to be appreciated, thanked, praised, respected, looked up to, to make someone proud of you, to get recognition (especially if not received at work or home), to receive social approval (selfish people are not approved), social esteem.

Expectation of Future Rewards

"Some day I may need help," having others in your debt, the feeling of being owed, belief that in helping others we avert being in need ourselves, fear of punishment or being judged (receiving punishment for being selfish), that our behavior returns to us.

The Need to Achieve

The sense of power in making things happen, to sense completion, an end, closure (assembly line workers often do not get this feeling), to get feedback, goal oriented, being able to feel proud of a job, good workmanship, satisfy a creative urge, to see and experience change, to prove or demonstrate perfection in a task.

The next step in this study was to develop an instrument that would accurately and objectively measure the relative strength of each of these needs. For a complete discussion of how this was accomplished and how the instrument was tested for validity and reliability, see Francies (1982). Numerous tests were made, including test-retest, Student's t test for the discrimination power of each statement, tests for internal consistency using Cronbach's Alpha, and several tests for construct validity. After nearly 18 months of testing, it was concluded that the instrument was reasonably valid and reliable. It was called the *Motivation Profile* at first, then changed to *The Volunteer Needs Profile* and more recently to *The Volunteer Motivation-Needs Profile* to more accurately describe what is actually being measured.

The instrument consists of 35 statements. The answers are rated from 1 (weak need) to 4 (strong need). The instrument contains seven subscales, corresponding to the seven needs discussed earlier. There are five statements for each subscale. Thus a subject's score for each subscale may range between 5 and 20. Only scores of 15 or more are considered in making a match to a task to meet those needs. Generally we found that from one to three subscales are involved in making a match. The instrument is scored and the results are immmediately shared with the volunteer for his or her response and in order to discuss the meaning *for that individual* of the higher scores.

THE NEED-SATISFACTION RELATIONSHIP

Our main support for this relationship is a series of studies in vocational rehabilitation at the University of Minnesota called the Work Adjustment Model (Lofquist & Dawis, 1969). The basic premise of this theory is that individuals will seek to achieve and maintain a "fit" or correspondence between themselves and their environment. In the work setting, this consists of personal abilities that must correspond to the ability requirements of the job, and personal needs that must correspond to the reward potential of the job to meet those needs, i.e., the reinforcer system. This may take effort on the part of both the individual and the work environment to adjust to the other, hence the concept of *work adjustment*.

Our concern was with two main propositions of this model: that satisfaction is a function of the correspondence between a worker's needs and the reinforcer system, i.e., job characteristics, and that the probability that a worker will quit is inversely related to his or her satisfaction. It is upon these basic concepts that this study was conducted. We had two concerns: would our instrument effectively identify a volunteer's motivational needs, and, second, would matching the volunteer to a task that had the potential to meet those needs make it more likely that the volunteer would stay with the task. The experiment which is now discussed was intended to answer those questions. Three hypotheses were tested which addressed these questions.

TESTING THE VOLUNTEER MOTIVATION-NEEDS PROFILE

Hypothesis One. Using the *Volunteer Needs Profile* to assign volunteers to a task will result in higher degrees of match than using the interview method alone.

Hypothesis Two. A high degree of match will lead to greater work satisfaction than a low degree of match of the volunteer's needs to the work assignment.

Hypothesis Three. The mortality rate (those dropping out) will be higher for a low degree of match than for those with a high degree of match.

FIGURE 1

INTRODUCTORY PAGE TO THE VOLUNTEER MOTIVATION-NEEDS PROFILE

Introduction to the Needs Profile

Please relax. This is not a test. There are no right answers or wrong answers. The Needs Profile measures several areas in which people may be motivated. The Profile gives feedback as to which needs most strongly motivate a particular individual. There are no GOOD OR BAD motivations.

Please be as honest as possible in your answers. Only by being honest can an accurate profile of your needs be obtained. The results will be used to better match you in a volunteer assignment.

INSTRUCTIONS

First: Each statement has two sides. Decide which side is *most* like you. Even if neither side is much like you, pick the side that comes the closest.

Second: On that side only, decide whether that side is "Almost Always True" for you or only "Sometimes True" for you. Please mark the corresponding box below.

Only mark one box for each entire statement.

Do not skip any statements.

You will find several statements that are very similar, but they are slightly different, so your answers may not always be the same.

Below are two examples of how another person answered the items. Please note that only one box per statement has been checked.

Almost Always True For Me	Some- times True For Me				Some- times True For Me	Almost Always True For Me
1. ☑	☐	Some people volunteer to gain experience to help them get a job.	-BUT-	Doing volunteer work for experience for a job is not important for other people.	☐	☐
2. ☐	☐	Some people feel they have so much that they should share.	-BUT-	Other people are not concerned about having more than someone else.	☑	☐

METHODS

A 2 x 3 design was used, with volunteers assigned to one of two groups (control or experimental) each with three levels of match (low, medium, or high). Subjects for this experiment were all volunteers newly recruited since January 1, 1982. They were recruited by the ordinary means by both BCDSS and the Voluntary Action Center. Every other volunteer was assigned to the experimental group with the rest in the control group. All volunteers took the Profile, but it was not scored for the control group until after they were assigned to a task. The experimental volunteer's Profile was scored, and the results were used in the interview and in making the task assignment. (See Francies, 1982, for complete details of this experiment.)

INSTRUMENTATION

The instruments used, in addition to the Profile, were the *Job Questionnaire* (JQ) (Brayfield & Rothe, 1951) and the *Satisfaction With Volunteer Assignment Evaluation* (SWVAE) (Francies, 1982) which were used to make an assessment of satisfaction. The SWVAE was developed to assess satisfaction specific to the seven subscales of the Profile. The JQ is more general. The reliability of the SWVAE, using Cronbach's Alpha, was $r = .92$. Satisfaction instruments were mailed between 10 and 12 weeks after the task was assigned.

RESULTS

Hypothesis One stated that there would be more high-degree matches when the Profile was used to make assignments than using the interview method alone. The hypothesis was supported. As can be seen in the following table, the distribution of the control group is nearly normal, while the experimental group is skewed toward a high degree of match. *Using the profile significantly improved the likelihood of obtaining a suitable assignment as compared to the interview method alone.*

Hypothesis Two stated that those in the high degree of match condition will be more satisfied than those in the low degree of match. Of the 120 volunteers in the experiment, two had moved and left no forwarding address and three refused to complete the evaluations. Of the remaining 115, 44 did not follow through on their assignment and so could not evaluate the task. The distribution of

176

these 44 are shown below. Note that 57% of the low group did not follow through as compared to 43% of the medium group, and 24% of the high group, suggesting they may not have felt the assignment was what they wanted. Of the 71 who did complete the questionnaires, 70 SWVAE's were useable and 64 of the JQ's. The remaining were incomplete, or, in the case of the JQ's, five had been completed in terms of the volunteer's paid employment and so could not be used.

Student's t was used to test the mean satisfaction scores of the low and high groups. Since the groups were so unequal in size, the low and medium groups were collapsed in a second test. This was done for the SWVAE and the JQ separately, and then the two measures were combined. The SWVAE was weighted equal to the JQ. (See Francies, 1982, for the details).

Hypothesis Two was supported (see Table 3). The results of every test indicated that the high degree of match subjects were significantly more satisfied with their volunteer work than the low condition or the low and medium combined conditions. *It is concluded that the degree of match does affect the volunteer's satisfaction in a positive direction.*

TABLE 1

DISTRIBUTION OF DEGREE OF MATCH OF VOLUNTEER X CONDITION

	Low	Medium	High	Totals
Control Group	n = 14	n = 26	n = 20	60
Experimental Group	n = 7	n = 18	n = 35	60
				120

Hypothesis Three predicted volunteers in the high degree of match condition would stay longer than those in the low degree of match condition. Volunteers were contacted as indicated between ten and twelve weeks after being assigned to a task. Telephone follow-up was made for those not responding. The agencies were contacted for the two volunteers that had moved. We were able to ascertain one of two conditions for each volunteer: "active" (still involved at time of contact) or "inactive" (had terminated prior to our contact). The results are shown in Table 4.

The reader will notice that the proportion of active to inactive volunteers reverses as one goes from the low to the high degree of match. The result of the Chi-square test is $X^2 = 13.21$, $p < .005$. Sixty-nine percent of the high match group remained active as compared to 29% of the low match group. *It is concluded that the degree of match does influence the likelihood of a volunteer remaining at the task for at least ten weeks.*

TABLE 2
RESPONSE TO EVALUATION QUESTIONNAIRES

	n	Control	Experimental	Low	Medium	High
Returned	71	32	39	9	23	39
No basis for evaluation	44	26	18	12	19	13
Unable to contact subject	2	—	2	—	—	2
Refused	3	2	1	—	2	1
Totals	120	60	60	21	44	55

DISCUSSION

All hypotheses were strongly supported. As predicted, using the Profile *increased the likelihood of obtaining a high degree of match between the needs of the volunteer and the task as compared to the interview method alone*. Volunteers in the control group displayed a normal distribution, while those in the experimental group were strongly skewed toward the high degree of match. Using the Chi-square test, we found $X^2 = 7.88$, $p < .025$.

Further, volunteers who were matched to a high degree to their task were significantly more satisfied. The results show that for the SWVAE measure, $t = 1.82$, $p < .05$ when compared to the low match group, and $t = 2.00$, $p < .025$ when the low and medium groups were collapsed. Using the same procedure for the JQ, the results were $t = 3.47$, $p < .005$ and $t = 3.28$, $p < .005$ respectively. And combining the two measures gave $t = 2.78$, $p < .005$ and $t = 2.65$, $p < .01$. *These results indicate that volunteers who were well matched to the task are more satisfied than volunteers whose needs are not addressed by the work*. These findings, as predicted by the Work Adjustment Model, indicate that the Profile has predictive validity.

And finally, 69% of those matched to a high degree were active after ten weeks as compared to 29% for those matched to a low degree. This is strong support for the validity of the Volunteer

TABLE 4

DEGREE OF MATCH X ACTIVE OR INACTIVE AT 10 WEEKS

	Low	Medium	High	Totals
Active	6	18	38	62
Inactive	15	26	17	58

Needs Profile, but it is also strong support for its utility. Using the Profile did conserve volunteers and reduce turnover to a greater extent than using the interview method alone to place volunteers in a job. *The high-matched volunteers as a group became involved to a greater extent and stayed longer than those not well matched to the job.*

Field experiments are especially difficult to control. There may well have been experimenter effects since the staff all knew the nature of the experiment. Whether conscious or unconscious, they may have tried to "help." That effect, if present, would have been partly overcome by a new staff person who was employed about half way through the experiment. She did not know the nature of the test, but may have at least partly guessed. However, the staff at the Voluntary Action Center *always* try to make the very best placements possible with the tools they have. Their enthusiasm over the results seems to indicate that they had confidence in the procedures they used. Although the effect cannot be ruled out, it would seem to be minor.

One challenge that might be raised is that the initial motivation of the control and experimental groups was different. This was tested and it was found that the mean scores (measured by points over 14) of the two groups were statistically the same: 7.167 for the control group and 6.533 for the experimental. If anything, the bias would favor the control group. The author has considerable confidence in the outcome, and these results should easily be replicated in similar settings. The conditions under which this experiment took place would be similar to that in which the Profile might be used in actual practice. Unlike laboratory experiments, this one will readily generalize to the field.

The implications and applications of this research are obvious in the area of assigning volunteers to a task. Placement coaches in VAC and RSVP programs should find their percentages of persons staying on the job increased when the Profile is used in conjunction with the interview. It should also be easily adaptable to other agencies where there is a variety of assignments from which to choose to place volunteers.

Further, the reliability and validity are great enough to suggest that the Profile may be useful in further research, such as determining if there are indeed differences between other popula-

TABLE 3
DEGREE OF MATCH X SATISFACTION SCORES

	SWVAE (n = 70)				JQ (n = 64)				Combined (n = 63)			
	Low	Med.	(L&M)	High	Low	Med.	(L&M)	High	Low	Med.	(L&M)	High
n	9	23	32	38	10	21	31	33	9	21	30	33
$\bar{x}$	56.4	59.0	58.3	65.5	59.1	64.1	62.5	70.0	57.1	61.2	60.0	67.4
Σ	508	1358	1865	2490	591	1347	1938	2311	514	1285	1799	2223
$\Sigma(\Sigma x2)$	30704	87270	117974	169240	36453	88307	124760	163423	30666	82140	112806	152273
Low X High		t = 1.82, p < .05				t = 3.47, p < .005				t = 2.78, p < .005		
(L&M) X High		t = 2.00, p < .025 (One-tailed test)				t = 3.28, p < .005 (One-tailed test)				t = 2.65, p < .01 (One-tailed test)		

tions of non-volunteers and volunteers, or between different types of volunteer workers, as for example, volunteers in human service and volunteers in policy-making positions. The instrument may also be useful in monitoring trends. For example, are more volunteers today looking for experience, and will this trend continue; or is the heightened sense of social responsibility a temporary experience of students, or will this continue into their later adult years. It could also be used to determine if a volunteer's needs change over time, for example, after one year on the job.

We have not tested the usefulness of this tool in matching to individuals rather than jobs, such as is necessary in a Big Brother program. An objective and practical way needs to be developed to assess the potential of a task to meet specific needs of volunteers. The *Minnesota Satisfaction Questionnaire* (Weisse et al., 1967) does this by asking workers directly about the level of satisfaction received from specific jobs. Such an instrument could be developed to assess volunteer jobs in relation to the seven needs that have been identified. One weakness in this study is that we needed to use staff to judge the tasks. Having workers involved with that task to assess its potential to satisfy needs would be a superior method since the assessment would come from those who have experienced the task.

A further limitation of the Profile is in its psychometric abilities. The Profile does not give an absolute score that can be compared to national norms. Instead, it yields a score that only estimates relative strength of one need as compared to other needs *within the same individual*. We did not find the total score of all seven subscales to have any significance in predicting turnover. Only the degree of match with the task was predictive in this regard, and the degree of match was based on the high scores for that individual. The absolute score may be lower than for other individuals, but if these others were mismatched, we could predict failure to stay with the task for them. In short, users of this instrument should not attempt to derive valid information from the scores in any absolute sense, but only in relation to the other subscales for that person. For that reason, it is not recommended that norms be established.

The Volunteer Motivation-Needs Profile is a tool that depends upon the user's ability to follow the leads it provides. The Need for Experience, for example, may mean simply to get out of the house and do something different, or it may mean the volunteer is in need of an experience that can help prepare for future employment. It is the user's task to discover the meaning of each high score for that individual.

This study has been concerned with volunteer turnover due for the most part to volunteers quitting their jobs, usually within the first three months. The *Volunteer Motivation-Needs Profile*, when used with the interview in placing volunteers in their jobs, does help to solve the problem. Using the instrument, it is possible to get a higher degree of match between the volunteer's needs and the task's potential to meet those needs. This leads to more satisfaction on the part of the volunteer. Because they are more satisfied with their work, they stay on the job longer. Thus the instrument helps solve the problem of volunteer turnover.

REFERENCES

Brayfield, Arthur H. and Harold F. Rothe
  1951 "An Index of Job Satisfaction," *Journal of Applied Psychology* 35: 307-311.
Cronbach, Lee J.
  1951 "Coefficient Alpha and the Internal Structure of Tests," *Psychometrika* XVI: 297-334.
Darley, John M. and Bibb Latané
  1970 "Norms and Normative Behavior: Field Studies of Social Interdependence," in Macaulay and Berkowitz, eds., *Altruism and Helping Behavior*. New York: Academic Press.
Francies, George Ray
  1982 *The Volunteer Needs Profile: Development and Testing a Seven Scale Profile For Use in Placing Volunteers in Human Service Agencies*. Unpublished thesis. Green Bay: University of Wisconsin.
Gidron, Benjamin
  1976 *Rewards from Sustained Volunteer Work: A Study of Volunteers in Four Health and Mental Health Institutions*. Unpublished dissertation. University of Maryland Baltimore Professional Schools.
Kennett, David A.
  1980 "Altruism and Economic Behavior, I: Developments in the Theory of Public and Private Redistribution," *The American Journal of Economics and Sociology* 39: 183-198.

Lofquist, Lloyd and Rene Dawis

1969 *Adjustment to Work: A Psychological View of Man's Problems in a Work Oriented Society*. Englewood Cliffs, NJ: Prentice-Hall.

Scheier, Ivan H.

1980 *Exploring Volunteer Space*. Washington, DC: Volunteer Press.

Walster, Elaine, G. William Walster, and Ellen Berscheid

1978 *Equity: Theory and Research*. Boston: Allyn and Bacon, Inc.

Weiss, David J., Rene V. Dawis, George W. England, and Lloyd H. Lofquist

1967 *Manual for the Minnesota Satisfaction Questionnaire*. University of Minnesota.

Winer, B. J.

1971 *Statistical Principles In Experimental Design*. (2nd ed.) New York: McGraw-Hill Book Co.

Selected Paper 3

NEED SATISFACTION OF PAID AND VOLUNTEER WORKERS IN HEALTH SERVICE OCCUPATIONS

Larry F. Moore and John C. Anderson

Probably from the beginning of time, the field of health service has made extensive use of volunteer (unpaid) persons to augment and assist the paid medical practitioners in providing appropriate care for patients. In hospitals and extended care agencies, volunteers perform many roles similar to paid persons and thus are occupied in direct patient care activities and in a variety of administrative and clerical duties, often reporting to the same supervisor as their paid co-workers.

Like paid workers, volunteer workers are motivated to participate in work activity in order to satisfy their human needs.

To date, little research has been published on the needs and need satisfaction levels of the unpaid worker, the volunteer, yet citizen participation in voluntary programs and activities has increased dramatically. "Voluntarism" — giving time and energy to do work for non-remunerative reasons — likely provides a rich source of opportunity for human need satisfaction and the need hierarchy theory has been singled out as conceptually useful when discussing the motivation of volunteers (Kappell, 1968; Knowles, 1972).

In recent years the topic of need satisfaction on the job has been extensively researched and reviewed (Hinrichs, 1970). One frequently used conceptual framework is that of Maslow (1943, 1970). The theory postulates a hierarchy of needs arranged in order of their prepotency, and investigations using this general construct to study work motivation have examined samples of managerial (Porter, 1961; Wanous and Lawler, 1972), union (Miller, 1966), operative (Slocum, Topichak, and Kuhn, 1968), clerical (Beer, 1968), government (Paine, Carroll and Leete, 1966), and military personnel (Porter and Mitchell, 1967) with mixed results (cf. Wahba and Bridwell, 1983). Mitchell and Moudgill (1976) demonstrated the operationality of the Maslow conceptual framework using oblique factor rotation methods.

The question of need satisfaction and its role in work motivation becomes crucial when the individual is employed in a voluntary rather than a paid capacity. Traditional methods, such as salary and fringe benefits, commonly used as inducements of work contributions, by definition, do not apply to volunteer workers. On the other hand, it has been argued that tangible rewards primarily satisfy "lower-order" needs and do not take account of "higher-order" needs for self-esteem and self-actualization (Maslow, 1943, 1970). Deci (1975) stresses the importance of the human need for obtaining intrinsic job satisfaction through becoming ego involved in work and committed to doing it well. Much research on the motivation of volunteers suggests that volunteers perform their work roles in order to obtain intrinsic job satisfaction associated with "higher-order" needs (Anderson and Moore, 1978; Flynn and Webb, 1975; Gidron, 1983; Gluck, 1975; Jenner, 1982; Qureshi, Davies, and Challis, 1979; Sharp, 1978). The purpose of this study is to identify the extent of need satisfaction for health service volunteer workers and to compare the need pattern of volunteers to that of paid employees performing similar functions in a health care setting. Specifically, it is hypothesized that health service volunteer workers have higher levels of higher-order need satisfaction than do paid workers in similar occupations.

METHOD
The Instrument

In separate studies, questionnaires were administered to three samples in order to measure need satisfaction and to provide demo-

TABLE 1

QUESTIONNAIRE ITEMS GROUPED BY MASLOW NEED CATEGORY

Need Category and Item Description	Questionnaire Item
Security	
Sec. 1	The feeling of security I have in my volunteer position.
Sec. 2	The amount of predictability and order in my volunteer position.
Sec. 3	The extent to which my supervisors let me know just what is expected of me in my volunteer position.
Social	
Soc. 1	The opportunity in my volunteer position for developing close personal friendships.
Soc. 2	The opportunity in my volunteer position for conversation and exchange of ideas with my co-workers.
Soc. 3	The opportunity I have in my volunteer position to help other people.
Esteem	
Est. 1	The feeling of self-esteem I get from being in my volunteer position.
Est. 2	The importance and appreciation I receive from my co-workers in my volunteer position.
Est. 3	The recognition or credit I receive from my supervisors in my volunteer position.

Autonomy	
Aut. 1	The opportunity in my volunteer position for independent thought and action.
Aut. 2	The opportunity in my volunteer position to participate in the setting of goals.
Aut. 3	The freedom and power I have to make decisions in my volunteer position.

Self-Actualization	
S.A. 1	The opportunity for personal growth and development in my volunteer position.
S.A. 2	The feeling of really worthwhile accomplishment in my volunteer position.
S.A. 3	The opportunity I have in my volunteer position for doing original and creative kinds of work.

graphic data. As shown in Table 1, need satisfaction was gauged by 15 items classified according to five need categories using a format similar to the Porter (1961) instrument. Three items were randomly presented for each of the security, social, esteem, autonomy, and self-actualization need categories.

Respondents were asked to indicate on a 7-point scale how much of each characteristic there *is now* in their job. Although *should be* and *importance* scores were collected on two samples, for the following reasons only *is now* scale scores are reported here. A six month test-retest of the instrument by R. W. Miller (1970) found *is* scores to be acceptably reliable (average r = .63) and significantly more reliable than *should be, discrepancy*, or *importance* measures. In addition, Alderfer (1967), employing multi-method procedures (Campbell and Fiske, 1959), concluded that a questionnaire of this type had satisfactory convergent and discriminant validities. Similarly, Wanous and Lawler (1972) found that *is* scores correlated most highly with a single item measuring respondents' total job satisfaction. Thus, the 15-item instrument is taken to have acceptable reliability and validity as a measure of job need satisfaction.

SAMPLE AND PROCEDURE

Sample Selection

As the purpose of the research was to compare voluntary workers and conventionally employed persons, the selection of comparison groups was important to the external validity of the study. In selecting appropriate comparison samples, consideration was given to the similarity of work environments and duties performed. The volunteer sample respondents were involved in a variety of jobs and agencies, but all performed patient or client service functions in hospitals and health related agencies. Moreover, most of the volunteers performed more than one type of service. In general, the types of activities performed were closely comparable to those of paid hospital staff personnel. In a hospital setting, the volunteer is typically supervised by or working with the nursing staff while contact with the administrative staff is limited to receiving directions for performing clerical activities. Two comparison samples were studied, representing as closely as possible, paid employees performing occupational activities generally similar to those performed by the sample of volunteer workers. The third comparison sample, administrative staff, was included not because of occupational similarities but because previous studies indicated that senior administrators tend to achieve a greater degree of job satisfaction than do less senior employees (Porter, 1962; Porter and Mitchell, 1967). Hence this group was regarded as a possible "bench-mark."

Volunteer Sample

Initial contact was gained through Canada's 49 Volunteer Bureaus, which were requested to suggest a representative sample of agencies using volunteers who would be interested in participating in a research study. Each Volunteer Bureau then relayed to the researchers its list of agencies, addresses, volunteer coordinators' names, and number of questionnaires required. Questionnaires were sent to 198 agencies in 30 Canadian urban centres with instructions for distribution to a random sample of each agency's volunteers. A self-addressed, stamped envelope accompanied each questionnaire to facilitate rapid return directly to the investigators. Respondents were informed that participation was voluntary and anonymity was assured. When non-responding agencies were deleted, the overall response rate was 37%. No follow-up was attempted. The return yielded 1,062 usable responses, of which 263 were from health service volunteers.

Because of the moderate response rate, a comparison of demographic characteristics was made with results of several other studies of characteristics of volunteers (Caldwell, Katz and Levine, 1972; Gallup, 1981; Payne and Reddy, 1972; Statistics Canada, 1980). Although differences exist between samples, the patterns are not significantly different in terms of age, sex, education, marital status, occupational background, and amount of time spent per week in volunteer work. Therefore, the volunteer sample appears to be representative of people who do volunteer work.

Samples of Hospital Employees

Initial contact with a large hospital was made and permission to undertake the research was obtained. Meetings with department heads and supervisors were called to clarify the nature of the project and the intent and means of the survey. Of 1,400 questionnaires distributed, 744 responses (53%) were returned.

For purposes of comparison, three subsamples were chosen: the nurse aides, the nursing staff (both registered and licensed practical nurses), and senior administrative personnel (assistant department heads and above). This group composed 670 of the 744 responses.

Demographic Comparison of Subsamples

As demographic characteristics have been found to be related to need fulfillment of volunteer workers (Anderson and Moore, 1974), it is important to be aware of possible systematic biases in the results due to differences in sample composition. A comparison of selected demographic variables of the three samples is presented in Table 2. Inter-sample differences in age, education, and marital status are unlikely to have a biasing effect; however, the greater proportion of females in the volunteer sample could slightly inflate any differences in esteem, autonomy, and self-actualization scores when making comparisons with the administrative sample. Although Anderson and Moore (1974) found that female volunteers reported higher levels of esteem need satisfaction and lower levels of autonomy and self-actualization than did males, this possible bias does not seem important to the present analysis.

To test for overall differences in need satisfaction across samples, one-way analyses of variance were computed on the mean scores for the five need categories. Several pair-wise comparisons among sample groups were made in order to test the hypothesis that volunteer workers have higher levels of higher-order need satisfaction than do paid workers in similar occupations.

RESULTS

The mean need satisfaction scores by group are shown in Table 3. One-way analyses of variance showed overall significant differences beyond the .01 level in each of the five need categories (security $F = 5.84$, df $= 3/929$; social $F = 8.85$, df $= 3/929$; esteem $F = 40.25$,

TABLE 2

DEMOGRAPHIC ANALYSIS OF THE SAMPLES

Characteristics	Canadian Volunteers 1062	Nurses Aides 153	Nursing Staff 361	Administrative Staff 156
Sex:				
Male	11.8%	12.00%	14.7%	42.9%
Female	88.2%	88.00%	85.3%	57.1%
Marital Status:				
Single	21.3%	39.00%	43.9%	33.5%
Married & Other	78.7%	61.00%	56.1%	66.5%
Age:				
M	41.7%	27.30%	30.0%	37.8%
SD	—	7.60%	8.2%	6.9%
Education:				
M	13.2%	11.46%	14.1%	17.6%
SD	—	—	—	—

NOTE: Means presented for volunteer sample on age and education, from grouped data.

df = 3/929; autonomy F = 35.91, df = 3/929; self-actualization F = 36.28, df = 3/929).

Using the Scheffé test for multiple comparisons of means (Ferguson, 1971), the mean need satisfaction score for the volunteer sample was compared with the mean scores of the nursing staff, nursing aides, and administrative staff for the five need categories. The results are given in Table 4.

Mean scores for the volunteer sample were significantly higher than both the nursing staff and nursing aide samples at

TABLE 3

NEED CATEGORY MEANS AND STANDARD DEVIATIONS OF HEALTH SERVICE VOLUNTEERS AND PAID PERSONNEL

Need Category	Canadian Volunteers 263	Nurses Aides 361	Nursing Staff 153	Administrative Staff 156
Security:				
M	4.99	4.49	4.99	4.77
SD	1.87	1.55	1.38	1.99
Social:				
M	4.95	5.35	4.65	5.49
SD	2.07	1.54	1.51	1.83
Esteem:				
M	5.25	4.00	4.20	5.08
SD	1.78	1.42	1.80	1.38
Autonomy:				
M	4.41	3.63	3.25	5.09
SD	2.10	1.84	1.64	1.60
Self-Actualization:				
M	4.69	3.57	3.31	4.93
SD	2.03	1.79	2.27	1.57

the .01 level for esteem, autonomy, and self-actualization, supporting the hypothesis. Interestingly, the volunteer sample had a significantly higher need score on the social dimension than did the nursing staff group, although the volunteer and nursing aide sample means on social are identical. Difference in sample size accounts for the discrepancy in significance.

The nursing staff and nursing aides had remarkably similar need patterns across the five categories, differing significantly only on the social dimension, where the nursing staff is higher.

Finally, the comparison between the administrator and volunteer sample means for each of the five need categories revealed only one significant difference. The administrator group, as might be expected, had a higher score for autonomy satisfaction.

DISCUSSION

The central focus of this investigation has been to compare the need satisfaction levels of volunteer workers with those of paid workers

TABLE 4

SCHEFFÉ TEST FOR MULTIPLE COMPARISONS OF MEANS FOR FIVE NEED CATEGORIES
(Significant values only)*

Need Category	Volunteers vs. Nursing Staff	Volunteers vs. Nursing Aides	Nursing vs. Nursing Aides	Volunteers vs. Administrative Staff
Security	13.18			
Social			16.89	
Esteem	93.90	43.03		
Autonomy	27.04	37.33		13.25
Self-Actualization	49.00	50.55		

* $p < .01$, $F' = 11.40$

holding similar occupational positions in health care settings. As predicted, volunteers appear to derive more higher-order need satisfaction from their jobs than their paid counterparts. Since the task requirements were similar for the paid and volunteer workers, the observed differences in need satisfaction are likely related to differences in the way in which volunteer and paid workers are rewarded for their work. Since the opportunity for volunteers to receive extrinsic rewards is, by definition, low or nonexistent, they must obtain intrinsic rewards from their work, e.g., opportunity for self-expression, personal challenge, helping others, the job itself, etc. As Deci (1975) points out, these rewards focus on higher-order needs and are mediated by the person himself. On the other hand, the paid worker, even when classified as a paraprofessional, is much more likely to receive externally mediated tangible rewards such as money, promotion, and fringe benefits from his job. Thus, engaging in voluntary activity, in addition to providing useful services for the recipient organization, provides a rich source of job-related need satisfaction.

The observed difference in need satisfaction between the nursing staff and the nurse aides on the social dimension may be related to occupational differences. Registered nurses are expected to exercise considerable initiative in caring for patients and have far greater opportunity to socialize, both with patients and with other members of the nursing staff, than do nurse aides, who are engaged chiefly in "housekeeping" activities.

Finally, the contrast between the bench-mark sample of administrative personnel and the volunteer illustrates that volunteer work in health care settings as a source of need satisfaction, compares favorably in all categories except autonomy. Higher administrator scores in this category may be due to the socially elite and more autonomous nature of the administrative role compared to the occupationally less prestigious and demanding roles performed by the volunteers in this study

REFERENCES

Alderfer, C. P.
1967 "Convergent and Discriminant Validation of Satisfaction and Desire Measures by Interviews and Questionnaires," *Journal of Applied Psychology* 51: 509-520.

Anderson, J. C. and L. F. Moore
1974 "Individual Correlates of the Motivation of Canadian Volunteers," University of British Columbia. Unpublished paper.
1978 "The Motivation to Volunteer," *Journal of Voluntary Action Research* 7: 120-129.

Beer, M.
1968 "Needs and Need Satisfaction Among Clerical Workers in Complex and Routine Jobs," *Personnel Psychology* 21: 29-222.

Caldwell, M., M. Katz, and D. Levine
1972 "Characteristics of Volunteers in a State Mental Hospital," *Volunteer Administration* 6: 4-10.

Campbell, D. T. and D. W. Fiske
1959 "Convergent and Discriminant Validation by the Multi-Trait Multi-Method Matrix," *Psychological Bulletin* 58: 81-105.

Deci, E. L.
1975 *Intrinsic Motivation*. New York: Plenum.

Ferguson, G.A.
1971 *Statistical Analysis in Psychology and Education* (3rd ed.) New York: McGraw-Hill.

Flynn, J. P. and G. E. Webb
1975 "Women's Incentives for Community Participation in Policy Issues," *Journal of Voluntary Action Research* 4: 137-145.

Gallup Organization
1981 *Americans Volunteer*. Washington, DC: Independent Sector.

Gidron, B.
1983 "Sources of Job Satisfaction Among Service Volunteers," *Journal of Voluntary Action Research* 12: 20-35.

Gluck, P. R.
1975 "An Exchange Theory of Incentives of Urban Political Party Organizations," *Journal of Voluntary Action Research* 4: 104-115.

Hinrichs, J. R.

    1970 "Psychology of Men at Work," *Annual Review of Psychology* 21: 519-554.

Jenner, J. R.

    1982 "Participation, Leadership, and the Role of Volunteerism Among Selected Women Volunteers," *Journal of Voluntary Action Research* 11: 27-38.

Kappell, B. M.

    1968 "The Volunteer Movement in the United States," *Volunteer Administration* 2: 11-28.

Knowles, M. S.

    1972 "Motivation in Volunteerism: Synopsis of a Theory," *Journal of Voluntary Action Research* 1: 27-29.

Maslow, A. H.

    1943 "A Theory of Human Motivation," *Psychological Review* 50: 370-396.

    1970 *Motivation and Personality* (2nd ed.) New York: Harper and Row.

Miller, E. L.

    1966 "Job Satisfaction of National Union Officials," *Personnel Psychology* 19: 261-274.

Miller, R. W.

    1970 "Job Level and Life Area as Sources of Maslow-Type Needs," University of British Columbia. Unpublished paper.

Mitchell, V. F. and P. Moudgill

    1976 "Measurement of Maslow's Need Hierarchy," *Organizational Behavior and Human Performance* 16: 334-349.

Paine, F., S. Carroll, and B. Leete

    1966 "Need Satisfaction of Managerial Level Personnel in a Government Agency," *Journal of Applied Psychology* 50: 247-249.

Payne, R., B. Payne, and R. Reddy

    1972 "Social background and Role Determinants of Individual Participation in Organized Voluntary Action," in D. H. Smith et al., eds. *Voluntary Action Research*. Lexington, MA: D. C. Heath's Co.

Porter, L. W.

    1961 "A Study of Perceived Need Satisfaction in Bottom and Middle Management Jobs," *Journal of Applied Psychology* 45: 1-10.

198

1962 "Job Attitudes in Management: 1. Perceived Deficiencies in Need Fulfillment as a Function of Job Level," *Journal of Applied Psychology* 46: 375-384.

Porter, L. W. and V. F. Mitchell
1967 "Comparative Study of Need Satisfaction in Military and Business Hierarchies," *Journal of Applied Psychology* 51: 139-144.

Qureshi, H., B. Davies, and D. Challis
1979 "Motivations and Rewards of Volunteers and Informal Care Givers," *Journal of Voluntary Action Research* 8: 47-55.

Sharp, Elaine B.
1978 "Citizen Organization in Policing Issues and Crime Prevention: Incentives for Participation," *Journal of Voluntary Action Research* 7: 45-58.

Slocum, J., P. Topichak, and D. Kuhn
1971 "A Cross-Cultural Study of Need Satisfaction and Need Importance for Operative Employees," *Personnel Psychology* 24: 435-445.

Statistics Canada
1980 *Overview of Volunteer Workers in Canada*. Ottawa: Government of Canada, Catalogue No. 71-530.

Wahba, M. A. and L. G. Bridwell
1983 "Maslow Reconsidered: A Review of Research on the Need Hierarchy Theory," in R. M. Steers and L. W. Porter, eds. *Motivation and Work Behavior* (3rd ed.) New York: McGraw-Hill, 34-41.

Wanous, J. P. and E. E. Lawler, III
1972 "Measurement and Meaning of Job Satisfaction," *Journal of Applied Psychology* 56: 93-105.

Selected Paper 4

INSUFFICIENT JUSTIFICATION AND VOLUNTEER MOTIVATION

Jone L. Pearce

Human motivation is one of the most important, and baffling, of mysteries. Motivation is of critical importance to all of those who are concerned with the behavior of others: teachers worry about the best way to motivate students, therapists analyze patients' motives, and supervisors seek to motivate subordinates. As troubling as motivation is for these professionals, it becomes almost overwhelming when it is the motivation of volunteers that is considered. After all, students seek good grades, patients want to feel better, and employees are paid for their efforts. But why do volunteers volunteer? Why do they continue to contribute year after year?

There is ample evidence that volunteer motivation remains a mystery to volunteers and to those who work with them. Pearce (1978: 174) quotes a volunteer in a poverty relief agency reflecting on her uncertainty about her own and others' motivation to volunteer:

> "[What are the major differences between volunteer and employing organizations?] There seems to be a spirit there [among volunteers] that people have. It's probably not there if people are paid. It's hard to say exactly why. They [volunteers] probably decide they are doing it for a good reason so they assume a positive attitude about it. If you are paid you probably don't question it; you assume you are doing it for a living. Volunteers don't know why they are working; they don't know the answer. I guess they assume they do it because they want to do good. These assumptions lead to different ways of doing things. Not that paid people aren't cheerful; it's just that it's not needed."

In the same study Pearce (1978) describes the frustrations experienced by managers of volunteers who strive to provide rewards that in fact have no appeal to their volunteers. An example is offered from the same poverty relief agency cited above:

> A voluntary poverty relief agency provided food and emergency transportation to those who called to ask for assistance. The agency was designed to provide temporary, immediate emergency assistance to those in need. Volunteers answered the phones, delivered the food to the requester's door, and provided needed transportation. . . . The board decided to institute a 'pot luck dinner' to thank the volunteers and provide a social occasion in which they could get to know one another. This dinner was considered a failure, since less than ten percent of the volunteers attended. The leadership was frustrated and angry, muttering about 'apathetic volunteers.' Yet, when volunteers were asked why they didn't attend the dinner they indicated they were reluctant to go to a gathering in which they wouldn't know anyone else. They volunteered for this organization because they wanted to make a small contribution in the fight against hunger, not to meet other people. Since the dinner wasn't seen as 'real work,' and might be socially uncomfortable, they saw no reason to attend. The planners of the dinner didn't anticipate this perception, and so went to a lot of effort to put on a 'failure.' Such experiences appear to be common among managers of voluntary organizations, who must continually experiment to find something that works for at least some of their volunteers. (Pearce, 1983a : 89)

These examples illustrate that volunteer motivation is frequently uncertain to both the volunteers and those who work with them.

In the face of this mystery, and the discomfort it implies, Deci's (1975) theory of intrinsic and extrinsic motivation has been seen as the long-awaited solution. Deci (1975: 23) suggests that people's motives can be categorized as being either intrinsic or extrinsic:

> Intrinsically motivated activities are ones for which there is no apparent reward except the activity itself. People seem to engage in the activities for their own sake and not because they lead to an extrinsic reward. The activities are ends in themselves rather than means to an end.

202

By contrast, extrinsically motivated activities are those performed in order to obtain some benefit; some reward given by another, hence extrinsic to the work itself. This work offered a plausible explanation for volunteers' efforts. Based on Deci's (1975) theoretical perspective, volunteers and those concerned with their motivation, could claim that volunteers are intrinsically rather than extrinsically motivated.

As attractive as it is to have a name for our mystery, it will be suggested that acceptance of Deci's (1975) theory has rather striking practical implications. These flow from Deci's (1975) arguments about the relationship between extrinsic and intrinsic motivation: that the addition of extrinsic rewards to a task that is already intrinsically motivating will result in an actual decrease in intrinsic motivation. He presents persuasive laboratory evidence that the addition of extrinsic rewards often leads to a *decrease* in people's intrinsic motivation to perform the work. Furthermore, he suggests that a person's intrinsic motivation can be enhanced to justify the performance of a dull activity for insufficient extrinsic rewards. That is, the person will ask him or herself, "Why am I doing this? It certainly isn't for the money!" This feeling is uncomfortable — producing "dissonance" — which the questioner can reduce by answering, "I must be doing this because I like the activity itself." Under conditions of insufficient justification for an activity, relatively higher intrinsic motivation might be expected than if the work is adequately compensated by extrinsic rewards.

This has been called the "sufficiency of justification hypothesis" and has been taken out of the laboratory and applied to workplace motivation by Staw (1976). He proposes that when both extrinsic and intrinsic organizational rewards are abundant, individuals experience "overjustification" for the work and are likely to reduce dissonance by devaluing the less tangible intrinsic rewards. Similarly, when individuals perform work for which the rewards are few, they experience "insufficient justification" which leads them to enhance the importance of intrinsic rewards.

If this hypothesis is true, it has several practical implications for volunteers. First, it would suggest that "paying" volunteers for their work would simply substitute one kind of motivation — extrinsic — for another — intrinsic. In other words, if volunteers are reimbursed, say for travel expenses, this will not increase their motivation but simply shift their attention from the work itself to the reimbursement. Secondly, it would suggest that volunteer motivation can only be maintained through challenging or intrinsically interesting tasks. We would not expect volunteers to remain at routine or dull jobs, since it is the work itself that is motivating them. Finally, it implies that the "volunteer spirit" may be more the result of underpayment than commitment to the mission of the organization. The volunteer quoted at the beginning of this paper, in fact, suggested just that. Therefore, if Deci's (1975) and Staw's (1976) theories are appropriate to volunteer motivation, they have far-reaching implications for the management of volunteers.

Yet there is substantial research evidence raising questions about the sufficiency of justification hypothesis. The research developing from this hypothesis has been reviewed by Staw (1976) and Guzzo (1979) who find mixed support in actual work settings. Although a diminution of intrinsic motivation has been produced in laboratories, none of the field studies reported this effect (Dermer, 1975; Eden, 1975). In addition, Guzzo (1979) has called the basic intrinsic/extrinsic dichotomy of organizational rewards, itself, into question. He presents convincing evidence that organizational rewards may vary simultaneously along several attributes. Further, the only studies in actual organizations that demonstrated support for the operation of sufficiency of justification are not dependent on the intrinsic/extrinsic dichotomy of organizational rewards. Staw (1974) examined cadets' attitudes toward ROTC before and after the draft lottery. After the lottery those with high lottery numbers were assured they would not be drafted and would now be hypothesized to experience insufficient justification for participation in ROTC. Those of this group without committing contracts dropped out, while committed cadets who would not now be drafted developed more favorable attitudes toward ROTC than did the other cadets. Note that these cadets were not necessarily more intrinsically motivated, since participation was enforced by a contract; simply, those cadets with less compelling justification for participation developed more positive attitudes toward the organization. Pfeffer and Lawler's (1980) results are also consistent with the sufficient justification hypothesis using a national sample of college and university professors. Uncommitted professors showed a positive relationship between salary and job satisfaction. Committed professors did not show this relationship, and these two effects were stronger for those who had job alternatives. Again, these differences are consistent with experienced insufficient justification, but they appear in attitudes toward the task, not in any difference in the motivation for engaging in the task.

In summary, there is some evidence that individuals may have more positive feelings about their organizations when their reasons for participating are less compelling. There have been, however, no studies outside of the laboratory that demonstrate that intrinsic motivation is higher if the extrinsic rewards are meager. That is, volunteers may like their organizations more because they are insufficiently paid, but we still have no evidence about what might motivate them.

In the present paper the results of a field study comparing the motivation and attitudes of volunteers with employees doing similar tasks are briefly reported. These results indicate that volunteers may very well experience insufficient justification for their participation, but their work motivation does not appear to be the intrinsic motivation predicted by Deci (1975) and Staw (1978). The practical implications of these results for the design of volunteer jobs are developed in the concluding section.

THE STUDY
Sample

Organizations staffed predominantly by volunteers and those staffed entirely by employees working on the same or similar tasks were paired. Four matched sets, or eight organizations, were sampled; these are two newspapers, two poverty relief agencies, two family planning clinics, and two municipal fire departments.

1) The volunteer-staffed newspaper is the student newspaper for a medium-sized private university located in a northeastern U.S. suburb. Each week 4,000 copies of the 10 to 12 page paper are distributed free on campus newsstands.

2) The employing newspaper is distributed free once a week in apartment building lobbies and shops in an affluent residential neighborhood of a large metropolitan city. Each week 50,000 copies of this 12-page community newspaper are distributed. The paper is owned by the editor and publisher.

3) The voluntary poverty relief agency is a non-denominational Christian relief organization in a medium-sized northeastern city. Its primary task is the distribution of food to those who request it (13,245 deliveries in the previous year), but it occasionally provides transportation to medical appointments as well. If clients want food they call a number monitored by an answering service; the answering service calls the telephone volunteer on duty (two shifts a day of about four hours each), and leaves the clients' names and phone numbers. The telephone volunteer calls the clients, collects information (address, number of people to be fed, etc.), and tells the clients when to expect the deliveries. The telephone volunteer then calls the driving volunteer or leaves a message at the central office. The volunteers work a one-half day shift each month and elect the governing committee which hires the two part-time paid coordinators to staff the central office.

4) The employing poverty relief agency is a municipal welfare department of a medium-sized New England city that is statutorily required to provide emergency relief to those who do not qualify for any of the state or federal relief programs. In practice, most of their clients are chronic, usually men with drug- or alcohol-related problems. Clients must appear weekly to personally receive their checks from their social workers, and usually attend a work or counselling program.

5) The voluntary family planning clinic provides gynecological, contraceptive, and related counselling services to women in a New England town. The current patient load is 200 women with pregnancy testing done once a week, and clinics held two evenings a month; the office is staffed during weekdays by a salaried secretary. The clinic is run by a core group of fourteen female volunteers who work anywhere from 4 hours a month to over 40 a week and who elect their own governing body.

6) The employing family planning clinic provides sex education, gynecological, contraceptive, and related counselling services to women in a large northeastern city. Clinics are held four days and one evening a week, and the case load is 4,000 women. This clinic is a component of a municipal health department.

7) The volunteer fire department provides emergency medical technicians, fire prevention, and fire fighting services to a rural New England town of about 15,000. They responded to over 500 alarms in the previous year. In an emergency, the town despatcher is called; she makes an announcement through the radio and blasts a horn so others will get to their radios. The closest firefighter goes to the station to take the apparatus (engine, hook and ladder, or ambulance) to the destination, while other volunteers proceed there directly in their own cars. The department is composed of four companies — three pump, and one hook and ladder. Each company elects a house administrative group and its officers; the department as a whole elects the chief and two assistant chiefs.

8) The employing fire department provides fire prevention and fighting services to a northeastern suburb of 26,000. The department answers an average of 200 calls a month. There is a central firehouse in which five firefighters and the chiefs are stationed, and two outlying stations.

Procedures

The data collection procedures followed the same pattern in each organization. Entry began with a telephone call, followed by one or more site visits to secure participation. Data collection began with interviews with a random sample (with oversampling of office holders and supervisors) of organizational members, followed by distribution and collection of questionnaires.

Measures

All data for this study were taken from a single questionnaire. The motivation scales are based on Guzzo's (1979) critique of the intrinsic/extrinsic dichotomy of organizational rewards, with a wide variety of reward items chosen based on the work of Pearce (1983b). The nine work reward items formed three scales: Intrinsic, Social, and Service Work Rewards. Questions concerning pay, fringe benefits, and promotions are not included because they are unavailable to the volunteers.

Three job attitude scales are used in the present analyses. Job Satisfaction and Intent to Leave were used by Pfeffer and Lawler (1980). However, an additional variable has been added which is a better approximation of likely sufficient justification cognitions; it is called Job Praiseworthiness. More detailed information about the sample, procedures, and measures used in this report are available in Pearce (1978; 1983c).

Results

The tests were completed using voluntary/employing by task type (2 x 4) analysis of variance; that is, each of the eight organizations is placed in a cell corresponding to its voluntary or employing membership and its task type (newspaper, poverty relief, family planning, or firefighting). For the motivation scales, there is no statistically significant difference in reported Intrinsic Motivation. However, volunteers are more likely to report that they work for the rewards of Social Interaction than are employees ($F = 7.11, p < .01$). Most interesting is the substantial difference between the Service Motivation reported by volunteers and employees ($F = 16.78, p < .01$). There is a significant Service Motivation interaction reflecting relatively less Service Motivation among both newspaper volunteers and employees than among those performing the more purely "service" tasks of poverty relief, family planning, and firefighting.

Regarding job attitudes, volunteers report greater Job Satisfaction ($F = 17.39, p < .001$), less Intent to Leave ($F = 31.25, p < .001$), and greater reported Praiseworthiness of their work ($F = 5.75, p < .01$) than do comparable employees. There is a significant task-type effect for Job Satisfaction which is the result of lower Job Satisfaction among newspaper and poverty relief workers when compared to family planners and firefighters.

In summary, volunteers doing the same work as employees are more likely to report that they work for the rewards of social interaction and service to others, that their work is more praiseworthy, and that they are more satisfied and less likely to leave their organizations.

Study Limitations

That these reports were produced by experienced sufficiency of justification must be assumed, since sufficiency of justification cognitions in this study, as in all of the field studies cited above, were not directly measured. Alternative hypotheses include differential selection into volunteer work and employment, or some effect of the very different nature of "spare time" volunteer work and holding a job. Regarding differential selection, for this sample there were no differences between these groups in age or gender, and virtually all of the volunteers were employed and many of the employees had been volunteers. This indicates that the volunteers and employees in this sample do not represent different "social classes", but does not address the concern that "volunteering" and "going to work" may represent vastly different psychological approaches to organizational participation. This paper presents attitudinal differences consistent with sufficiency of justification but offers no evidence that this is the only, or even most important, difference.

Differential retention is a real threat to the interpretation of the job attitude differences. It is much less costly for dissatisfied volunteers to quit than it is for employees who derive their incomes from their jobs. Therefore, the employee sample may contain a broad range of satisfied and dissatisfied members, but the volunteer sample is probably "restricted" to the satisfied. However, this argument is less plausible for the motivation results. Employees who remain working because they depend on their salaries should not be more likely to report less social and service motivation than unsalaried volunteers, since the same service and social rewards are available to both groups; unlikely, that is, unless they are experiencing oversufficient justification and therefore de-emphasizing these job rewards.

IMPLICATIONS

These results suggest important implications for the understanding of volunteer motivation. Most important, perhaps, is the striking finding of insignificant differences in working for intrinsic rewards. This is particularly interesting since Staw (1976) and Deci (1975) proposed that it would be intrinsic motivation that would be affected by extrinsic rewards. Thus, this study indicates that unpaid volunteers are not necessarily more intrinsically motivated by the work itself.

It is suggested that Staw's (1976) proposition is overly narrow. Why should individuals experiencing insufficient justification necessarily emphasize the interestingness of their jobs? Why not attend to the ways in which saving lives and property from fire is serving the community? Individuals can increase the sufficiency of the justification for their activities by enhancing the importance of any number of rewards, and the targets of this enhancement will depend on the nature of the work. Producing newspapers, poverty relief, staffing clinics, and fighting fires are, after all, services to their respective communities. In addition, most of these volunteers had developed close friendships over the years. In contrast, most laboratory experiments provide few opportunities for meaningful social contact, and most laboratory tasks cannot be reasonably regarded as services to others. There really is nothing other than the work itself in the setting subjects can use to increase sufficiency of justification.

These results do suggest that volunteers probably search about for a sufficiently plausible reason for working without pay. Further, they suggest that the interestingness of their actual job responsibilities is not as frequently chosen as service to others and sociability rewards. The presence of this sufficiency of justification effect has practical implications for volunteer compensation, for assessing the role of altruism in motivating volunteers, and in the etiology of the "volunteer spirit."

First, the results of this study suggest that paying for work does seem to lead the salaried to de-emphasize the service and social rewards of their jobs to a greater extent than those doing the same work without pay. This suggests that managers who evoke service and social goals in motivating their employees may have less success, simply because employees are not as likely to perceive themselves as working for these rewards as are volunteers. It is important to emphasize, however, that this difference in motivation will

210

not necessarily reflect differences in actual job performance. Volunteers may see themselves as more motivated by service and sociability, but the direct impact of motivation on job performance is muted by such factors as individuals' skills and experience, time commitments to other leisure and family activities, and so forth. Therefore, paying volunteers may well have the effect of replacing social and service motivation with monetary motivation, but this "reduction" in motivation does not necessarily imply lowered job performance.

Second, since there is evidence that volunteers choose to enhance the importance of service in an attempt to retrospectively build sufficient justification for their volunteer work, it becomes very difficult to assess the actual role of "service" or altruism in the decision to volunteer. That is, when volunteers say thay volunteer to serve others we cannot distinguish between the *a priori* desire to serve that led them to volunteer and the retrospective choosing of a socially acceptable "reason" for their actions. The results of this study echo Smith (1981) who has argued that society condemns using charitable activities for the pursuit of selfish goals such as diversion or sociability; thus, we find a severe social desirability bias in volunteers' stated reasons for volunteering. This would imply that recruitment appeals to service motives may not be as effective as might be assumed.

Finally, the results of this study help us to understand the development of the "volunteer spirit" — that frequently praised feature of volunteer-run organizations — that seems to be lacking in organizations dedicated to the same goals but staffed by salaried professionals. To quote that perceptive volunteer again: "Volunteers don't know why they are working; they don't know the answer. I guess they assume they do it because they want to do good." It could very well be the mystery of volunteer motivation, itself, that fosters the "volunteer spirit." The same uncertainty that makes volunteers so difficult to "manage" as organizational workers (Pearce, 1983a) is also the source of their greatest organizational strength. Perhaps we should accept the inherent mystery of volunteer motivation — recognizing its benefits as well as its costs — rather than searching for an "explanation" that will never really fit.

REFERENCES

Deci, E. L.
1975   *Intrinsic Motivation*. New York: Plenum.

Dermer, J.
1975   "The Interrelationship of Intrinsic and Extrinsic Rewards,"
        Academy of Management Journal 18: 125-129.

Eden, A.
1975   "Intrinsic and Extrinsic Rewards and Motives: Replication
        and Extension with Kibbutz Workers," *Journal of Applied
        Social Psychology* 5: 348-361.

Guzzo, R. A.
1979   "Types of Rewards, Cognitions, and Work Motivation,"
        Academy of Management Review 4: 75-86.

Pearce, J. L.
1978   "Something For Nothing: An Empirical Examination of the
        Structures and Norms of Volunteer Organizations."
        Unpublished dissertation, Yale University.
1983a   "Labor That Is Worth Nothing: The Paradox of Volunteers,"
        in Mel Moyer, ed., *Managing Voluntary Organizations*.
        Toronto: York University, 84-97.
1983b   "Participation in Voluntary Associations: How Membership
        in Formal Organizations Changes the Rewards of Participa-
        tion," in D. H. Smith et al., eds., *International Perspectives in
        Voluntary Action Research*. Washington, DC: University
        Press of America, 148-156.
1983c   "Job Attitude and Motivation Differences Between Volun-
        teers and Employees From Comparable Organizations,"
        Journal of Applied Psychology 68: 546-652.

Pfeffer, J. and J. Lawler
1980   "Effects of Job Alternatives, Extrinsic Rewards and
        Behavioral Commitment on Attitude Toward the Organiza-
        tion: A Field Test of the Insufficient Justification Paradigm,"
        Administrative Science Quarterly 25: 38-56.

Smith, D. H.
1981   "Altruism, Volunteers, and Volunteerism," *Journal of Volun-
        tary Action Research* 10: 21-36.

212

Staw, B. M.

1974 "Attitudinal and Behavioral Consequences of Changing a Major Organizational Reward: A Natural Field Experiment," *Journal of Personality and Social Psychology* 29: 742-751.

1976 *Intrinsic and Extrinsic Motivation*. Morristown, NJ: General Learning Press.

Selected Paper 5
HOW ART THOU MOTIVATED? LET ME COUNT THE WAYS!

James I. Grieshop

How are thou motivated? Let me count the ways! With apologies to Browning, the apoetical alteration of these famous lines highlights one significant dimension of the issue of volunteers and motivation. The issue, from an organizational perspective is not simply "how I (the organization) motivate thee," but "how thou (the volunteer) motivate yourself."

Obviously, any extended interaction between an organization and its personnel involves exchanges of some type. This really is no less a fact for organizations with volunteers than it is for organizations with paid employees. In the case of volunteers, the nature of this exchange may be less noticeable or concrete than for the latter (paid professionals do receive salary and fringe benefits in exchange for their time). The volunteer-organization "exchange economy" (Boulding, 1970) operates with different currency; it is in fact a barter system. Since the system's currency may not necessarily be known for each situation, it must be determined. The motivation dimension seems to offer one way to understand and to catalogue this currency and, most importantly, to specify at least one domain of the operating exchange system ledger.

The following research study describes and analyzes the motivation and participation of volunteers in a Master Gardener program. Concurrent with the implementation in 1980 of the described Master Gardener volunteer programs, a long-term action research program was undertaken. In this effort, specific research activities were designed to assess and monitor individual motivations, incentives, and volunteer satisfactions and to understand some aspects of the nature of the operating exchange system. Results obtained over a three-year period involved nearly 600 volunteers and 15 programs in one state. Of particular significance are the findings of the types, strength, and durability of volunteer motivations.

The research literature on motivation and voluntarism in the past three decades includes at least two areas important to this study. Much of the literature on the motivation of volunteers concludes that there are many reasons to explain a volunteer's participation. While altruism has sometimes been over-identified as a motivator (see Schindler-Rainman, 1977, and Ellis and Noyes, 1978, for examples), Smith (1981) argues that, in general, volunteers are motivated by a complex of reasons, of which altruism is only a minor one. Several theoretical schemes have been put forward to portray this complex: Sills (1957) and Gidron (1978) used the concept of self-oriented motives; Naylor (1967) poses self-interest (learning, self-actualization, and increased status) motives; Pearce (1982) focuses on intrinsic/extrinsic dichotomy (intrinsic, social, and service motivations); and Smith (1981) suggests that the categories of Material, Solidary, and Purposive Incentives are of potential use.

The issue of an "exchange economy" also bears importance in reference to this study. Do volunteers operate in a system with strong expectations of giving and getting? Booth and Babchuck (1969) concluded that volunteers' affiliation with volunteer associations does constitute an exchange between the individual and the association. Phillips (1982) argues that motivation and expectation must be seen in the context of a social exchange between the volunteer and the organization.

Multiple motivation and an exchange economy were both central to the implementation of the Master Gardener *volunteer program* and the *action research activities*. For program purposes it was "hypothesized" that volunteers would participate because of a variety of reasons/expectations/motivations, the least of which would be a desire to "do good." An aim was to create, in a sense, an exchange or barter economy within a highly complex, but decentralized state-wide program, in which the volunteers and the organization would be partners. Central to the research program were the questions of what motivated the volunteers, what incentives were operational, how strong were they, and would they last over a period of intensive volunteer work.

216

Clark and Wilson's Incentive Theory (1961) provided a framework for analyzing volunteers' incentives and expectations for participation. In their theory, three categories or types of incentives are identified: Material Incentives (tangible rewards such as money, goods, services and their equivalents); Solidary Incentives (intangible rewards such as fellowships, group affiliation, friendship, and prestige); and Purposive Incentives (also intangible, but including such rewards as feelings of making important contributions and of satisfaction for achieving an important goal). Although the Master Gardener volunteers' motivations were measured, no attempt was made to formally test and measure the organizational incentive system. It was, however, taken into account in terms of the operating "exchange economy." The essential action research questions were: What types of incentive motivated the 600 volunteers to participate, and how strong and durable were these incentives? Poetically speaking, "...let me count the ways I and thou art motivated."

MASTER GARDENER PROGRAM

The purpose of the Master Gardener Program is to train and utilize adult volunteers as educators and extenders of information, specifically in the subject areas of practical horticulture and gardening (Grieshop, 1982a). Since 1972, Cooperative Extension Services in over 30 states, each a branch of the United States' Land Grant Universities, have organized Master Gardener Programs. In California, on which case this study is based, the Master Gardener Program was begun in 1980. In three years that program grew from two counties and 90 volunteers to approximately 19 counties and nearly 1,000 volunteers.

A primary reason (or incentive) for developing a volunteer program in the area of gardening was organizational "enlightened self-interest." In California's urban areas, professional, paid staff were inundated with requests for information, material, and gardening educational programs. The demand far exceeded the ability to respond. Prior to 1980, Cooperative Extension's practical horticulture and gardening program operated solely with a paid staff. With the inception of the Master Gardener Program, this one component became a volunteer organization in which volunteers acted as the primary means for meeting organizational goals. Due to the above-mentioned conditions, the program was designed to use the principle of an "exchange economy" — it was assumed that individuals and organizations operate for their own best self-interest but that fair and equitable exchanges (or bartering) between the volunteers and the organization are feasible. In this barter system volunteers GAVE, directly or indirectly, time, expertise, money, goods and service while RECEIVING access to training, knowledge, information and personnel, and the opportunity to share and provide service. The organization GAVE training, time of personnel, recognition, certification, and materials and RECEIVED in exchange more effective and efficient ways to meet the organizational goals of education and service.

Individuals who ultimately became certified Master Gardener Volunteers were recruited, selected via an application and screening process, and received 50 hours of training, as a group, over a three-month period. The volunteer commitment was explicit: in exchange for the training, each person was expected to volunteer an equal number of hours to the organization. Volunteers were representative of the communities in which they lived (average age was 42 and ranged from 22 to 80; 46% were male, 54% female; 10% were minority; occupationally they represented professional, service, blue-collar and white-collar sectors) and of a 1981 profile of U.S. volunteers (Independent Sector, 1981).

METHODOLOGY:
Instruments and Procedures

During the research phase, information on attrition, hours volunteered, types of activities, cost benefits, etc., was gathered. An Incentive Questionnaire was also developed, field tested and revised for use with each group of trainees. The 13-statement questionnaire was administered to each group on the first day of training during the years 1980, 1981, and 1982. Ten raters independently judged the 13 statements as representative of one of the three Incentive Categories: Material, Solidary, or Purposive. Inter-rater reliability for each statement was determined by ten raters (values ranged from 1.00 to 0.60). Each question was answered on a six-point scale ranging from "An extremely important reason" (value 5) to "Not a reason" (value 0). Since in 1981 the program expanded from two counties to nine counties and over 200 volunteers, the 1981 volunteers were targeted for more inclusive study. In addition to completing the

Incentive Questionnaire prior to beginning training, a modified 13-item Post Incentive Questionnaire was mailed to and completed by 123 of the volunteers in September 1981. These 123 volunteers comprised a "Pre" and "Post" Incentive Questionnaire subgroup.

Pre and Post Questionnaires were scored and average scores and rankings were calculated for each of the three groups (1980-82). Scores and rankings were also determined for the 1981 subgroup and a One-Way Analysis of Variance was performed on the mean values. In addition, less intrusive methods were used to collect other important data: the application form completed by each trainee was used to determine other stated reasons for participation and information on attrition, and professional staff collected statistics and information on hours worked and volunteer characteristics.

Finally, during mid-1982, an in-depth Master Gardener Survey was designed, field tested and mailed to the 264 Master Gardener Volunteers. Two hundred and two questionnaires were returned; 199 were usable, a response rate of 74.5%. Of particular interest to this study were the questions related to benefits of participation. In one-section of the survey, respondents were asked to indicate, via a forced-choice format, their level of agreement with 23 benefit statements categorized as either Material, Solidary, or Purposive. Each statement was independently categorized by ten raters using a Q-sort method; inter-rater agreements ranged from 1.00 to 0.60. Scores ranged from 4.00 (Totally agreed) to 1.00 (Totally disagree).

RESULTS

Incentive Questionnaire. The ranking and average scores for each group of Master Gardener trainees for the three years are listed in Table 1A. For each year, the most powerful incentives (as represented by average values exceeding 3.75) are a mix of Material (3), Solidary (1), and Purposive (2) [see Table 1A]. No significant differences on average scores were indicated on the basis of residence, ethnicity, sex, or age. In the first two cases, too few respondents were represented in each category to merit a meaningful analysis. In the latter two cases, age and sex apparently made no difference in motivation scores. The same six incentives are ranked highest in each case, albeit with some minor but insignificant order rearrangement. In each, Material Incentives (i.e. Increase knowledge, Gain new skills,

Receive useful training), Solidary Incentives (i.e. Share knowledge), and Purposive Incentives (i.e. Provide a service, Gain personal satisfaction) are clearly the most "powerful" incentives. The remaining seven incentives were consistently valued much lower — ranging from 3.37 ("Creatively use free time" — a Purposive Incentive) to 0.35 ("Receive a tax credit" — Material Incentive). These latter seven, for all three years, must be viewed as weak, low-level, or unimportant incentives. The first six, with consistently high values, suggest that individuals who enter the program are similarly motivated by a complex mix of incentives, characterized by the expectation of specific material rewards. These results contrast with information gathered from application forms completed by each trainee/volunteer, which included the question: "Why do you want to become a Master Gardener?" In both groups from 1980 and 1981, the majority of respondents (75% to 80%) gave a specific answer that was judged to be "altruistic." Most answers were of the types "to do good, to help my community, or to be of needed service." Far fewer responses and respondents stated reasons that could be identified as "Material."

   Pre and Post Incentive Questionnaires. Table 1B details results of tabulation and analysis of the scores for the Pre and Post Incentive Questionnaire completed by 1981 volunteers. Results similar to those described in the previous section were found. The same six incentives were reported as being the most powerful (values exceeding 3.75) both prior to beginning the training program and eight months after participation in the training and intensive volunteer work. In general, the Post Incentive Questionnaire average values were lower than the Pre values. Results of the One-Way Analysis of Variance revealed only one significant difference ("Opportunity to share knowledge" $p < .01$). Two other sets of average values were statistically significant ("Creatively use free time" $p < .008$ and "Gain practical experience" $p < .03$). Since these incentives were originally considered as low strength or unimportant, their statistical significance has little meaning. Therefore, interpretation of these differences would appear to be misleading.

   Results suggest that the incentive factors for these volunteers are, for the most part, durable. Thus, over the course of the volunteer's experience of nearly one year, some reward expectations are maintained and at approximately the same level of strength.

Data on participation, used as one indicator of "incentives met," are also instructive [see Table 2]. Before an individual could call him/herself a Master Gardener Volunteer, each was expected to complete the 50-hour training program conducted over an 8- to 12-week period and then be certified as a Master Gardener. Consequently, the attrition rate can serve as one indicator of motivation, or at least of satisfaction with the program. The attrition rate during the training periods (9% for 1980 and 5% for 1981) and during the volunteer phase (20% for 1980 and 14% for 1981) are extremely low. The criterion for the volunteer phase attrition rested on whether or not the individual completed the full 50 hours of volunteer work. In fact, a number of volunteers completed some (20 to 45 hours) but not all of the hours and were nevertheless classified as "drop-outs". These data suggest two things: (1) that the volunteers were initially highly motivated to actively participate in the program and (2) that, in all likelihood, their most important expectation/ incentives (i.e. to increase knowledge, to receive training, to gain personal satisfaction, to provide a service, to gain skills, and to share knowledge) were met to a satisfactory degree. One additional indicator of volunteer satisfaction is available: 64% of the 1980 volunteers reentered the 1981 program. Reentry required them to participate anew in the training and to perform the volunteer work.

Master Gardener Survey: Benefits Section. Results from the Benefits Section indicate that the Material Benefits were most often selected as the strongest (i.e. with a value of at least 3.00), followed by Purposive and Solidary ones. Table 3 lists results on the basis of mean value rank and percent of respondents who strongly agreed or disagreed with the statement. Other analyses (not reported here) on the basis of sex, ethnicity, previous volunteer experience, income, and marital status all show that same consistent pattern with no differences attributable to the various independent variables. As seen in the table, Material Benefits related to the currency of the economic exchange system (i.e. information, access to information, and knowledge) are the strongest. Other Material Benefits, along with Purposive Benefits (including altruistic ones such as "opportunity to help" and "opportunity to do something useful") are also significant. Furthermore, results, on the basis of percent of agreement, reveal that respondents believed the Material Benefits were the strongest. Over 95% of all respondents "agree" or "strongly agree" that "new sources of information," "new knowledge," and "access to experts and information" are important benefits of participation.

TABLE 3
BENEFITS OF PARTICIPATION

N = Ranged from 199 to 160

Benefit	Mean Value	% Agree or Strongly Agree
1. New sources of information (M)	3.56	97.4
2. New gardening knowledge (M)	3.49	97.4
3. Access to experts and information (M)	3.48	95.9
4. Opportunity to help (P)	3.28	94.4
5. It was fun, made me feel good (P)	3.25	94.2
6. New gardening skills (M)	3.23	93.2
7. Certification by university (M)	3.21	91.7
8. Taught me about Cooperative Extension (M)	3.19	90.6
9. Opportunity to apply what was learned (P)	3.19	89.2
10. Something useful to do (P)	3.16	90.6
11. Provided sense of accomplishment (P)	3.13	90.9
12. Provided broader education (M)	3.11	87.0
13. Made new friends (S)	3.05	91.1
14. Provided creative outlet (P)	3.01	81.5
15. New way to study and learn (P)	2.76	66.1
16. Developed skills to work with public (M)	2.72	63.5
17. Learned about my community (P)	2.70	64.5
18. Provided leisure time outlet (P)	2.67	61.8
19. Improved self-confidence (P)	2.55	53.7
20. Developed new status among friends (S)	2.52	51.6
21. Reached educational goals (M)	2.42	43.2
22. New professional contacts (S)	2.39	44.6
23. Helped get a job (M)	1.77	8.7

(M = Material; P = Purposive; S = Solidary)

DISCUSSIONS

Results from action research projects usually cannot be as confidently interpreted as results from carefully designed research utilizing comparison group and controlled interventions/treatments. An action research gap — between what can be gained and what can be claimed — underscores the problem of how best to interpret and discuss these results. The results may be best understood in relationship to other work. "Altruism, Volunteers, and Volunteerism," a JVAR article by David Horton Smith, is of particular use. In this provocative article, Smith (1981) attempts to synthesize the literature and criticize much of the prevailing wisdom on the subject of motivation and volunteers. In some cases Smith substantiates his arguments through research (his and others). In other cases, however, the weight of evidence is less overwhelming and arguments tend to become assertions. Nevertheless, his article, along with others, provides a useful framework against which this study's results can be both interpreted and discussed, and, in turn, these results may be used to augment, confirm, or support some of the assertions.

In discussing "relative altruism" and absolute selfishness, Smith states: "There is more relative altruism to the extent that the individual is acting in a 'grants economy' mode rather than in a market or 'exchange economy' mode." (Smith, 1981: 24) This study's results suggest that, at least in terms of an "exchange or barter economy" — programs like the Master Gardener Program — altruism is but one of several incentives operating, and a relatively minor one at that. Over the three years measured, both at the beginning of the program and in the Pre/Post situation, non-altruistic incentives (i.e. Material and Solidary as well as certain Purposive ones) tended to be selected more often and at higher levels than altruistic ones. If the results are reliable, then the "exchange economy" operates but it operates with a non-altruistic medium of exchange. It appears that although most Master Gardener Volunteers are motivated by multiple incentives, with altruism as only one factor, they do like to say that "altruism" is the reason for involvement. Results from content analysis of answers to the open-ended application question "Why do you want to be a Master Gardener?" confirm Smith's belief that: "Not surprisingly, the giving of altruistic reasons for involvement is fairly popular." (Smith, 1981: 25) Volunteers give an answer which they must believe program personnel want to

TABLE 1
INCENTIVE QUESTIONNAIRE RESULTS
1980-1981-1982

Incentive Type To become a Master Gardener is important to me because:	A. 1980-81-82 Volunteers Rank (and Mean Score)*			B. 1981 Pre-Post Questionnaires Range (Mean)		Significance
	1980 N = 95	1981 N = 218	1982 N = 162	Pre N = 123	Post N = 123	
I will be able to increase my knowledge in the area of gardening. (M)	1 (4.64)	1 (4.69)	1 (4.77)	1 (4.68)	1 (4.52)	n.s.
I will be able to gain new skills as a gardener. (M)	2 (4.60)	6 (4.00)	3 (4.44)	6 (3.89)	5 (3.99)	n.s.
I will have the opportunity to receive useful training. (M)	3 (4.59)	2 (4.49)	2 (4.65)	2 (4.51)	2 (4.37)	n.s.
I will be able to provide a service to other people in my community and/or neighborhood. (P)	4 (4.26)	4 (4.17)	5 (4.13)	4 (4.14)	4 (4.02)	n.s.
I will have the opportunity to share my knowledge with other gardeners. (S)	5 (4.20)	5 (4.12)	6 (4.07)	5 (4.00)	6 (3.65)	p < .01
I will gain a great deal of personal satisfaction. (P)	6 (4.15)	3 (4.25)	4 (4.36)	3 (4.27)	3 (4.07)	n.s.
I will be able to creatively use my free time. (P)	7 (3.34)	7 (3.34)	7 (3.37)	7 (3.78)	7 (2.80)	p < .008
I will be certified by the University of California Cooperative Extension. (M)	8 (2.76)	9 (2.14)	8 (2.74)	9 (2.13)	9 (2.30)	n.s.
I will receive free instruction and materials. (M)	9 (1.93)	8 (2.39)	9 (2.47)	8 (2.43)	8 (2.79)	n.s.
I will gain practical experience that can help me get a job. (M)	10 (1.73)	10 (1.73)	10 (1.80)	11 (1.70)	12 (1.26)	p < .03
I will become part of the University of California. (S)	11 (1.65)	12 (1.66)	11 (1.70)	12 (1.66)	11 (1.97)	n.s.

I will be recognized by the people of my community. (S)	12 (1.19)	11 (1.72)	12 (1.56)	10 (1.80) 10 (1.93)	n.s.
I can get a tax credit for my volunteer work. (M)	13 (0.34)	13 (0.57)	13 (0.55)	13 (0.54) 13 (0.41)	n.s.

* Response scores ranged from a high of 5 (extremely important factor) to 0 (not a factor).

(M = Material Incentive; P = Purposive Incentive; S = Solidary Incentive)

TABLE 2
PROGRAM PARTICIPATION FACTS

	1980	1981
Number (%) of trained/volunteers:		
At beginning of training	95	230
At conclusion of training	86 (91%)	218 (95%)
Who completed at least 50 hours of volunteer work	69 (80%)	187 (86%)
Who continued work in 1981	—	57 (64%)
Average number of reported hours/volunteer	82	71

hear, an acceptable altruistic answer. When asked in this simplistic manner, few note their real reasons and expectations of enlightened self-interest.

Results from other studies support this conclusion (Grieshop, 1982b). Similar action research was conducted by the author on two other volunteer programs with the subject foci of food preservation/nutrition and forestry. These results revealed the same unmistakable pattern: volunteers give altruism as the reason for their wish to participate, when asked directly, whereas responses to a more in-depth questionnaire show the same mix of incentives, with Material Incentives most prominent.

These volunteers participate with the expectations of specific rewards and benefits and of fulfilling their responsibility to the exchange/barter system. From the organizational perspective, a primary aim during both training and volunteer phases was to deliver or make available Material rewards (i.e. information, skills, access to experts, and certification), Solidary rewards (i.e. fellowship and affiliation), and Purposive rewards (i.e. opportunity to be of service and to gain personal satisfaction). These organizational aims coincided almost perfectly with volunteer reported benefits. The degree of fit and satisfaction, in turn, was revealed by the low attrition rate and the high continuation rate (64% in 1981). Obviously, a well-functioning exchange system, based on the premise of specific motivations, incentives, and rewards is indicated by these results. From the perspective of costs and benefits, these appear to be, as Phillips (1982) argues, at least in balance. It may be that not only are these in balance but the rewards have far exceeded the costs to both volunteers and the Cooperative Extension.

The issue of incentive or motivation categories is still open to discussion. In truth, the question is only partially related to whether the Material-Solidary-Purposive model or the Extrinsic-Intrinsic (cf. Pearce, 1982) or Self-Oriented/Personal Growth (cf. Jenner, 1982) or an Altruistic/Non-Altruistic model is best. All need to be tested. The question also revolves around the need to explore expectations and rewards, costs and benefits, and motivations and satisfactions. To exclude one element or component may distort our understanding of the reality of volunteer and organization exchange systems.

This study suggests some future directions for

researchers and programmatic personnel alike. The Master Gardener Program is characterized by a cycle of recruitment, selection, training, and volunteer work. Although the procedure is not unique to this program, the incorporation of a relatively long-term and formalized training program distinguishes it from many other volunteer programs. Does this feature attract a particular type of volunteer with a unique incentive configuration? Does the gardening focus exert a particular and strong pull on certain volunteers, and is this pull stronger than similar attractions of social service (or other) volunteer programs? What effect does this cycle create for the characteristic "exchange economy"? This question of an "exchange economy" in general needs far more study.

From a programmatic perspective, the nature of this exchange between volunteer and the organization, as shaped by motivations and benefits, must be addressed. The significance of the exchange angle will become increasingly important, particularly as many resources are reduced and organizations look to volunteers as a solution. Program personnel must be sensitive to the multiple mix of motivations and work to create and deliver a smorgasbord of benefits. These personnel need not only count the motives that drive volunteers but structure the organizations for the mutual benefit of volunteers, organization, and clients.

REFERENCES

Booth, A. and N. Babchuk
   1969   "Personal Influence Networks and Voluntary Association
          Affiliation," *Sociological Inquiry* 39: 179-188.
Boulding, K.
   1970   *The Economy of Love and Fear*. Belmont, CA: Wadworths.
Clark, P.B. and J.O. Wilson
   1961   "Incentive Systems: A Theory of Organization," *Administration
          Science Quarterly* 6: 129-166.
Ellis, S.J. and K.H. Noyes
   1978   *By the People: A History of Americans as Volunteers*.
          Philadelphia: Energize.
Gidron, B.
   1978   "Volunteer Work and Its Rewards," *Volunteer Administration* 11:
          18-32.

Grieshop, J.I.

1982a "Growing with Master Gardener," *California Agriculture* 36: 17-19.

1982b "Statistical Report on the University of California Cooperative Extension Adult Volunteers in Community Education Programs." Unpublished report.

1982c "Preliminary Statistical Results: Master Gardener Survey — 1981."

Jenner, J.R.

1982 "The Role of Voluntarism Among Selected Women Volunteers," *Journal of Voluntary Action Research* 11: 27-37.

Naylor, H.H.

1967 *Volunteers Today*. New York: Associated Press.

Pearce. J.

1982 "Does Paying for Work Reduce Motivation? Results of a Field Test Comparison Volunteers and Employees." Paper read at Annual Conference Associated for Voluntary Action Scholars, Michigan State University, August 1982.

Phillips, M.

1982 "Motivation and Expectation in Successful Volunteerism," *Journal of Voluntary Action Research* 11: 118-125.

Schindler-Rainman, E. and R. Lippett

1977 *The Volunteer Community*. La Jolla, CA: University Associates.

Sills, D.

1957 *The Volunteers: Means and End in a National Organization*. Glencoe: The Free Press.

Smith, D.H.

1981 "Altruism, Volunteers, and Volunteerism," *Journal of Voluntary Action Research* 11: 21-36.

Selected Paper 6
MOTIVATION IN UNIVERSITY STUDENT VOLUNTEERING

Terry H. Chapman

BACKGROUND

Voluntary action, as defined by David Horton Smith, is "that which gives personal meaning to life. It is [action] which one freely chooses to do whether for enjoyment in the short term and/or from commitment to some longer-term goal that is not merely a manifestation of biosocial man, socio-political man, or economic man." (Smith, 1973: 163)

Smith then provides a comprehensive model for examining various factors which may influence voluntary action and summarizes the types of variables as contextual — generally the historical and bio-physical factors; the personal — generally the social background, social roles, personality and capacities, and attitudes of the individual; and the situation factors — i.e. the specific, situational, stimuli perceptions relevant to individual action.

Motivation is meant as "reasons why a person volunteers or decides to volunteer" in this article and the discussion is limited to human service or social service-type volunteering as a specific type of voluntary action. This context will be most helpful in understanding volunteering behavior in college and university students.

Volunteering by college and university students has been a significantly important activity since the 1960s when the ferment of dissent spilled over into social action causes and projects. By 1971, approximately 400,000 student volunteers were providing volunteer assistance to a wide variety of educational, political action, social action, and health-related programs (Peterson, 1971). Also, the idea of experiential learning whereby the student learns by both class and outside-class experiences started to be recognized and such institutions as Antioch College and Northeastern University provided specific cooperative education opportunities for students. These two developments furthered student interest in exploration of "real life" endeavors while still enrolled in higher education.

MOTIVATION-RELATED RESEARCH

Most of the research to date has tended toward broad descriptive treatments of volunteer programs — their participants, the program, or a demographic picture of the volunteers themselves. Ken Allen (1971), in the premier issue of the *Synergist*, presented a thought-provoking article entitled "What motivates volunteers?," in which he suggested that the lack of research on volunteer programs can be understood in part because their main concern has been survival. Another interesting point was that in considering motivations for Peace Corps volunteering (admittedly volunteering of a different order) two main types of motivation appeared: the desire to serve and help others; and an inquisitiveness about the world, including the desire to resolve questions of future careers. Later research would seem to corroborate these two types as at least part of the motivational complex underlying "short-term" social service volunteer experiences of college and university students.

Coles and Brenner (1968) participated with a group of college volunteers in Virginia, West Virginia, Kentucky, and Tennessee in a VISTA associates program of teaching in Appalachia. They stated that the students' participation could be seen as part of the general need of college students to "come to terms with themselves, their wishes, and purposes."

Earlier, in 1967, Block and Smith discussed reasons for volunteering and not volunteering by University of Minnesota students and found that the most important reasons given for volunteering were, "desire for personal experience," and fulfillment of "moral conviction." Less important were to "meet new friends," "political conviction," and "rebellion against society," respectively. Williams in 1972 studied a sample of University of Mississippi students and found that their major reasons for choosing to volunteer included "desire to help others" (47%); "desire for vocational experi-

232

ence" (24%); "recognition of need" (20%); "anticipated personal benefits" (4%); and "other reasons" (5%).

Jane S. Smith in 1978 reported a Michigan State University survey of 2,544 of their students from 15 colleges and 136 different departments (majors) and found that 70.2% had volunteered to gain career experiences and that 15.8% had volunteered for job contacts. Sixty-three percent stated that their volunteering had an effect on their career plans and 17.6% actually considered or did change their previous career decision.

A National Council of YMCA study in 1979 of college and high school volunteers cited the five most important items in "becoming involved in volunteer activities" were: "being very interested in the program of the activity" (83.1%); "feeling that I will grow and improve myself by participation" (70.1%); "feeling that I will be doing something important, making a real contribution to society" (68.2%); "knowing that I will receive training and support so that I can succeed in the activity" (63.6%); and "being very interested in the participants in the activity" (53.9%).

Serventi (1980) studied student volunteers at the University of Virginia, who had participated in "service-oriented student volunteer programs" and found an association between the volunteer program and the types of benefits that students perceived they had gained by volunteering. Volunteers' motivations were also found to be the best prediction of benefits that volunteers were likely to acquire.

Chapman (1980) studied university students' reasons for deciding to volunteer in social service-related agencies and utilized several statistical methods to identify types of reasons and any relationships between demographic characteristics and the type of reason given for deciding to volunteer.

The Likert-type questionnaire asked subjects to rate the relative importance of 32 reasons, based upon a review of the literature and the researcher's professional experience in advising and placing college and university students in volunteer positions.

Factor analysis subsequently identified nine types of reasons or factors and the Scree test (Cattell, 1966) yielded five substantive factors:

1. *Experiential*: reasons based upon responding to active participation in a volunteer assignment to gain work experience and/or to

test ideas or career intentions.

2. *Community Need*: reasons based upon responding to social, educational, or health-related community needs as expressed by agencies, programs, or media.

3. *Personal*: reasons based upon responding to "self-directed" needs: increasing self-confidence, making new friends, gaining experience different from school, desire to have fun.

4. *Adult Influence*: reasons based upon input or influence of an adult including parents, other relatives, or other adults excluding teachers.

5. *Academic*: reasons based upon learning such as "opportunity to learn new ideas" or "volunteering was a course option."

The relationship of these five factors to selected demographics was then calculated and several significant relationships were identified ($<.05$): Sex of student and student score on the Personal factor; sex of student and student score on the Academic factor. Also found was a significant relationship between student major and student score on the Experiential factor and also the Community Need factor. Previous work experience was significantly related to student score on the Adult Influence factor. University course requirement was significantly related to student score on the Academic factor. Career interest was significantly related to student score on Community Need and Experiential factors. School classification, i.e., Freshman, Sophomore, Junior, Senior, was significantly related to the Personal factor. Student status, i.e., part-time or full-time student, was significantly related to student score on the Adult Influence factor.

What do these significant relationships tell us about student behaviors? Those students who volunteered in an area related to their own career interests rated Experiential and Community Need reasons more important than those who volunteered in a new or different area. Human service majors rated Experiential reasons higher than other majors. Humanities majors rated Community Need reasons higher than technical, human services, social science, or biological majors.

Sophomores rated Personal reasons higher in importance than freshmen, followed by juniors, seniors, and graduate students respectively. Female students rated Personal reasons higher than male students.

Full-time students rated Adult Influence reasons higher than did part-time students. Those students with no prior work experience rated Adult Influence reasons higher than those who had prior work experience.

Students who volunteered as a course requirement rated Academic reasons higher than those who had not volunteered as a course requirement. Female students rated Academic reasons higher in importance than male students.

Tables 1-5 show the proportion of variance (R^2) (in student scores on the five dependent variables) which can be explained or associated with the respective independent demographic variables. These measures of association are first steps toward understanding apparent relationships between sex, major, etc., and how important the five factors were in the student's decision to volunteer. For example, 35% of the variance in student scores on the Experiential factor can be associated with the Career Interest

---

TABLE 1

ANALYSIS OF VARIANCE FOR INDEPENDENT VARIABLES ON FACTOR 1 —Experiential

Independent Variables	MS_b	MS Error	F	R^2	PROB>F
1. University Course Requirement	3.3607	.9830	3.42	.023	.0666
2. Career Interests	49.8357	.6579	75.74	.351	.0001*
3. Work Experience	.1556	1.0059	.15	.001	.6947
4. Marital Status	.7619	1.0024	.76	.005	.3848
5. Sex	.8652	1.0009	.86	.006	.3541
6. Student Status	.4101	1.0155	.40	.003	.5261
7. Place of Residence	.9093	.9924	.92	.007	.3402
8. Major	5.1947	.8814	5.89	.147	.0002*
9. School Classification	.6515	1.0100	.65	.018	.6313

* Significant at <.05 level

independent variable. Specifically, knowing whether the student volunteered in an area related to his or her career interests will explain 35% of the variance in student score on the Experiential factor or experiential type of reasons for deciding to volunteer. The (PROB>F) values show the probability of student score differences resulting from chance.

The five reasons cited by university students from a list of 32 reasons as "the one most important reason I originally decided to volunteer" were in order of frequency:
1. Volunteering offered me opportunity to work in preferred career field.
2. Volunteering offered me opportunity to learn by doing.
3. I wanted to help other people.
4. Volunteering offered me opportunity to explore a career field.
5. Volunteering would give me experience with specific client group such as aged, gifted, retarded, youth, women, men, etc.

TABLE 2

ANALYSIS OF VARIANCE FOR INDEPENDENT VARIABLES ON FACTOR 2 — Community Need

Independent Variables	MS_b	MS Error	F	R^2	PROB>F
1. University Course Requirement	.0838	1.0064	.08	.001	.7733
2. Career Interests	6.4949	.9365	6.93	.047	.0094*
3. Work Experience	.1311	1.0061	.13	.001	.7186
4. Marital Status	.1482	1.0100	.15	.001	.7022
5. Sex	.3726	1.0044	.37	.003	.5435
6. Student Status	1.5577	.9891	1.57	.011	.2116
7. Place of Residence	.5308	1.0097	.53	.004	.4697
8. Major	3.4562	.9120	3.79	.100	.0059*
9. School Classification	.4496	1.0159	.44	.013	.7776

* Significant at <.05 level

The desire to gain career work experience, help other people, and learn by doing seem to characterize why university students decide to volunteer in social service. Further research needs to examine each of these five reasons to differentiate their specific "motivational power."

RESEARCH IMPLICATIONS

Research on university and college volunteering has been able to characterize some of the reasons why students volunteer. Next steps should include replication studies of the apparent relation between selected demographics and different types of reasons for volunteering. Another objective should be longitudinal studies which would include reasons for volunteering and how those relate to the student's opinions and feelings at various time intervals after the volunteer experience. Once these studies have been accomplished and replicated with diverse populations of university and college

TABLE 3

ANALYSIS OF VARIANCE FOR INDEPENDENT VARIABLES ON FACTOR 3 — Personal

Independent Variables	MS_b	MS Error	F	R^2	PROB>F
1. University Course Requirement	1.6370	.99540	1.64	.012	.2018
2. Career Interests	3.4227	.98910	3.64	.024	.0650
3. Work Experience	.1998	1.00560	.20	.001	.6564
4. Marital Status	2.7235	.97200	2.80	.020	.0964
5. Sex	8.0546	.94990	8.48	.057	.0042*
6. Student Status	.6737	1.01240	.67	.005	.4160
7. Place of Residence	1.6354	1.00620	1.63	.012	.2045
8. Major	1.8196	.98320	1.85	.051	.1227
9. School Classification	3.7410	.92054	4.06	.105	.0038*

* Significant at $<.05$ level

students and with widely differing volunteer programs, progress will have been made toward establishing basic cause and effect relationships. This level of knowledge would then enable theoreticians and practitioners to predict how students will learn and contribute to society on one stage in the incredibly complex arena of voluntary action.

APPLIED IMPLICATIONS

University and college students seem to desire specific opportunities to gain work experience. The fact that they also appear to desire altruistic settings where they can test out ideas and learn new ideas means that teachers, advisors, and administrators should consider these needs when developing plans for curricula, counseling alternatives, and financial commitment for student development. No longer can it be said that off-campus activities such as volunteering do not contribute to the student's learning.

TABLE 4

ANALYSIS OF VARIANCE FOR INDEPENDENT VARIABLES ON FACTOR 4 — Adult Influence

Independent Variables	MS_b	MS Error	F	R^2	PROB>F
1. University Course Requirement	1.7700	.9945	1.78	.012	.1843
2. Career Interests	.6846	1.0092	.68	.005	.4115
3. Work Experience	4.1669	.9775	4.26	.029	.0408*
4. Marital Status	.6971	1.0024	.70	.005	.4057
5. Sex	.7405	1.0018	.74	.005	.3914
6. Student Status	4.5520	.9852	4.62	.032	.0333*
7. Place of Residence	2.4656	1.0180	2.42	.017	.1220
8. Major	2.2050	.9686	2.28	.062	.0642
9. School Classification	2.4116	.9590	2.51	.066	.0679

* Significant at <.05 level

The student who wishes to experientially test an inclination to enter a specific or general career field can find out whether his or her interest is temporary or long lasting. Also, the student who has a firm idea of career direction can gain valuable work experience by comparing and contrasting the actual experience with the theory presented in the classroom.

Agencies, including colleges and universities, can utilize motivational research findings in designing their recruitment and outreach for student volunteer support by including career experience, helping others, and testing ideas as benefits. These benefits can then become motivators to an individual student given the appropriate time, place, and need pattern.

Agencies which utilize student assistance can expect a generally high level of energy, sincerity, and desire to help but must realize that students' availability will usually be semester-related and scheduling needs to be mutually agreed upon before the

---

TABLE 5

ANALYSIS OF VARIANCE FOR INDEPENDENT VARIABLES ON FACTOR 5 — Academic

---

Independent Variables	MS_b	MS Error	F	R^2	PROB>F
1. University Course Requirement	5.2188	.9700	5.38	.037	.0218*
2. Career Interests	.2807	1.0118	.28	.002	.5992
3. Work Experience	.0080	1.0070	.01	.000	.9288
4. Marital Status	.2123	1.0106	.21	.001	.6474
5. Sex	3.9787	.9788	4.06	.029	.0457*
6. Student Status	.3285	1.0176	.32	.002	.5708
7. Place of Residence	.0363	1.0162	.04	.000	.8502
8. Major	.6855	1.0121	.68	.019	.6088
9. School Classification	.8252	1.0050	.82	.023	.5138

---

* Significant at <.05 level

assignment begins.

Professors might consider adding a volunteer option when curriculum building and observe differences in performance by students who try this experiential type of learning. A journal or written report of the volunteer experience could provide insight for the student and an opportunity to integrate experience with theory. It might also serve as a motivation for the professor to re-test concepts, principles, and career values thereby strengthening the learning for everyone.

REFERENCES

Allen, Ken
1971 "What Motivates Volunteers," *Synergist* 1: 49-54.
Block, J.H., N. Haan, and M.B. Smith
1967 "Activism and Apathy in Contemporary Adolescents," in J.F. Adams, ed., *Contributions to the Understanding of Adolescents*. Boston: Allyn and Bacon.
Chapman, Terry H.
1980 "University Students' Reasons for Volunteering." Unpublished Ph.D. dissertation. University of Missouri-Columbia.
Coles, Robert and Joseph Brenner
1968 "American Youth in a Social Struggle (II): The Appalachian Volunteers," *American Journal of Orthopsychiatry* 38: 31-46.
Peterson, Virgil
1973 "Trends in U.S. Collegiate Voluntary Associations in the Twentieth Century," in David Horton Smith, ed., *Voluntary Action Research: 1973*. Lexington, MA: Lexington Books.
Serventi, Debra Lou
1980 "Perceived Motivations and Benefits of Students Participating in a University Student Volunteer Program." Unpublished Ph.D. dissertation. University of Virginia.
Smith, David Horton, ed.
1973 *Voluntary Action Research: 1973*. Lexington, MA: Lexington Books.

Smith Jane S., Mary I. Edens and Christiana A. Dolen
1978 "The Relationship of Service-Learning Experiences to Career Decision Making," *Volunteer Administration* XII92: 28-33, from Jane Smith, *1977-78 Annual Report: Office of Volunteer Programs*, Michigan State University, East Lansing.
Williams, Polly Franklin
1972 "A Study of College Volunteers: Characteristics, Analysis of Activities, and Perceived Participation Effects." Unpublished Ph.D. dissertation. University of Mississippi.

Selected Paper 7
MIXED MOTIVES:

RESIDUES OF ALTRUISM IN AN AGE OF NARCISSISM

Jon Van Til

(Reprinted with permission from *Working Papers for the Spring Research Forum: Since the Filer Commission* (1983), published by The Independent Sector, 1828 L Street NW, Washington, DC 20036.)

We Americans have never quite believed Emerson, when he wrote:

> "It is one of the most beautiful compensations in life that no man can sincerely help another without helping himself."

We rather have struggled with ideas of self-denial and altruism in the quest to find what Richard Sennett would call a "purified identity" for volunteering. We seem to need to be able to distinguish between the self-sacrifice of the volunteer and the avariciousness of our pursuit of economic self-interest.

The intellectual historian will be required to help us fully understand our eagerness to accept the theory of the "invisible hand" in economics, while being so uncomfortable with it when it comes to voluntarism. Perhaps it is the Manichean side of the Protestant Ethic, or perhaps a yearning for a golden age of simplicity and goodness. Whatever its base, however, it is the point of departure for all studies of the "non-economic" motivation of the volunteer, the topic assigned to this author in the deliberations of the present Forum. Thus we begin, as did the Filer Commission in its study of the current meanings of giving, with our ambivalent national legacy of "sincerely trying to help another."

I. "CHANGING MOTIVATIONS": THE REPORT OF THE FILER COMMISSION

The Filer Commission recognized with clarity and sensitivity the ambiguous legacy of volunteering in America (1975:62). "Personal sacrifice for the community good has probably always been esteemed," they wrote, "and, in some eyes suspect — and underlying motivations have perhaps always been complicated."

In its discussion, the Commission ranged over the history of giving from tribal society through the Middle Ages and Puritan America. Particular attention is paid to the thinking of Cotton Mather and Andrew Carnegie in their review. Mather is viewed as articulating "an exceedingly broad philosophy of giving and one that covers the wide spectrum of motivations that have been and often still are attributed to giving." Carnegie, on the other hand, is seen to have focused on the ways in which conspicuous giving by "administrators of surplus wealth" could contribute to the philanthropist's own rise to prominence in his community and nation.

The Commission proceeds from its historical review of the motivation of giving to an almost entirely institutional analysis. The institutionalization of philanthropy receives detailed attention in their study, as does the emergence of the state as a "major 'philanthropist.'"

The Commission directed little attention to the current disposition of Americans toward giving and volunteering. Although they commissioned a study of "non-economic motivational factors in philanthropic giving," they cite only at one point (Commission, 1975: 62) any contemporary research, and that parenthetically (a finding introduced with the observation that "some social scientists feel" that there is not as much individual volition involved in giving "as we might pretend"). The lonesome finding is that the Commission's survey finds that 30% of higher income givers feel pressured into giving more than they would otherwise choose to.

The curious treatment of this datum by the Commission speaks both to its uncertainty in interpreting social science and in confronting directly the ambiguous legacy of volunteer motivation. There is a faint derogation in the observation that some social scientists "feel" about a matter on which "we" (The Commission?) "pretend."

The Commission clearly finds itself on firmer ground when it addressed institutional change or economic data, and the remainder of their report is based almost entirely on such research. The behavioral sciences, having been given their parenthesis, receive no further attention on the question of motivation in their pages.

II. WHAT RECENT RESEARCH TELLS US ABOUT THE MOTIVATION OF VOLUNTEERS

The motivation of giving and volunteering is a topic not dissimilar to the weather: everybody talks about it, but few give it systematic study. For the purposes of the present paper, I have reviewed every article published in the Journal of Voluntary Action Research (JVAR) for a discussion of the motivation of voluntary action. This review, encompassing papers published over the past 12 years in the major international journal in its field, yields a manageable number of papers for individual review. Additional material on motivation research may be found in a number of major recent publications, and these are selectively reviewed in this section.

A grand total of 20 papers centrally focusing on the motivation of voluntary action have been published, or are currently in the process of being published, in the Journal of Voluntary Action Research. These papers have varied widely in their theoretical and methodological approaches, as well as in the types of voluntary activity they have investigated.

The first of the twenty, for example, was a brilliant application of Maslow's celebrated "hierarchy of human needs" to the question of volunteer motivation. The author, the distinguished community educator Malcolm Knowles, noted that "institutional volunteerism has been structured in this country, on the whole, on fairly low-level and static assumptions" about why people volunteer (1972:27). In Maslow's terms, Knowles argues, organizations usually cast their appeals in terms of needs for safety, belonging, and esteem.

"What," Knowles (1972:28) asks in this seminal article, "would volunteerism in America (or elsewhere) look like if it were structured around self-actualization as its motivational mode?" And he answers: it would involve both service and learning; it would be developmental; it would provide growth for the volunteer; it would treat clients as collaborators in mutual self-development, and not mere objects of service; and, finally, it would place volunteering at the centre of a national education enterprise, rather than the periphery of the national welfare enterprise.

Knowles concludes:

> My prediction is that if service-oriented volunteer programs were to be organized around this developmental concept of motivation: (1) individuals would enter into volunteer service in an ego-extending frame of mind; (2) they would see the field as offering a rich variety of resources rather than as a set of parochial fiefdoms; (3) they would relate to volunteer agencies and their clients as partners in a process of mutual change and development; and (4) they would engage in volunteer service as an aspect of a lifelong process of continuing self-development. (1972:29)

Knowles' focus on the self-enhancing aspect of giving sets a useful context for discussing a range of later studies that have focused on just what it is that one "gets" from volunteering.

In a dramatic demonstration of Knowles' point regarding the institutionalization of low-level motives in appealing to volunteers, sociologist Richard Ofshee and five research colleagues studied the motivation of participants in Synanon, an intentional community initially formed around goals of drug rehabilitation. Three categories of motives are found to explain the attraction of new members to Synanon: (1) direct ties to a present resident of the community; (2) attraction to the "social movement aspects of Synanon (the drug-free environment or the communal lifestyle)"; or (3) the search for help on a personal problem, be it the need for "simple companionship" or the alleviation of emotional distress (Ofshee et al, 1974:69). Only the second category approaches the level of self-actualization, and that in the dubious context of a "total community."

246

David Gottlieb, in a study of volunteering in a very different context, that of what motivated VISTA volunteers, finds a similar mix of motives. "Females," Gottlieb's data indicate, "tend to be more altruistic than male volunteers; and younger volunteers, particularly females, are most likely to view VISTA as a relevant and useful activity - an activity which allows one to get away from it all and at the same time provides an opportunity for learning about oneself and contemplating one's future" (1974:4). Males, on the other hand, more often cite motives of "escape" — "to get away from what I was doing" — in explaining their volunteering.

John Flynn and Gene Webb, in a study of women volunteers in Kalamazoo, lent further credence to the "multiple motives" explanation. "When asked what had led the participants to work on policy campaign issues, responses centered upon the primary beneficiary of their own participation. Almost one half of the actors indicated that 'self-oriented' needs were served by their activism." However, the same women also spoke of the importance of "self-maintenance needs" such as the need to keep busy or to "escape," and self-actualizing goals such as self-education and personal growth (Flynn and Webb, 1975:140).

These studies, each of which indicates that motivational multiplicity is the usual pattern among volunteers, lead to the conclusion so clearly drawn by Gidron (1977) that "contrary to common beliefs which relate volunteer work solely to altruistic motives, people have both other and self-oriented reasons for volunteering." The implications of this motivational multiplicity include, Gidron writes in a recent JVAR article (1983), "that in order to be satisfied, a volunteer needs, above all, a task in which self-expression is possible — a task which gives the volunteer the opportunity to develop abilities and skills, a task which is seen as a challenge, a task where achievements can be seen."

Organizationally, Gidron continues, his findings "imply that the work conditions should enable the volunteer to receive from the job what it has to offer. The volunteer should not have to waste precious time getting to work, looking for tools, arguing with officials about what to do and how to do it. These findings call for clear policies on the role of volunteers in the organization and the means to implement these policies."

The research summarized above, then, leads to the

first of several summary propositions regarding what we do know about volunteer motivation. This proposition is:

A) PEOPLE VOLUNTEER FOR MULTIPLE REASONS, AMONG WHICH ARE THEIR OWN PERSONAL AND SOCIAL GOALS AND NEEDS.

The discovery of the "non-altruistic" volunteer in the mid-1970s led to the application of theories of rational self-interest to the world of volunteering. Thus in 1975, Peter Gluck applied "exchange theory" to the study of volunteers in an urban political organization. Gluck (1975:104) summarized this theory as follows:

> The theory is based upon the following basic assumptions: (1) individuals have a variety of needs, drives, and goals which they seek to attain; (2) some of these can best be achieved within the context of organizational participation; (3) organizations need some mechanism to influence the behavior [of their activists].

Gluck proceeded to distinguish between two dimensions of motivation. On the one hand he found two sets of objects of incentives, self- and other-regarding motives. On a second dimension he distinguished between tangible and intangible rewards. Only among one group of political activists, those who were young and college educated, did Gluck find substantial expression of other-oriented motives. Most of the political volunteers he studied were in it for themselves (1975:107).

More recently, exchange theory has been employed by Phillips (1982) to understand how volunteers evaluate their continuing participation. Studying hosts of a "Fresh Air" placement program for city children, Phillips finds that host motivation develops in predictable stages. In Stage 1, "exposure to the idea that one might be a host," altruistic motivation clearly prevails. In Stage 2, "preliminary decision to be a host," altruism is mixed up with "egoistic" motives as arrangements begin to be made for a two-week visit by a child. Stage 3, "final decision to be a host," brings the commitment to a family decision, typically made on the basis of benefits (companionship, exposure to a different lifestyle) perceived from hosting.

In Stage 4, the child actually comes for the visit, and altruism returns to prominence as a motive, particularly when expectations are not met and the visit turns out to be more difficult than anticipated. In Stage 5, the family decides whether or not to invite a child for the following summer. Here the question of the degree to which the visit fulfilled the mixed altruistic-egoistic motivations of the family becomes critical.

The logic of exchange theory, that pluses need to outweigh minuses if an action is to be undertaken, was stated formally by Stinson and Stam (1976) in economic terms in their "Toward an Economic Model of Voluntarism." The two economists conclude that citizens facing the decision whether or not to volunteer in local governmental programs make their decisions "based both on the amount of satisfaction derived from [the] volunteer work and the shadow wage, or tax savings, obtained from having the service provided by volunteers rather than paid professionals" (1976:58).

The applicability of exchange theory to the study of the decision to volunteer suggests a second generalization from the literature:

B) THE INDIVIDUAL WHO VOLUNTEERS TYPICALLY DOES SO ONLY AFTER WEIGHING ALTERNATIVES IN DELIBERATE FASHION.

Elaine Sharp's JVAR paper (1978) usefully identifies three major forms of incentives which may motivate volunteers: material (e.g. goods or service); solidary (e.g. status, enjoyment, or sociability); and expressive (e.g. the chance to act out certain values).

Sharp concludes that different motivational configurations seem particularly suited to different organizational challenges. Thus, if citizens are volunteering to "coproduce" a desired outcome with officials (say by organizing a neighborhood crime watch), the appeal to solidary incentives is most successful. But if advocacy (protest, legislative change) is the goal, two alternative models seem most viable. One focuses on adversarial politics — here material motives seem most effective in generating volunteering. A second advocacy style involves achieving an advisory credibility, and here solidary motives are most prominent.

A similar finding emerges from the study of a midwestern opera guild, the "Angels," as studied by Marilyn and Richard Wilmeth. Two distinct groups of participants are found within the single organization: "one very pointedly instrumental and the other, probably more typical group, an instrument-expressive one" (1979:24). The instrumental group is older and evinces an "almost religious" dedication to the advancement of opera and to the role of volunteers within that mission. One member put the matter clearly to the Wilmeths (1979:24): "The reason for the success of the Opera is the people who kept up the public interest before the "Angels" decided it was SOCIALLY fun and ruined it!"

The papers by Sharp and the Wilmeths suggest a third important lesson that may be drawn from the JVAR studies:

C) THAT THE REALM OF VOLUNTARY ACTION ITSELF IS A COMPLEX AND MANY FACETED ONE, IN WHICH DIFFERENT ORGANIZATIONAL TASKS APPEAL TO DIFFERENT MOTIVATION FORCES.

Laurie Davidson Cummings illustrates this third law in her study of can and bottle recyclers (1977). She finds that recyclers are often "one-timers" responding to a small cash return from their recycling. Nonetheless, the recyclers, when asked about their reasons for recycling, overwhelmingly cited the need "to help the environment." Cummings observes that "Recyclers, perhaps like other volunteers, believe that altruistic rather than economic incentives should be given as the major reason why they volunteer" (1977:154).

Cummings' work suggests that the ideology of giving may mask the more "real" motives of self-interest. Perhaps, one may be tempted to conclude, such realism also must force a re-assessment of the vaunted American willingness to participate in voluntary action. Greta Salem addressed this issue in her study (1978) of local political participation in Chicago. "There is a popular tendency to assume that apathy is an innate characteristic of American citizens who prefer to focus on private rather than public affairs. However, another explanation is possible" — the system may not provide adequate opportunities for the development of participatory skills and culture (1978:18).

250

Salem's study of the 44th Ward Assembly lends substance to the structural explanation. Given the chance to participate, Salem finds urbanites actively engrossed in local decision making. Some volunteers become even more dedicated to their activity, as Ross' memoir on the New Left Movement of the 1960s indicates. Ross writes: Through personal ties which legitimately carry affective expression, primary groups . . . offer a series of secondary gains which support movement participants emotionally and help to mold them intellectually. Primary groups become the locus of an individual's collective orientation" (1977:149).

Zurcher's observation that many voluntary roles are "ephemeral" (i.e. transitory, ad hoc in nature) gives further fullness to the nature of voluntary participation in complex society. (Zurcher, 1978) Those who work together in disasters, or in bowling groups, or in the Naval Reserve, all move quickly into and out of roles that take on great meaning and structure for them. The participants may be active in several forms of action, each with a fulsome structure and culture within the context of the "ephemeral role."

What, then, of altruism as a motive for volunteer service? Is it merely one more "ephemeral role," to be discounted as so much ideology? Or does it form one, albeit of many, force that continues to impel people to participate as volunteers?

Jessica Jenner addresses this question in her study (1982) of women volunteers in a national organization. She carefully distinguishes between three major motivating configurations (1982:30-31):

- PRIMARY — "Volunteer work is my main career or work activity . . ."
- SUPPLEMENTAL — "Volunteer work is a supplement to the other parts of my work life."
- CAREER INSTRUMENTAL — "Volunteer work is a way to prepare me for a new (or changed) career, or to maintain skills and contacts in a career I am not actively pursuing at this time."

Just about three in five of the volunteers studied by Jenner fitted the "supplemental" category, the others evenly divided between the remaining categories. For the supplemental volunteers, motives of community service, association, and personal growth

251

were almost equally prevalent. Jenner draws the conclusion from her study that "altruism and self-actualization were about equally important motivators. For organizations this suggests that not only must the cause be worthy, but the role played in the organizational context must also be meaningful: (1982:35).

In a comprehensive review of the role of altruism as a motivator of voluntary action, David Horton Smith (1981:23) finds "literally no evidence to justify a belief in some 'absolute' form of human altruism, in which the motivation for an action is utterly without some form of selfishness." Smith concludes that:

> The essence of volunteerism is not altruism, but rather the contribution of services, goods, or money to help accomplish some desired end, without substantial coercion or direct remuneration. It is the voluntariness and unremunerated character of volunteerism that is distinctive . . . . Altruism is a variable both among volunteers and among voluntary organizations. Failure to admit this constitutes a failure to face human social and individual reality. (1981:33)

In a recent JVAR article, Natalie Allen and William Rushton (1983) put Smith's concepts to a rigorous empirical test. They review all available studies of the altruism of volunteers and conclude that the concept of the "altruistic personality" is a valid one. Thus, community volunteers "appear to have more positive attitudes toward themselves and others and, as such, possess greater feelings of self-efficacy. Compared to non-volunteers, these individuals can be characterized as being more emotionally stable."

From these studies, we may draw a fourth major conclusion, to wit:

D) CONCERN FOR OTHERS, WHILE NOT ALWAYS PURELY ALTRUISTIC, REMAINS AN IMPORTANT MOTIVATING FORCE FOR MUCH VOLUNTARY ACTION.

Anderson and Moore (1978:120), in a study of Canadian volunteers, see altruism as the leading motive of those who perform voluntary action. "It appears that people do volunteer for a variety of reasons but that the humanitarian motive — to help others — and the desire to feel useful and needed quite consistently outweigh other reasons given."

252

If pure altruism does not exist, it is not the case that altruism has lost its appeal. It remains a critical force in the motivation of those who practice voluntarism.

One further point may be derived from the literature, and it harkens back to Salem's observation regarding the ways in which structures may retard active participation. In a remarkable pair of papers that appeared in the 1980 Special Issue of JVAR, Jone Pearce and David Adams explored two little-studied facets of voluntary organizations.

Pearce examined the ways in which volunteers often seek to avoid leadership roles. Comparing the rates at which leadership is sought in employing, as against volunteer, organizations, Pearce finds that few rewards are available to the volunteer leader. She concludes that if "voluntary organizations are to remain viable, they must find ways to increase the attractiveness of leadership positions" (1980:92).

Adams' paper explores another structural factor within many voluntary organizations — their tendency to segregate volunteers into "elite" and "lower" roles. Studying a Red Cross chapter, Adams finds that what Board members do and what serving volunteers do are quite different tasks. Moreover, the twain rarely meet, nor is there much mobility between their separate organizational roles. Voluntary organizations seem quite able, Adams suggests, to create miniature class systems within them, or at least to reflect the class divisions prominent in the world beyond.

The research of Pearce and Adams implies that we carefully attend to the structural realities that form the societal context of giving and volunteering. This theme, that voluntarism is itself a social activity highly dependent upon the "turbulent environment" of today's social realities, was a central one in the significant research that emerged from the National Forum on Volunteerism (1980, 1981).

Writing for this Forum, Gordon Manser (1980:6) observed with his customary acuity emergent patterns of volunteer development:

> Many volunteers have transferred their loyalty from so-called traditional organizations to small, neighborhood or block groups, where cause and effect, (effort and outcome), are more closely linked and more manageable. Others, especially younger people, have moved into cause and advocacy groups as a reaction to the powerlessness of politics.

The interaction of these fast-changing social currents and the "multiple motives" of volunteers (recognized as demonstrated fact by all the Forum's consulting writers — see Scheier, 1980:19-20; Van Til, 1980:8-10; and Trecker, 1980:37) is well summarized by Manser (1980:7):

> On the one hand, enlightened self-interest includes a desire to make a significant impact on a community problem. On the other hand, it includes a desire to have an experience which is meaningful in terms of one's personal career or skills goals. Because this represents a symbiotic balance between altruism and self-interest, volunteers thus motivated are found to be highly committed and responsible in their work. They also have greater expectations from the organizations for which they work. At the same time, volunteers may tend to have more commitment to an issue than to an organization. If the organization does not live up to the volunteer's expectations, the volunteer will move to another interest and another organization.

Above these shifting organizational challenges and opportunities stands our inability, as a society and as a planet, to assure our own survival. Dean Harleigh Trecker puts the matter powerfully in his essay for the National Forum on Volunteerism (1980:37):

> Perhaps of greater significance than anything else is our failure as a people to articulate, enunciate and work for common national and international goals. One searches in vain for any agreement on the need for a universal quality of life goal meaningful to most people. No doubt four decades of life under the "balance of terror" approach of the great powers in their defense structure has had a subliminal effect on people. Unconsciously, "survival" is the real, though not necessarily spoken, goal. If this is true, it is lamentable, because it eliminates, or at least delays, the immense opportunities for world betterment and more satisfying lives for humanity.

Trecker's observation that our failure to deal with issues of planetary survival retards our ability to create a voluntary society suggests the wording of our final generalization from the literature:

E) THE MOTIVATION TO GIVE AND TO VOLUNTEER IS SHAPED AND CONSTRAINED BY BROADER SOCIAL REALITIES, AND PARTICULARLY BY THE OMNIPRESENT REALITY OF WORLD CHAOS AND DESTRUCTION.

This generalization goes far to explain the success of the "nuclear freeze" movement in recent years, as well as the continuing prominence of narcissism in American culture. After all, if the world can end at any moment in a frenzy of nuclear destruction, it often seems to make just as much sense to ignore the possibility as it does to try to do something about it, or anything else.

III. WHAT WE STILL NEED TO KNOW

What, then, is left to learn about volunteer motivation? Our review of a significant portion of the literature on the subject, drawn in large part from the major journal in the field, would suggest that we probably know at least as much as we need to about the multiple motives of most volunteers. Further studies should keep us updated on any changes in these patterns, but the basic work has been done.

Much more problematic are the questions raised by Pearce, Adams and the consulting writers to the National Forum on Volunteerism — questions of the impact of vast and uncontrollable social forces upon the decisions that each of us make as we plan our daily lives and actions.

What is left to learn, I submit, is how we each choose, and how our institutions select, between the forces of narcissistic self-indulgence and those of realistic societal reconstruction. We need to learn, in short, how to relate ourselves both to persons and to societal forces.

Richard Sennett has shown us, in the brilliant corpus of his work, how important it is for us to make this dual connection. He has also shown us how particularly difficult that connection is, for we are the heirs of a Protestant Ethic which has confounded our sense of social responsibility. Sennett explains why (1978:334):

> Worldly asceticism (the denial of gratification for the purpose of validating the self — the hallmark of the Protestant Ethic) and narcissism have much in common. In both, "What am I feeling?" becomes an obsession. In both, showing to others the checks

and impulses of oneself feeling is a way of showing that one does have a worthy self. In both, there is a projection of the self onto the world, rather than an engagement in worldly experience beyond one's control.

In our patterns of giving and volunteering, most Americans surely remain heirs of the Protestant Ethic. We perform our community service with the same stolid quest for respectability with which we play out our economic and family lives. And, if Sennett's surmise is indeed correct, we give and volunteer ourselves with the narcissist's wish to avoid confronting forces beyond our control.

Here we come face to face with the limits of contemporary voluntarism and its inability to deal directly with issues of distribution and inequality, corporate and governmental irresponsibility, war and peace. Like the narcissist, paralyzed by the fear of missing an experience that may prove gratifying — and like the ascetic, aiming desperately to interact only with those forces that will validate self-worth — we tend to limit the range of our volunteering to what is safe, respectable, and consonant with the limits of our economic and political lives.

The frontier of motivational studies, then, may be seen to consist in searching for, and nourishing, the courage to create, and act upon, visions of voluntarism that directly meet the challenges of a world in flux and turmoil.

What are such visions? Time does not permit their full elaboration in these pages, but among them are:

— Amitai Etzioni's brilliant construct of the "active society" (1968), in which individuals and communities identify needs and proceed to resolve problems with the confidence that both they and what they do matters.

— Ron Lippitt and Eva Schindler-Rainman's vision of the "collaborative community" (1980), in which the barriers that separate us are removed in a collective process of trust-building and problem-resolution. (It should also be noted that this volume contains an extremely wise chapter on "the motivational dynamics of voluntarism.")

— Willis Harman's image of "societal transformation" (1978), in which the basic longings of persons for meaning are harnessed to the powerful engines of science and communications.

— Marilyn Ferguson's recognition that an "aquarian conspiracy" (1980) is afoot in this land, by which individuals find both ways to connect with each other and to regain control of the organizational forces that threaten both sanity and civility in a world in chaos.

— John Naisbitt's identification of "megatrends" (1982), many of which presage a future in which individual and group decisions will prove more significant than the travails of multinational corporate machinations or the paralysis of central government.

— My own argument that "citizen coproduction" — the emerging partnerships between individuals and communities, on the one hand, and economic and political organizations, on the other, both to define what is needed and how it can most sensibly be produced — will characterize much of our energy, food, security, and social peace processes in the years ahead (Van Til, 1982).

These, I believe, and other visions like them which connect the theory and practice of voluntarism, are the "cutting edge" issues of our time. These are the issues that will need to be understood before we can make the connection between what we want life to be and what we can do to make it better.

IV. A RESEARCH AGENDA FOR THE YEARS AHEAD

I shall be very brief. The argument of this paper leads to the identification of four major lines of research.

Firstly, we need to know more about the lives of extraordinary volunteers, those who identify tasks beyond the routine and accomplish beyond the norm. We need, in short, a study of volunteer "Profiles in Courage" that details what it is that people can do to serve others, challenge injustice, and build a better society.

I suspect that far too many of our diurnal pronouncements on volunteering consist in fact as mere boosterism. Abstractions such as "private-sector initiatives" or "independent sector activity" are often only distantly related to the reality of the lives of those who actually practice volunteering. These concepts need to be rooted firmly in reality lest they remain mere ideological fluff in an age of image, display, and "PR."

Secondly, we need to learn from those who have succeeded in building effective volunteer communities and organizations. We need to know how people can learn both to enjoy each other's company and to achieve valued ends. Volunteering is not merely "unpaid work"; nor is it pure socializing. Rather, it is a unique combination of the two, and we need to know more about its organizational chemistry and how to produce it more regularly.

Thirdly, we need to develop methods of "action research" which identify the needs and aspirations of those who volunteer, and feed back to those individuals and their organizations useful information and assistance. Such research might give us a fuller picture of the size and power of the voluntary sector within a city or state. It could also provide an invaluable means of building effective collaborative networks among discrete organizations (cf. Lippitt and Van Til, 1981).

Finally, we need to pay much more attention to what it means to aspire toward the creation of an "active society." As the potential citizen volunteer faces the manifold decisions to act or not to act, he and she will benefit from reviewing summaries of the thinking and action of others (by which I mean research) that are concrete, reality-based, and actionable.

We need to be able to know how it is possible to act responsibly in an interdependent world. We need to know how to maintain individual autonomy in an era of corporate and political megastructures. And we need to learn how to sustain the sense that if we are to survive, we need to care about each other as well as about ourselves.

Perhaps when we know these things, then we will be able to build a society as good as our remarkably enduring and admirable motives to volunteer.

REFERENCES

Adams, David
> 1980 "Elite and Lower Volunteers in a Voluntary Association: A Study of an American Red Cross Chapter," *Journal of Voluntary Action Research* 9: 95-108.

Allen, Natalie and William Rushton
> 1983 "Personality Characteristics of Community Mental Health Volunteers: A Review," *Journal of Voluntary Action Research* 12: 36-49.

Anderson, John C. and Larry F. Moore
> 1978 "The Motivation to Volunteer," *Journal of Voluntary Action*

Research 7: 120-129.

Commission on Private Philanthropy and Public Need
1975 *Giving in America: Toward a Stronger Voluntary Sector*, published by Commission.

Cummings, Laurie Davidson
1977 "Voluntary Strategies in the Environmental Movement: Recycling as Cooptation," *Journal of Voluntary Action Research* 6: 153-160.

Etzioni, Amitai
1968 *The Active Society*. New York: The Free Press.

Ferguson, Marilyn
1980 *The Aquarian Conspiracy: Personal and Social Transformation in the 1980s*. Los Angeles: J.P. Tarcher.

Flynn, John P. and Gene E. Webb
1975 "Women's Incentives for Community Participation in Policy Issues," *Journal of Voluntary Action Research* 4: 137-146.

Gidron, Benjamin
1983 "Sources of Job Satisfaction Among Service Volunteers," *Journal of Voluntary Action Research* 12: 20-35.
1977 "Volunteer Work and Its Rewards," *Volunteer Adminstration* 11: 18-32.

Gluck, Peter R.
1975 "An Exchange Theory of Incentives of Urban Political Party Organization," *Journal of Voluntary Action Research* 4: 104-118.

Gottlieb, David
1974 "The Socialization and Politization of VISTA Volunteers: Sex and Generational Differences," *Journal of Voluntary Action Research* 3: 1-9.

Jenner, Jessica Reynolds
1982 "Participation Leadership and the Role of Volunteerism Among Selected Women Volunteers," *Journal of Voluntary Action Research* 11: 30-31.

Knowles, Malcolm S.
1972 "Motivation in Volunteerism: Synopsis of a Theory," *Journal of Voluntary Action Research* 1: 27-29.

Naisbitt, John
1982 *Megatrends: Ten New Directions Transforming Our Lives*. New York: Warner Books, Inc.

National Forum on Volunteerism

1980 *A Look at the Eighties: Critical Environmental Factors Affecting Volunteerism*. Appleton, WI: Aid Association for Lutherans.

Ofshee, Richard, et al

1974 "Social Structure and Social Control in Synanon," *Journal of Voluntary Action Research* 3: 67-76.

Pearce, Jone L.

1980 "Apathy or Self-Interest?: The Volunteer's Avoidance of Leadership Roles," *Journal of Voluntary Action Research* 9: 85-94.

Phillips, Michael H.

1982 "Motivation and Expectation in Successful Volunteerism," *Journal of Voluntary Action Research* 11: 118-125.

Ross, Robert J.

1979 "Primary Groups in Social Movements: A Memoir and Interpretation," *Journal of Voluntary Action Research* 6: 139-152.

Salem, Greta W.

1978 "Maintaining Participation in Community Organizations," *Journal of Voluntary Action Research* 7: 18-27.

Schinder-Rainman, Eva and Ronald Lippitt

1980 *Building the Collaborative Community: Mobilizing Citizens for Action*. Riverside, CA: University of California Extension.

Sennett, Richard

1978 *The Fall of the Public Man*. New York: Random House.

Sharp, Elaine B,

1978 "Citizen Organization in Policing Issues and Crime Prevention: Incentives for Participation," *Journal of Voluntary Action Research* 7: 45-58.

Smith, David Horton

1981 "Altruism, Volunteers and Volunteerism," *Journal of Voluntary Action Research* 10: 21-36.

Stinson, Thomas F. and Jerome M. Stam

1976 "Toward an Economic Model of Volunteerism: The Case of Participation in Local Government," *Journal of Voluntary Action Research* 5: 52-60.

Van Til, Jon

1982 *Living with Energy Shortfall: A Future for American Town and Cities*. Boulder, CO: Westview Press.

Wilmeth, Marlyn Walton and J. Richard Wilmeth
   1979 "Lesser Angels and Minor Profits: The Supporting Group Behind One Professional Opera Company," *Journal of Voluntary Action Research* 8: 21-32.
Zurcher, Louis A.
   1978 "Ephemeral Roles, Voluntary Action and Voluntary Associations," *Journal of Voluntary Action Research* 7: 65-74.

CHAPTER AUTHORS

Valerie A. Ahwee is currently the Resource Materials Coordinator at the Vancouver Volunteer Centre. She is involved in marketing publications, editing newsletters, and managing a resource library for community organizations.

Ronald J. Burke is currently Professor of Organizational Behavior in the Faculty of Administrative Studies at York University. He received his B.A. at the University of Manitoba and his M.A. and Ph.D. at the University of Michigan. Dr. Burke is currently studying burnout among men and women in police work, the effects of the current economic recession on the satisfactions and experiences of school-based educators, and mentoring relationships in organizations.

Lary Lindsay is currently an independent consultant engaged in organizational and financial research. She received both her B.A. and M.B.A. from York University. She is an active volunteer in several organizations and is currently involved with the Faculty of Administrative Studies Alumni Association.

Larry F. Moore holds an M.B.A. and a Doctorate in Business Administration from the University of Colorado where he specialized in management studies. His current research interests include occupational attitudes of people at work, human resource planning, organizational design and development, employment interviewing, and organizational theory. He is Associate Professor of Industrial Relations Management in the Faculty of Commerce and Business Administration at the University of British Columbia.

Craig C. Pinder is currently an Associate Professor of Industrial Relations Management in the Faculty of Commerce and Business Administration at the University of British Columbia. He received his B.A. at the University of B.C., his M.A. at the University of Minnesota, and his Ph.D. at Cornell University. His research interests include the role of personnel transfers in employee development. Dr. Pinder has recently published a book on work motivation.

Ivan H. Scheier, Ph.D., is a consultant, trainer, and author in the field of volunteer leadership. He has written over 100 publications, including ten books. Dr. Scheier is the past director of the National Information Center on Voluntarism and the president of Yellowfire Press.

Eva Schindler-Rainman, Ph.D., is a national and international consultant, trainer, and behavioral scientist with special expertise in the areas of voluntarism, human resource development, and non-traditional organizational design and development. She has authored and co-authored numerous books and articles.

Vicki R. Schram is an Assistant Professor of Family Economics in the Department of Family and Child Ecology at Michigan State University. She received her Ph.D. from the University of Illinois, specializing in family and consumption economics. Her doctoral research focused on the influences of volunteer work participation of married women. Subsequent research in the volunteer work area include the investigation of job skill development in volunteer work and volunteer work participation in dual-earner families, family financial management, and the influences of time spent in housework.

SELECTED PAPERS AUTHORS

John C. Anderson, Ph.D., is an Associate Professor in the Graduate School of Business Administration, Columbia University.

Terry H. Chapman, Ph.D., is Manager of Education, Meeting Planners International, Middletown, Ohio.

Robert Flashman, Ph.D., is a Family Resource Management Specialist, Kentucky Cooperative Extension Service, University of Kentucky.

George Ray Francies, Ph.D., is a Coordinator of Volunteer Services, Brown County Department of Social Services, Green Bay, Wisconsin.

James I. Grieshop, Ph.D., is a Lecturer and Specialist in Community Education, Cooperative Extension, University of California, Irvine.

Jone L. Pearce, Ph.D., is an Assistant Professor in the Graduate School of Management, University of California, Irvine.

Sam Quick, Ph.D., is a Human Development and Family Relations Specialist, Kentucky Cooperative Extension Service, University of Kentucky.

Jon Van Til, Ph.D., is the Editor of the Journal of Voluntary Action Research, and is an Associate Professor in the Department of Urban Studies and Community Development, Rutgers University.